BECOMING A
BELOVED
DISCIPLE

10 STEPS TO A DEEPER RELATIONSHIP WITH JESUS

STEFANI YORGES

CROWN
PRESS

With deep love and gratitude
for all those who encouraged this butterfly
to leave the cocoon

◆

Jesus,
For Thine is the kingdom,
and the power, and the glory
forever

CONTENTS

◆

PREFACE

Everyone knows that John was the disciple whom Jesus loved. At the Last Supper, he sat closer to the heart of Jesus than anyone else. Wouldn't you love to be that close to Jesus?

You can be one of His beloved disciples too! He has made a way for everyone to be as close to Him as they want to be. *You* determine how close you will be, not Him.

Some want it badly enough to give **everything** to have it, laying aside anything that hinders their intimacy with Jesus. They will have what they seek. He draws near to those who draw near to Him.

"Why do some people "find" Jesus in a way that others do not? Why does He manifest His presence to some and let multitudes of others struggle along in the half-light of an imperfect Christian experience?

*Of course, the will of God is the same for all. He has no favorites within His household. All He has ever done for any of His children He will do for all His children. **The difference lies not with God but with us.***

The difference is a spiritual receptivity, an inward longing, and a corresponding determination to do something about it. These people differ from the average Christian because they went on to cultivate it until it became the biggest thing in their lives."

A.W. Tozer

Perhaps you haven't been satisfied for a while now. It's not that He's not enough, or that you are ungrateful, but you can sense there is MORE – more of His glory, more of His love, more of His untapped vastness – that you are not yet experiencing.

This book is for thirsty souls who are determined to follow Jesus. He is calling you out of stagnation and "church as usual." He is calling you away from the shores of spiritual mediocrity and complacency, and into the depths of a more victorious life in Jesus. He's calling you to be powerfully awakened to your destiny and purpose. He is asking you to sit at His feet and listen to His heartbeat. Jeremiah 33:3 says, *"Come unto Me and I'll show you great and unsearchable things you do not know."*

You have the same invitation John the beloved disciple had – to call yourself "the one Jesus loves." In this study, you are invited to really believe it and to live your life from that perspective. Are you ready to get started?

10 Steps to a Deeper Relationship with Jesus

This book provides ten steps to become a beloved disciple, but it's not about a program or a method. It's about *building a progressively deeper relationship with Jesus.*

God typically works in sequence to accomplish His divine purposes. He will build your character and strengthen your relationship with Him in an orderly fashion. Throughout this journey, you will:

➤ Surrender to Him – Steps 1, 2, and 3

Jesus laid down his life for you.[1] You will now be invited to lay down your life to demonstrate your love for Him. Steps 1, 2, and 3 are about surrendering your "old ways" and cutting ties that bind you to other things. He is looking for disciples who put their own world on hold for the sake of the Kingdom – those who lay down their agendas, plans, and decide to be "all in" for Jesus.

➤ Wait upon Him – Steps 4, 5, and 6

You will learn more about Jesus as you spend more time with Him. Going beyond the norms of ritual and duty, you will become saturated in His abiding presence and power. You will be invited to pray and worship at a deeper level than you've known before. Steps 4, 5, and 6 are about waiting on Him – intertwining your life with His Spirit and establishing a firm foundation. These steps require you to form new habits; to put on "new ways."

➤ Bear Fruit for Him – Steps 7 and 8

Once you are firmly established, you will be better able to discern His plans and purposes for your life. You will begin to care about what He cares about. He chose and appointed you to bear fruit – fruit that will last.[2] You will be invited to join His Kingdom work in ways you've never experienced before. Steps 7 and 8 help prepare you to make a difference in this world. Living a deeper life dedicated to the Lord will activate your destiny and purpose for eternity.

➢ Abide in Him – Steps 9 and 10

He is the vine; you are the branch. You must *remain* in Him – apart from Him you can do nothing.[3] You will be invited to experience His peace, contentment, and rest like never before. Steps 9 and 10 represent a life lived with a strong, calm balance that only the Lord can provide. This is the result of allowing Him to satisfy every area of your life to its fullest.

While these ten steps are presented in an orderly fashion, it's likely that you will proceed through each one at a different pace, make more progress in some than others, and need to revisit certain steps throughout the rest of your life.

Study Tools

At the end of each chapter, you will find several supplemental study tools that can help you make further transformational changes in your life:

➢ Workbook Discussion Questions

A journey is always better when it is shared so it is best to get some friends to join you in this study. Ecclesiastes 4:9 says that *"two are better than one – they can help each other."* By doing this study in a small group you can discuss what you have read and the implications for your life. You can pray for, encourage, and support each other as you walk through each step. Real spiritual growth is never an isolated, solitary pursuit. Maturity is best accomplished through relationships.

➢ Worship Meditations

Music can often touch the soul more deeply than words on a page. Take your time with the songs provided in the sample playlists. Sometimes you may want to leave a song on repeat for days until you grasp what He intends for you. The worship list can be used individually for private meditation or as part of your small group discussion.

➢ Prayers

Confessing truth in prayer is a powerful tool. It's important that God hears your voice and that you give Him permission to change you. We are told in Proverbs 18:21 that *life* and *death* are in the power of what we speak. As you say these prayers, you align yourself with His will and ask for His plans and purposes to be set in motion, which will help you experience life to the fullest.

➢ Spiritual Markers

A spiritual marker represents a transition, decision, or direction guided by God. When significant transformation has taken place, it can be helpful to identify a spiritual marker at that point. Over time you can look back at the spiritual markers in your life and see how God has faithfully guided you. Each step in this study has a spiritual marker associated with it – a sign that you are moving closer to the heart of Jesus.

➢ Verses to Remember

Each step has a Bible verse that teaches a truth from that chapter. If you really want to transform your life, memorizing Scripture is an important place to start. Carry each verse with you until you have sealed it into your heart and mind.

This book is a path for growing closer to Jesus. Given all the resources available in it, this study is not something you will sit down and read straight through in a short period of time. Doing a full chapter each week would allow you to complete the study in eleven weeks. However, that would still be a very intensive pace for the depth and amount of content available here. Slowing down might mean reading the chapter one week, and then working on the discussion questions and other materials the second week. Another option is reading half of the chapter and doing half of the discussion questions per week.

Dwelling in His Word

God promises that His Word will *"accomplish what He desires and will achieve the purpose for which He sent it."*[4] The Amplified Version of Hebrews 4:12 say that His Word is *"alive and full of power [making it active, operative, energizing, and effective]; it is sharper than any two-edged sword, penetrating to the dividing line of soul and spirit, exposing and sifting and analyzing and judging the very thoughts and purposes of the heart."*

For that reason, the Bible is quoted extensively throughout this study [emphasized by italics] and allowed to speak for itself. In fact, there are more than a thousand verses captured in these pages that are intended to *"dwell in you richly."*[5] Most commonly used are the English Standard Version and the original New International Version. However, if an important point is better expressed in another translation, occasionally other versions are used. These exceptions will be noted in the reference section at the end of the book.

———————◆———————

I am so excited to begin this journey with you! I hope that this study will convince you of one thing: by surrendering yourself totally to God's purposes, He will bring you the most pleasure in this life and the next. I hope it affirms your desire for "more of Jesus," even as you live in a culture where most feel they have "enough of Jesus."

I am convinced that most believers have no idea how great our God is. We ask for crumbs when He is a feast...we look at stars when He is a galaxy...we want a song when He is a symphony.[6] What God has prepared for you is more than your ears have heard before, more than your eyes have seen before, and more than your mind could possibly conceive![7]

"To have found God and still pursue Him is the soul's paradox of love, scorned by the too-easily-satisfied religionist, but justified by the children of the burning heart."

A.W. Tozer

INTRODUCTION

I remember the first time I heard Kari Jobe sing, *The More I Seek You*.[1] I thought, what on earth is she talking about? Sit with Him? Drink from the cup in His hand? Feel His heartbeat? I had never been so overwhelmed by Him that it was more than I could stand, while Kari said that she lays back against Him to breathe and melts in His peace.

I was raised in a church where a relationship with God was quite formal. I saw Him as holy and powerful, but not as my "friend." Growing up, our family went to church three times a week. We attended Sunday School classes, sang in the choir, and did all the right service activities. I gave my public testimony and was baptized at an early age. Once married, my husband and I joined a nondenominational church – serving on the Missions Committee and Deacon Board. But I soon found that simply *doing* the right Christian things did not bring deep, satisfying joy. I wasn't melting in His peace.

I believed in Jesus as my Savior but was not enjoying an intimate relationship with Him. I was doing all that I thought God required but needed more of Him in my life. In fact, I wanted ALL that was available to me. If there was something I was missing (and clearly there was), I wanted it. If other people were sitting at His feet and drinking from the cup in His hand, I wanted to as well!

It took many years before I realized that true contentment, peace, and satisfaction can only come through an abiding and intimate relationship with Jesus. Fellowship with Him is what makes our joy complete.[2] Fullness of joy is truly found only in His presence.[3]

Going Through the Motions

Many Christians go through the motions of attending church and following all the rules. Armed with discipline and determination, they do the best they can to read their

Bibles and pray. But with little or no relationship with Jesus, they are left wondering, *is this all there is?*

There are far too many lukewarm believers experiencing dry, unfulfilled lives. Should we accept that *average* is all God wants for them? Where is the divine power that enables us to look different from the rest of the world? People should look at our lives and know there is something different about us – on the inside.

Adequate or Abundant Life?

He has promised us the same resurrection power that raised Jesus from the dead, an all-surpassing peace, and overflowing joy. Growing in the knowledge of who God is and pursuing an intimate relationship with Jesus is the key to experiencing this more *abundant life.*[4] You will never be satisfied just to know *about* God – you need more of God Himself, through real, personal experience. Daily fellowship with Him will release His anointing to accomplish His purposes for your life.

The Bible says, *"Be filled with the Holy Spirit."*[5] This means that you must remain full of the Spirit of God by pursuing Him on a daily basis. It's possible to have a glass of water that is not filled to capacity. It's possible to have a battery that is not completely charged. It's possible to have food in your stomach, but not feel completely full. You need to continually engage in your relationship with Jesus the same way you continually re-fill your stomach with food to survive.

God is looking for men and women who are willing to walk in moment-by-moment dependence on Him. His eyes *"range throughout the earth to strengthen those whose hearts are fully committed to Him."*[6] Jesus is looking for the kind of follower that is no longer content to "just get by" and instead wants to experience everything He has to offer in this life.

Perhaps you're doing this study because you are at a turning point in your life. Given that it is not "accidentally" in your hands today, let's trust that God plans to use it to draw you closer to Himself. Now you can either continue in an "adequate" Christian life, or you can get more and more on fire, becoming a *beloved disciple* that is passionately devoted to Him. Are you ready for more?

More is Available

If you only know the God of history, your God is not big enough. It is possible to know all the familiar Bible stories and still not really know Jesus. And you make little progress in a personal relationship with Him if you only absorb what you have read and been taught. He will not be found in textbooks.

You can only know Him more fully by going deeper in the Spirit. You will not be transformed by knowledge but by His love. This requires a transition from *head* to *heart*. He just needs your heart fully devoted and pliable in His hand.

"Nothing can prevent the spiritual rejuvenation of the soul that insists on having it."

A.W. Tozer

He is Calling

God's original plan was to have intimate fellowship with those He created. He created you for Himself – He wants a relationship with you more than anything! He said, *"I don't want your sacrifices – I want your love; I don't want your offerings – I want you to know me."*[7] He wants you, personally and individually and uniquely, to spend time with Him.

Even if you have strayed, He desires to draw you back to Himself. James 4:8 says, *"Draw near to God, and He will draw near to you."* While you have busied yourself with other interests, He has still been occupied with you. When you abandon all your other pursuits, you will see that He has never deserted you. His love is constant – unchanged by time, place, or circumstance. It is only you that has chosen to separate yourself from Him.

Seek and You Will Find

If you seek Him, you will find Him.[8] To *seek* means to "desire, pursue, and require something; to go after it with all of your strength." Jeremiah 29:13 says, *"You will find Me when you search for Me with all your heart."* The Amplified version says to seek Him as your *"first and vital necessity."*

No one has ever sought Him in vain. *"He is a rewarder of those who diligently seek*

Him."[9] Not those who are only half-heartedly wishing, but those who are intentional and determined in their pursuit of Him. The Lord said, *"I love those who love Me, and those who seek Me **diligently** will find Me."*[10]

Many people say they want guidance from God, but they don't passionately desire Him or lay aside other things to pursue Him with all their strength. Each day, you should desire to know Jesus more fully than you did the day before. You will need to forfeit all else to become a *beloved disciple.*

When you insist on having more of Him, you immediately attract the attention of the Holy Spirit. He has so much more in store for you. Could it even be *overwhelming,* as the Kari Jobe song said? Absolutely! Would you expect anything less from the God of the universe?

"Modern man can go everywhere, do everything. But only a rare person now and then is curious enough to want to know God."

A.W. Tozer

Through the Narrow Gate

There are so many people just lingering at the entrance to the Christian life – like a sheep standing at an open gate, gazing longingly at the fresh pasture available on the other side. Why? Jesus tells us the gate is open, but not wide. *"...Small is the gate and narrow the road that leads to life, and **only a few find it.**"*[11]

He offers His *"secret counsel to the righteous."*[12] Psalm 25:14 says, *"The Lord confides in those who fear Him."* Jesus also told His disciples, *"The knowledge of the secrets of the kingdom of heaven has been given to you, but **not to the crowds.**"*[13]

Not everyone is going to get it. I want to know the secrets of God – I want Him to confide in me! He has a deeper revelation of Himself to share with you too if you are open to receive it.

A Heart's Desire

Some people in the Bible clearly demonstrated a passion to know God more intimately than others around them. The great ones of the Kingdom have always been those who loved God more than others did. Those who pursued Him more intensely were rewarded with more of His presence:

- Moses talked with God face to face.[14]
- Abraham was called *"a friend of God."*[15]
- Enoch *"walked with God."*[16]
- Daniel was highly esteemed.[17] The King James version says he was *"greatly beloved."*
- Mary, the mother of Jesus, was highly favored. An angel of the Lord told her the *"Lord is with you."*[18]
- Job was a man who feared God. God Himself said, *"There is no one on earth like him; he is blameless and upright."*[19]
- David was described as *"a man after God's own heart."*[20]

Even today, it's obvious that some people are closer to God than others. They routinely talk of hearing from God, walking with God, and seeing God work in their lives. These "beloved disciples" speak about Jesus as if they know Him personally! They are sure of Him. They have a single-minded focus. Can you identify some people that seem to enjoy this kind of close, intimate relationship with Jesus? Thomas doubted the resurrected Savior until he saw the scars for himself.[21] Like him, do you stubbornly doubt the experience of these beloved disciples?

Intimate with Jesus

Why do some people seem to have a more intimate relationship than others? Does He just like them better? No – what is available to one is available to all. You can be as close to Jesus as you choose to be. The Bible teaches us that we have a lot to do with the level of intimacy we experience with Him. Like any relationship, you must work at it. It won't happen on its own. It will take your focused time and attention. You must ask for more and invest more. You must want it, pursue it, and chase after it.

Perhaps you feel that you are simply not one of those people capable of a deeper relationship with Jesus. Some Christians do not believe *they* have been called to a deep, intimate relationship with Him. But you must trust that you have been invited to experience the depths of Jesus Christ just as surely as you were invited to receive His salvation. Jesus prayed that we might be *one with Him, just as He is one with the Father."*[22] The whole purpose of this life is for us to enjoy the closest possible relationship with Jesus.

Consider where you have become spiritually sluggish. Jesus said, *"Come out from among them and be separate."*[23] Or are you so satisfied with your own experience that you want nothing more? It is dangerous to stop learning and growing in Him. Evaluate the stubbornness of your heart. Some would rather do anything than obey His command *"Come to Me."*[24] But a personal relationship with Him changes everything. Be willing to look foolish enough to come.

◆

You Set the Level

In your personal relationships, you are obviously closer to some people than others. You probably have a wide circle of family and friends, but you have an "inner circle" of closer friends and confidants. You share more with this small group than you would with everyone else. Do you think God treats us this same way?

God's Invitation to the Israelites

We see this pattern between God and the Israelites in Exodus 19-24. God wanted all the Israelites to consecrate themselves and gather at the foot of Mount Sinai for a very special event. Everyone was welcome to gather there, but no one was to go further up the mountain without specific invitation. On the third day, the Lord appeared in a thick cloud to all the people. Then He invited Moses, Aaron, and 70 of the elders to climb the mountain and eat a covenant meal with Him. They got to enjoy dinner in the presence of God! After the meal, Joshua and Moses were invited to climb up the mountain to an even higher level. Finally, Moses alone was invited to approach the Lord. There, God spoke with Moses *"as a man speaks with his friend."*[25]

Why would God let only some of the Israelites enjoy His presence for a meal, and then invite only Moses to meet with Him more closely? These levels of intimacy seem to correspond with *maturity* and *commitment*. Remember that the Israelites who were content to simply gather at the base of the mountain were the same ones that later pooled their jewelry to make a golden calf to worship. On the other hand, Moses and Joshua were both known for their courage, humility, and dedication to the Lord. Moses had personally sacrificed a life of luxury in Pharaoh's palace. He spent 40 years in the desert preparing for God to use him to set His people free. He took many risks to obey God in leading the Israelites out of Egypt. And we know that whenever Joshua wasn't serving Moses, he could be found praying in the tabernacle.[26] Sent ahead to spy on the Promised Land, Joshua was one of only two who came back with a good report that demonstrated great faith.[27] Eventually, God chose Joshua to replace Moses to lead the Israelites into their new homeland.

The Construction of God's Temple

It's interesting that God called for similar boundaries or levels of intimacy when His first temple was built. He provided Moses with clear instructions for how to create a place where He could dwell with the Israelites on earth saying, *"Make a sanctuary for me, and I will dwell among them."*[28] The specific layout of the tabernacle and its courtyard was significant because it illustrates God's prescribed way for man to approach Him. *"Make this tabernacle and all its furnishings exactly like the pattern I will show you."*[29]

In the outer court area, everyone was permitted to gather, worship, and make sacrifices to atone for their sins. But only priests were permitted to enter the "Holy Place," or inner court. Finally, the "Holy of Holies" was a place set apart for the Ark of the Covenant and mercy seat. Whoever entered into the Holy of Holies was entering the very presence of God. Only one high priest was permitted to enter this area once a year.

Thick curtains and veils separated the holy areas from the rest of the temple. The veil served as a barrier to make sure that no one carelessly and irreverently entered God's presence. Even when the high priest entered the Holy of Holies on the Day of Atonement, he had to meticulously prepare by washing himself, putting on special clothing, burning incense, and bringing a sacrifice to atone for sins.

It's clear there are some specific requirements for drawing near to such a holy God. While we all have direct access to God since the veil was torn,[30] His prescribed pattern calls for greater holiness, maturity, and commitment as we get closer and closer to His inner sanctuary.

Followers of Jesus

Jesus demonstrated the same pattern again in the New Testament. He enjoyed various levels of intimacy with the group that followed Him during His earthly ministry. Jesus allowed at least 70 people to travel with Him regularly.[31] And following His resurrection, we know that He took the time to personally appear to more than 500 followers.[32]

But from this larger group of followers, Jesus chose 12 disciples to share a deeper level of intimacy. They got to walk, talk, and eat with Him on a daily basis. Out of those 12, there were three (Peter, James, and John) that were allowed to experience several unique and special situations separate from the rest. But even among those three privileged disciples, only one was considered the *beloved* disciple. John described himself many times as the "one that Jesus loved." John felt comfortable enough to rest his head on

Jesus's chest at the Passover meal.[33] Perhaps to lay back against Him to breathe…and feel His heartbeat (as in the song at the start of this chapter).

Jesus loved them all, and they all loved Jesus, but some experienced Him more intimately than the rest. Today, not everyone is willing to pay the price to be close to Jesus. Not everyone is willing to commit the time to become a *beloved* disciple.

From the Shallows to the Depths

I love the ocean. Growing up in the center of the United States, I rarely had access to it. Now that I live near on the East coast, I go as often as I can. While spending long days at the beach, I have noticed that some people like to sit on the shore, basking in the sun. Others occasionally dip their toes in the water. Some study the scene cautiously and test the intensity of the water before venturing in, all the while holding the hand of another. And then there are those who dive straight into the crashing waves and enjoy the full refreshment and excitement of the adventure.

This parallels our own levels of intimacy with Jesus. The cautious ones who stay on the shore feel like they are still in charge. They are not willing to abandon themselves completely. It's true there are some real dangers in the ocean. I have been knocked around by a few big waves and seen others affected by riptides, not to mention the possibility of sharks, jellyfish, and stingrays in the water.

The roughest part of the ocean is right where the waves crash onto the shore. Once you get past that point, though, the depth of the ocean can be quite calm and peaceful. In our early walk with Jesus, it's not uncommon to encounter strong resistance from the enemy and those around us – just like trying to wade through those crashing waves. But continuing to pursue Him into the depths is very rewarding. You are not meant to remain on the safety of the shore forever. By "staying out" you are "missing out." It's time to dive in!

How Deep?

We determine what depth of God's presence we will experience in our lives by our degree of desire, commitment, and level of mature obedience to His instruction in our lives. You wouldn't put an immature infant in the crashing waves of the ocean. You don't share your deepest secrets with casual friends who haven't established that they are trustworthy with that personal information. In the same way, Jesus walked more closely with a select few while here on earth.

We see a consistent pattern throughout the Bible where everyone is welcome, but a few choose to go deeper and reach a higher level of spiritual maturity. I don't know about you, but I want to get as close to Jesus as I can! I want to become a *beloved disciple.*

———————◆———————

Choosing Discipleship

A disciple is someone willing to learn. At the time of Jesus, gifted teachers walked from town to town interpreting the Scriptures in the village synagogues. A term of respect for these teachers was *Rabbi.* It literally means "my master." The rabbi's goal was to raise up disciples who would later carry on his teaching. The Hebrew word for "disciple" is *talmidim,* meaning "one who is dedicated to learning a rabbi's understanding of Scripture and his way of living it out." Rabbis took on disciples who studied under their direction for years, traveling with them everywhere they went. Because the disciples traveled with their rabbi daily, lessons could be taught anywhere – in vineyards, marketplaces, or in open fields. The disciples would sit on the ground or on mats at the feet of the rabbi.[34]

The rabbi would serve as a living example of what it meant to apply God's word to everyday life. To follow a rabbi meant that the apprentice disciple would try to imitate their rabbi, learning not only from what he said but what he did. The task of the disciple was to become as much like the rabbi as possible. And given the amount of time spent together and the depth of issues discussed, the bond between a rabbi and his disciple would become very close.

One of the first recorded examples of the rabbi-disciple relationship is found in 1 Kings 19. Elijah, one of Israel's greatest prophets, called Elisha to become his disciple. The young man gave up a prosperous life to become Elijah's personal servant, traveling with him everywhere he went. He spent many years studying *from* Elijah, to become *like* Elijah. Through this prolonged intimate relationship with Elijah, Elisha was eventually able to carry on his ministry as a prophet to Israel.

Learning from Rabbi Jesus

The Bible makes it clear that this is the kind of relationship Jesus had with his own disciples. And as they walked and talked with Him, their hearts were transformed over time. The changes that Jesus worked in His disciple's lives did not come quickly or easily. There was no one-day "extreme makeover" that our culture has become accustomed to. Discipleship was a slow process of learning from the Rabbi. Even after walking with

Jesus for several years his disciples still messed up! But He never lost patience. He simply kept teaching and correcting them, allowing them time to grow.

As followers of Jesus, we are still called to be His disciples. And He works the same way in our lives. He wants us to mature through constant close connection with Him. Today, we sometimes confuse discipleship with "discipline." Both the vegan and the marathon runner exhibit tremendous discipline, but have they learned greater self-control or God-control? Of course, discipline is important in your spiritual life. But our goal for discipleship is not just to grow in self-discipline, but to be transformed into His likeness.

Discipleship requires personal, passionate devotion. Many who call themselves Christians today are not truly devoted to Jesus. To be a faithful follower requires complete commitment. Just like Elisha sacrificed everything to follow Elijah, most of Jesus' disciples dropped everything immediately to follow Him. Jesus reminded one hesitant potential disciple that *"No one who puts his hand to the plow and looks back is fit for service in the kingdom of God."*[35] Is there anything holding you back?

Discipleship has always been optional – *"If anyone would follow Me…"*[36] This is a deliberate choice and act of your will. It is not something that will happen accidentally. *"Choose for yourselves this day whom you will serve…"*[37] You will need to be in a daily, living relationship with Jesus as your Rabbi to become a beloved disciple. He doesn't expect perfection – just look at His first disciples! But He does expect you to sit at His feet so that you can learn how to live out His truth in your life.

In the Front Row

I have been teaching university students for more than 30 years. I always find it interesting which students choose to sit right in the front row and which prefer to sit as far in the back as possible. Everyone ends up hearing the same information, but the students in the front want to be right in the middle of the action – absorbing as much information and excitement as they can.

I found myself doing the same thing on a recent trip to Israel. In this case, I was the student looking for the front row seat! We had a fabulous tour guide named Erez. He was a believing Jew who could tell us all about the Jewish culture *and* about his Messiah. And though he had probably told the same stories hundreds of times, the excitement still poured out of him at every stop.

Erez talked all the time. The problem: the streets of Jerusalem are narrow. And the dusty paths in the mountains around the Sea of Galilee are narrow. You don't necessarily have to walk "single file", but you typically can't walk more than two abreast. So those who positioned themselves up close to him were going to hear more stories than the rest. You can be sure that's exactly where I wanted to be most of the time! I didn't want to miss a single detail.

I imagine that's how Peter, James, and John felt about their Rabbi. I'm guessing that as they walked all over Israel for those three years, they each followed Jesus as closely as they could. When He stopped to tell a parable, they probably put their mats down right at His feet. This would have set them apart from the other disciples. On the narrow paths, perhaps John jockeyed for the spot where he could hang onto every word. This would have allowed him to absorb every detail and not miss an opportunity to learn from the Master. As a student of your Rabbi Jesus, where will you position yourself?

John the Beloved Example

It is a joy to Jesus when a disciple desires to walk more intimately with Him. Describing himself as the "disciple whom Jesus loved,"[38] John provides us an example of what their intimate relationship looked like:

- He was among those first called to follow Jesus.[39]
- When Jesus called, John immediately dropped everything and followed.[40]
- He was included in the "inner circle" that got to witness special events like the Transfiguration[41] and the resurrection of Jairus' daughter.[42]
- He and Peter were given the responsibility to prepare the final Passover meal for Jesus.[43]
- John leaned His head on Jesus' chest during the Passover meal.[33]
- He was among the small group invited to pray with Jesus in the Garden of Gethsemane before His arrest.[44]
- Of the 12 disciples, only John stayed with Jesus for the entire crucifixion.[45]
- Jesus assigned John to care for His mother, Mary, after He was gone.[45]
- John wrote the Gospel that most people consider their favorite. He had more to say about the concept of love than anyone else in the New Testament, using the word more than 80 times.
- He was the only disciple spared a martyr's death.
- John was given the capstone ending, the grand finale, of the Bible – the Revelation of Jesus Christ.

Was John beloved because he was perfect? No – in fact, he has been described by various commentators as volatile, rash, aggressive, and overly ambitious. He argued with the other disciples over who was the greatest and asked Jesus for a special position in heaven.[46] His nickname was Son of Thunder…did he have a temper?[47] He once rebuked a man for casting out demons in Jesus' name without being a disciple[48]– did he prefer to keep such power to himself? He showed no mercy toward the Samaritans, suggesting that Jesus should burn them all up.[49] He fell asleep when Jesus asked him to pray the night before His death.[50] He still had some maturing to do…don't we all?

Fortunately, even with our own flaws, we can experience the very same intimate relationship with Jesus that John did. In fact, John says he wrote the Gospel for that very purpose! He said, *"We saw it, we heard it, and now we're telling you **so you can experience it along with us**, this experience of communion with the Father and His Son, Jesus Christ."*[51]

◆

That You May Know Him

Thankfully, many receive, but some receive more abundantly than others. I want to experience the same deep affection that Jesus and John shared. I want the relationship that God and David had. I want to feel as passionately about Jesus as Paul did. Jesus became their whole world! Anything less is just a dry old religion.

> *"What we need is a **zealous hunger** for God, an **avid thirst** for righteousness, a **pain-filled longing** to be Christ-like and holy. We need a zeal that is loving, self-effacing, and lowly. **No other kind will do.**"*
>
> A.W. Tozer

Jesus desires for you to be His beloved disciple, not just an ordinary one. Beloved means "something or someone counted precious; highly valued, rare and unique." This study is meant to show you how to experience a deeper and more precious relationship with Him.

The Conditions of Discipleship

In this study, ten steps have been laid out to guide you. They are progressive forward movements into a deeper relationship with Jesus. They involve reaching for more than you have already grasped. *"**Add** to your faith"*[52] means that you will likely be asked to do some new things you haven't done before. No matter where you are in your walk with Jesus, there is always room to grow. Paul said, *"Not that I have already attained, or am already perfected; but I press on..."*[53]

It is significant that John, who knew Jesus more intimately than most anyone else, still *"fell at His feet as though dead"*[54] when He appeared to him again on the island of Patmos. Remember John had already seen what the transfigured Christ looked like once before.[41] You may already know Jesus well, but I am convinced He will astound you in fresh, new ways!

While the prospect of ten steps may seem daunting, keep in mind that attaining excellence at anything worthwhile in this life is difficult. And if it's a goal worth achieving in your worldly affairs, the difficulty does not make you want to give up. Rather, it sharpens your focus with renewed energy and resolve.

The desirability of the end result will be sufficient to sustain you. You just need perseverance. The joy and peace of fellowship with Him will fill your life more and more. Sooner than you think, you will become convinced of His goodness, His love toward you, and His desire to reveal Himself to you – there are so many great things in store!

An All-Consuming Passion

Regardless of how superficial your Christian life has been up to now; you can experience the intimacy with Jesus that John did. You've seen that there are various levels to all relationships. How deep into the ocean are you willing to go? How far up the mountain do you want to climb? Do you want to sit at the feet of Jesus and drink from the cup in His hand? Don't settle for an ordinary journey through life.

It will require **diligent** seeking with **all** your heart. You take the time to do things that are important to you. You keep your appointments to visit the doctor, pick up your kids, and get a massage or a manicure. Do you keep your "appointments" with Him? If you say you don't have time to pursue Jesus, what else are you doing that is so important? You will have to fight distractions and *decide to protect the time* for fellowship with Jesus. If He truly is the most important thing in your life, He must have a place of priority in your schedule.

In the process of becoming a beloved disciple, you will be asked to give up other things to deepen your relationship with Him. In fact, the first three steps are all about yielding your heart more fully to Him. He may need to prune some things out of your life to make room. You might be asked to give up what you hold in one hand to embrace God's will in the other. Anything that causes you to lose your "first love" will threaten your relationship with Him.

Decide now to follow Christ, no matter the cost. Jesus said it would be worth giving up everything you have to gain entrance to His Kingdom. In fact, that is exactly what He demands.[55] You will need to deny yourself and yield everything to His Lordship to become a beloved disciple – but the benefits are well worth the cost. There is no bond on earth that compares to friendship with Him.

To Be All You're Called to Be

Remember His ultimate goal is to produce disciples that look like Him. Jesus said to His first disciples, *"Come, follow Me, and **I will make you...**"*[56] He will do the work. You don't produce the results – He does. It's more about *being* with Him than *doing* for Him. It's not about attending more conferences or taking more sermon notes. Well organized programs, tools, and books are valuable, but they cannot take the place of personal encounters with Him.

It's more about yielding; less about striving. It's about integrating Him into every part of your life. John 5:39–40 says, *"You diligently study the Scriptures because you think that by them you possess eternal life. These are the Scriptures that testify about Me, yet you refuse to **come to Me to have life**."*

Let Him know that you are seeking more in your relationship with Him; that you want to know more about Him. He will decide how and when to manifest His presence in your life. He deals with each of us in an individual and unique way – your relationship will not look the same as mine. I have never seen a burning bush like Moses or chariots of fire like Elijah, but I have been overwhelmed! I haven't seen physical walls come tumbling down as in Jericho, but my emotional walls have come down. I didn't confront Goliath with a stone, but I have learned to slay giant fears in my mind.

Stay patient. He is in control. He wants this more for you than you want it for yourself!

So I say to you, ask and keep on asking and it shall be given you;
seek and keep on seeking and you shall find;
knock and keep on knocking and the door shall be opened to you.
For everyone who asks and keeps on asking receives;
and he who seeks and keeps on seeking finds;
and to him who knocks and keeps on knocking, the door shall be opened.[57]

---◆---

Prayer

Jesus, touch me with fresh faith so I can experience You in new ways. Awaken dead parts of my heart so that I can more fully recognize the depth of Your love. I repent for pretending to be more spiritual than I am. Holy Spirit, intercede so that I will not drift aimlessly through this life. Lord, You say that You will spit out the "lukewarm" from Your mouth someday. I don't want to be lukewarm! I desire the passionate fire of God inside me. Fan the flame within me! Teach my heart what that looks like; feels like. Intensify my hunger and fire my devotion. Take away any indifference from my spirit. Fill up all that is lacking in me.

I want to be found in the Holy of Holies. I want my life to be lived at Your feet, drinking regularly from the cup in Your hand. I want to put my ear to Your chest and hear Your heartbeat. I want to rest against You, breathe You in, and experience Your overwhelming peace.

I am sorry for wandering away from You — for pursuing the riches of this world. They did not satisfy me. I want to be like Your first disciples who saw something about You that made them want to drop everything and follow You everywhere. There is no life apart from You. Pursue me when I fail to pursue You. Lift my head and turn my gaze back to You. Keep idols out of my heart and distractions out of my mind. Let me hear Your voice above all other noises demanding attention in my life. Capture my heart completely and make my affections be only for You.

You hold the world in the palm of Your hand, yet You see when a sparrow falls. The sparrows that You watch and the lilies that You clothe point to Your compassionate and personal care. You are Holy, Holy, Holy and the Maker of heaven and earth, yet Your ear is attentive to my call. I want to fully grasp that You love me…individually and uniquely. Everything I do matters to You. Guide my steps. Light my path. Show me how You are shaping my life.

I want to see the real You — not someone else's version of You. Open my eyes to see You more clearly. I will seek You with all my heart and soul. I dedicate myself to You. Refine me. Set me apart. Speak Your truth over me and into my life. Anoint my head with oil. Fill my cup until it overflows. Mold me, shape me, fashion me into Your likeness. Keep me teachable and trainable. Help Your Word and truth to fall on fertile soil in my heart. Soften my heart. Heal my soul. Your love washes over me, and I am renewed. I am Your beloved.

STUDY

1. In what way(s) are you currently "going through the motions" of a Christian life?

"I know your deeds, that you are neither cold nor hot. I wish you were either one or the other! So, because you are lukewarm--neither hot nor cold--I am about to spit you out of my mouth."

Revelation 3:15-16

---

2. What are some characteristics of "lukewarm" Christianity? Why is it so dissatisfying?

3. There is Christianity, and then there is Christian culture. Loving the church is not the same thing as loving Jesus. How would you distinguish the two?

4. The Pharisees loved religious culture—the public prayers, the fancy robes, the honor bestowed on them for their powerful position. But they hated Jesus. How can religion become a stumbling block to a dynamic, thriving, growing relationship with Jesus?

5. Can you describe your relationship with Jesus as *real* and *personal?* Why or why not?

He is Calling

6. What does it mean to *stray* from God? Why are we "prone to wander?"

7. Read John 6:44, 65 and John 15:16, 19. Why is it important to know that you have been specifically and individually *chosen* by Him?

8. John 14:21 says *"He who loves me will be loved by my Father, and I too will love him and show myself to him."* How does Jesus "show" Himself to you?

Seek and You Will Find

9. Hebrews 11:6 say that God *"rewards those who earnestly seek Him."* What does <u>earnestly</u> seeking look like?

10. What are some of the rewards you have already received through seeking Him?

11. What are the greatest obstacles to diligently seeking Him?

Intimate with Jesus

12. Do you know Christians who seem to have something you don't? What makes them different?

13. What are the best parts of being close to Jesus? What things draw you closer?

14. What do you miss most when you're not as close? What things pull you away from Him?

15. How is intimacy with Jesus different than striving to become "good enough" to please Him?

Choosing Discipleship

16. Why is it important to recognize Jesus as a Jewish Rabbi?

17. What do you think the early disciples saw in Jesus that made them want to immediately follow Him? What kept them committed to His leadership?

18. Discipleship under Rabbi Jesus involved gradual change over a period of many years. How have you changed and matured as a disciple of Christ over the past few years?

You Set the Level

19. Describe Peter's reaction to seeing Jesus in John 21:7. What are some possible consequences for those who never express their emotions to Jesus like that?

> *Jesus replied, "If anyone loves me, he will obey my teaching. My Father will love him, and we will come to him and make our home with him."*
>
> John 14:23

20. What kind of "home" are you inviting God into? Are there areas of your life that are off-limits?

To Be All You're Called to Be

21. A spiritual marker represents a new transition, decision, or direction guided by God. When significant transformation has taken place, it can be helpful to identify a spiritual marker at that point. Over time you can look back at the spiritual markers and see how God has faithfully guided you. What are some significant spiritual markers in your life?

22. What further transformations do you long for?

WORSHIP

The More I Seek You [Kari Jobe]

Oh Draw Me Lord [Selah]

In Over My Head [Bethel Music featuring Jenn Johnson]

Come to Me [Bethel Music featuring Jenn Johnson]

Oceans [Hillsong United]

Jesus, I Come [Elevation Worship]

With Lifted Hands [Ryan Stevenson]

The Motions [Matthew West]

I Say Yes [Kim Walker-Smith]

I Knew What I Was Getting Into [Misty Edwards]

Overwhelmed [Big Daddy Weave]

Living Hope [Phil Wickham]

Run to the Father [Cody Carnes]

O Come to the Altar [Elevation]

So You Would Come [Darlene Zschech]

ASK & IT WILL BE GIVEN TO YOU
SEEK & YOU WILL FIND
KNOCK & IT WILL BE OPENED TO YOU

MATTHEW 7:7

SURRENDER TO HIM

"Yield yourself to God… Surrender your whole being to be used for righteous purposes."[1]

Surrender is an essential part of becoming a beloved disciple. Jesus said, *"If anyone would come after Me, he must **deny himself** and take up his cross daily and follow Me."*[2] Dying to self means everything but Him is stripped away. God becomes all; you are nothing. Now this sounds unpleasant…

It is only by dying to self that He begins to truly live in you! *"For you have died, and your life is now hidden with Christ in God."*[3] And is it really "dying" when a caterpillar is transformed into a butterfly?

You surrender your whole being to Jesus and cease to live for yourself, so that He can become your All in All. He promised *"every spiritual blessing in the heavenly realms,"*[4] and to *"supply all your needs according to His riches in glory."*[5] He said, *"Open wide your mouth and I will fill it."*[6] He simply can't resist those who humbly confess how desperately they need Him.

Of course, this is optional. You have the privilege of *voluntarily* cooperating as He draws you deeper to Himself. The closer you are drawn to Jesus, the more you will be separated from your natural self. Your natural self will be opposed to this – so the struggle for control arises immediately. It requires a **continual choice** to surrender.

Bottom line: you can't have more of Him until there is less of you. So, right at the beginning of your commitment to this journey, you are put to the test. What will this look like in your life? In this unit, the first three steps in becoming a beloved disciple require laying down:

> your life through surrender,
> your heart through trials, and
> your rights through forgiveness.

Self de-throned. That is the process. Are you ready to get started?

YOUR LIFE IS NOT YOUR OWN

G od wants you to fully recognize His claim of ownership of you. *"The Lord has made everything for His own purposes."*[1] You are *"not your own... your body is the temple of the Holy Spirit."*[2] You were *"bought at a price."*[3] Acts 20:28 clarifies that Christ purchased more than our salvation on the cross; He purchased *us*. And Isaiah 43:1 says, *"I have called you by name, you are mine."*

In return for all He has done, you want to pour out your life as an offering. But the one and only thing you can truly give back to God is your right to yourself.[4] You don't really own anything else – it all came from Him and belongs to Him. Your income... He gave it to you. Your gifts and talents...He supplied them. Your house and clothes and food...He provided it all.

Job reminded us that *"Naked I came from my mother's womb, and naked I will depart."*[5] Anything He allows us to enjoy in between is just a bonus! The sooner you wrap your head around that concept, the sooner you can start to loosen your grip. You hold what He provides with open hands.

Laying It Down

You may feel you have already surrendered your life – after all, you're a Christian, right? When you became a Christian, you confessed that you believed in the Lord Jesus Christ as your Savior. Now He wants your life – *all of it*.

Salvation and Surrender

For missionary George Mueller, *salvation* was a separate decision from *surrender*. In a sermon given shortly after his 90th birthday, he said, "I was converted in 1825, but I only came to the *full surrender of the heart* four years later, in 1829. The love of money was gone, the love of place was gone, the love of position was gone, the love of worldly pleasures and engagements was gone. God, and God alone, became my portion. I found my all in all in Him; **I wanted nothing else.**"[6]

In salvation, you receive *His* life. In surrender, you give Him *yours*. Salvation is a gift; given instantly when you choose to believe. It will cost you nothing. But discipleship is a life-long process of giving yourself to Jesus. It will cost you everything. The scriptures that say, *"deny yourself,"* *"take up your cross,"* and *"hate your own life"*[7] all require a realignment of your priorities. It's no longer about you; it's all about Him. It is submission to Jesus no matter the risk or consequence. You tell Jesus that He can take your life and do with it whatever He wants.

Jesus came into this world to die. You are also called to die – to your sinful nature, your selfishness, and your pride. In saying, *"I am crucified with Christ..."*[8] you crucify your right to yourself, your demands for pleasure, even your tendency toward self-pity and self-righteousness.

Most believers have some idea of what it means to surrender but have never truly experienced it. You may have been a Christian for a long time, but is He really on the throne of your life?

Surrendering All

Some have what Oswald Chambers called "spiritual measles."[9] They look fine in the places where pride, self-sufficiency, and self-interest have been erased. When they are in a spiritual mood, everyone would think they are the highest quality saint. But don't dare let anyone see their spots!

Handing over parts of your life is not enough. He is asking you to abandon your *whole existence,* giving it up to God. Complete surrender means allowing Him access to "every room in the house." He doesn't want to be merely a guest or contained in a small closet. He wants to invade all of it! Upon your invitation, He will come in and take over more and more territory until all your life is completely His. You will soon find Him in areas where He had not previously been welcome. You will realize that some things are going to have to change. He may disrupt your reputation, identity, location, relationships, and finances. It can be exciting, but a little scary at the same time.

What will He ask you to lay down or surrender? I recently abandoned a lucrative business partnership without a clear idea of what I would be doing next. One of my friends put their house on the market without knowing where her family would be going next. Others quit their jobs without knowing what they were going to do next. Why? Because we all believed that is what He was asking us to lay down at the time. Yes, forfeiting security to go *wherever* for *whatever* seems crazy. And walking these things through was a tremendous test of faith for those involved. Sometimes directions about the "next thing" didn't come until the last minute, the 11th hour, or just before a deadline.

You might think you have surrendered all your life to Him, but there may be areas you aren't even aware of yet. You can only yield as much as you comprehend now. As you start to let go of one thing, He will show you what you need to surrender next. If you obey Him in the first thing He shows you, He will open the next truth to you. He won't reveal more until you have obeyed what you already know.

Where might you be insisting on your own way? Start to allow Him into the deep, hidden areas of your life. As you open the door, He will slowly reveal any misplaced affections and desires. You may be surprised at the things He will expose. Where have you been deceiving yourself?

"The blessed ones who possess the Kingdom are those who have rooted from their hearts all sense of possessing. These 'poor in spirit' are no longer slaves to the tyranny of things. They have broken the yoke of the oppressor; and this they have done not by fighting but by surrendering."

A.W. Tozer

An Unpopular Position

In *Experiencing the Depths of Jesus Christ*, Jeanne Guyon proclaimed that **abandonment** is *"of greatest importance in making progress in knowing the Lord."* She was imprisoned for her opinion in the 1600's. Sadly, I don't think this message is much more popular today.

Church pews are filled on Sunday mornings with people who want to hear about prosperity and blessings, not dying to self. There are plenty of popular preachers who promote the notion that God is some sort of indulgent genie waiting to grant our every wish. There certainly are promised blessings in store, but not necessarily material ones; and they don't come with a guarantee of fulfillment in our lifetime. Any teaching that fails to present the Christian life as a way of sacrifice, surrender, and submission is deceptive.

We tend to avoid teachings about sacrifice and dying to self. There is a price to be paid, and for some it is greater than others. If you want to become a beloved disciple, you need to be totally sold out to Christ, to serve Him at any cost, even to death. This is a measure of the depth of your commitment. Paul said, *"To me the only important thing about living is Christ; dying would also be profit for me!"*[10] Peter said to his Lord, *"I will lay down my life for You."*[11] Many beloved disciples have laid down their lives as martyrs. Are you capable of making the same sacrifice that they did?

You are on a quest to know Him and become more like Him. The gospel message is that Jesus laid down His life for us, and the subsequent challenge is that we also lay down our lives for Him. *"He died for all, that those who live should no longer live for themselves but for Him who died for them."*[12] Anyone who claims to be His disciple must live as He lived, and He lived with the spirit of humility. "Take up your cross" implies there will be some suffering involved. This shatters the safe, comfortable way we prefer to live. It is at this point that many turn back, saying *"Lord, I will follow you, **but**...*"[13]

You started this book because you wanted to become a beloved disciple...set apart... one of the few. Remember the narrow gate? Do you love Him enough to let go of all your plans, hopes, and dreams? If you are to be a disciple of Jesus, you must truly lay down your life for Him.

"I leave to You the ordering of my whole life, and with Your help will follow wherever You lead. I submit my whole being, all that I am, all that I have, and all that I will be to Your complete control. I only ask that Your will be perfectly done in me, through me, and by me."

Hannah Whitall Smith

Who Will Be in Control?

Surrender did not come naturally to me. As a former Type A perfectionist, I can be quite an ambitious organizer and planner. And I prefer to schedule things far in advance so that I know exactly what will happen when, where, why, and how. For me, surrender meant tearing up every itinerary I had created for my journey through life. Now I wait and see what He is doing, rather than planning on my own first. I don't know what I will be doing a year from now, 5 years from now, or 10 years from now. At this point, there is no particular way my life has to look.

You must make a similar choice. Who are you going to live for – yourself or God? There will be times when your plans will conflict with His. Who will win? Are you willing to move? Change your career? Postpone starting a family? Not have a family at all?

Most of us don't even realize how attached we are to our own agenda. If you are interested in accomplishing your own goals, Jesus cannot help Himself to your life at any time. When you are completely abandoned, you have no goals of your own to attain. *"Submit yourself to God"*[14] means giving Him the driver's seat and taking your hands off the steering wheel. Not even any recommendations from the back seat!

You don't throw your life away, but you *willingly* lay it down for Him and His purposes. Surrender does not mean that you become a doormat, stop using the mind He gave you, or suppress your personality. He made each of us unique for a reason. C. S. Lewis said, *"The more we let God take us over, the more truly ourselves we become – because He made us."* Your individuality remains, but your primary motivation for living is radically altered.

Try to put yourself in a *surrendered state of mind*. You are the clay, not the Potter. You are the disciple, not the Rabbi. You are the sheep, not the Shepherd. It doesn't mean you never put anything on your calendar again. But you join with Him in planning, instead of doing it solo. You are willing to change your plans if He asks. You take small steps and check in with Him at every moment. You are flexible and adaptable to His leading. You don't dig in your heels and cling to your own way. You become more dependent on Him for everything.

Divine Dependence

I teach psychology classes at a university. Those of you who have taken a basic psychology course may remember a concept called **locus of control.** This is how much people believe they have power or control over their own lives. With a short personality test, you get categorized as having an *internal* or *external* locus of control.

Internals believe they have control over the events in their own lives. Internals are described as the strong, healthy ones – the "winners" in life. They are resilient problem solvers. When confronted with a challenge, they find a way to work around it. Externals are viewed as weak because they do not depend on their own strength. They believe outside forces control their outcomes. They feel helpless and hopeless when confronted with life's obstacles.

This popular concept has been around since the 1950's when it was introduced by

Julian Rotter. The underlying question is this…do you control your life or does someone/something else control it? Of course, most of the psychological research suggests that it is healthier to be responsible for your own success and control your own outcomes. Our society encourages an internal locus of control. The theory doesn't know what to do with intelligent and successful individuals who willingly place their trust in God to take over.

For many years, I took great pride in viewing myself as an "internal." Self-reliant and independent. So it went against everything in me to relinquish total control to somebody I couldn't see. It felt foreign to allow someone else to be completely responsible for me and my life.

People who are self-sufficient believe it is a sign of weakness to depend on God. As humans with free will, we like to be in charge. The oldest temptation since the Garden of Eden is to be in control; to be *"like God."*[15] To become a beloved disciple, you must break your independence and surrender your life to Jesus. No one can do this for you, you must choose it yourself. Are you willing to suffer the humiliation of being completely dependent on Him?

A Crisis of the Will

Surrender and submission tend to be negative words in our society. They imply defeat. In our competitive and individualistic culture, we prefer words like success, winning, and victory. We are taught to never give up and never give in. The thought of yielding and submitting makes us uncomfortable.

The surrender of your will is the *greatest crisis* you will ever face. Many want to surrender, but on their own terms. Many rise to the call to *"deny yourself and take up your cross"* emotionally, but don't demonstrate it with a corresponding change in their will and way of life. A.W. Tozer called this a *"waste of emotion."*

Where you are not fully surrendered to God, you are surrendered to something else – to the approval of others, the love of money, fear, or your own ego. Self-preservation is what keeps you from surrendering, although you rationalize it with all forms of other excuses. When you start to seriously consider what it will cost if you obey the call of Jesus, you bargain with God or tell Him that He just doesn't understand. But He does. Shut out every other thought and get determined to be entirely His and His alone. The Holy Spirit will keep bringing you back to the same point over and over again until you do.

Completely surrendering means saying, "I am willing, with a sound mind, to give up control of my own life. I want God to fully possess me and accomplish all that

He desires within me." Romans 12:1 describes surrender as your *"reasonable service."* Another version translates it the *"most intelligent way"* to serve God. The most rational, responsible, and sensible thing you can do with your life is to let go and let God work.

---

*"The reason why many are still troubled, still seeking, still making little forward progress is **because they haven't yet come to the end of themselves**. We're still trying to give orders and interfering with God's work within us."*

A.W. Tozer

Letting Go

Surrender involves letting go. It's more about *getting rid of* than *getting.* You must let go before you can take hold of something else. It will cost you everything that is not of God. Paul said, *"I consider everything a loss compared to the surpassing greatness of knowing Christ Jesus my Lord."*[16]

God needs to purify you of anything that is not of Him. Many of us are emotionally attached to possessions and relationships – our homes, children, spouse, friends, pets, and jobs. All of this hinders your attachment to Jesus. He will need you to break your allegiance to any other person or thing. The cost will not be just one or two small things, but everything. *"Anyone who holds on to life just as it is destroys that life. **But if you let it go**, you'll have it forever, real and eternal."*[17] It's not that you no longer possess anything, but no earthly thing possesses you.

Maybe He has already pointed out certain plans, desires, or relationships – asking you to yield them. Those who are in Christ *"crucify the flesh with all its passions and desires."*[18] You will be asked to rid yourself of everything that might be considered a possession until you are an empty vessel standing before Him.

Obviously, this is a sacrifice. It could even be called a crucifixion. *"For I have been crucified with Christ, it is no longer I who live…"*[8] You renounce possessions of all kinds, not for your salvation, but to strengthen your commitment to Jesus. Without this step, you'll live a divided life. Your flesh will continue to resist and defy the work of the Holy Spirit in you, producing turmoil. Once you are willing to sacrifice it, the Holy

Spirit will go to work immediately and your real life, the spiritual life, will have the opportunity to grow.

How do you begin? Start to loosen your grip on every other person and every other thing. Lay down every idea of what you think is best for your life. Drop every preconceived need. Give up sinful desires and habits. Forget yourself until you can stand in complete indifference to yourself and your own life. This won't happen overnight – it's a gradual process.

Life in the Spirit

The surrendered life is difficult, and it doesn't get easier with time. In John 16:7, Jesus said that when He went away, He would send a *Helper*. This shows that He knew we would need help! The strain of sacrifice that He demands of you will be impossible without the supernatural help of the Holy Spirit.

In Acts 1:4-8, Jesus told His disciples to wait until they received the power of the Holy Spirit before going out as His witnesses. He knew they would need more than their own effort and enthusiasm to fulfill this responsibility. Even after being personally trained by the Master, they were still missing something. If those disciples needed the Holy Spirit to fulfill their mission, how much more do we need Him? They were told not to make a move until they experienced His presence and power in their lives. How naive we are to rush into our day without giving Him a thought. No wonder our lives can be so frustrating!

The Holy Spirit has been provided to teach,[19] guide,[20] direct,[21] warn,[22] convict,[23] and intercede.[24] You are supposed to be led by the Spirit.[25] As part of the Trinity, the Holy Spirit knows the thoughts of God[26] and guides each of us to the truth.[27] We are told that the Spirit of God dwells in us.[28] In other words, He makes His home in you.

But the Holy Spirit is polite – He will wait for an invitation to intervene in your life. James 1:5-6 says, *"If any of you lacks wisdom, ask God what you should do."* All too often we don't get any help because we don't ask for any. *"In all your ways acknowledge Him, and He will direct your paths."*[29] If you ask to be guided, He will show you the next step. That doesn't mean He will always lay out the whole map. You will have to get comfortable with some uncertainty and ambiguity. He doesn't promise to explain His plan in advance; He just promised He has one. You can be uncertain of your future and certain of God at the same time.

His plan is to bring you to the end of yourself – the point of desperation for His help! He will often engineer your circumstances so that you find yourself with nowhere to turn but to Him. When you finally stop depending on yourself, you receive the help of the Holy Spirit. Instead of trying harder, you begin to trust. Surrender means you voluntarily put yourself under the guidance of the Holy Spirit. In Ephesians 5:18, Paul calls for total surrender to the gentle – yet firm – promptings of the Holy Spirit. And the more you empty yourself of other things, the more the Holy Spirit can fill your life.

Growing in love for Jesus is a lifelong process that can't be achieved through self-effort. You've got to learn how to cooperate with the Holy Spirit. If you are willing to submit to the Holy Spirit, you will become increasingly sensitive to His direction in your life. The Holy Spirit is meant to be your moral compass and personal guide. *"Walk by the Spirit, and you will not carry out the desires of the flesh."*[30] You will be given help to avoid those things which you have no business getting involved in. When you are doing what He likes, you will sense a "green light" from Him (peace in your spirit). When you are going in the wrong direction, you will sense a "red light" (a warning, check in your spirit). If you should pause and wait, you may sense a "caution signal" (some tension, restlessness, or indecisiveness). The more you stop and ask God for directions, the more attuned you will become to these signals from the Holy Spirit.

He doesn't yell for your attention; He leads with gentle whispers and subtle nudges. Romans 7:6 explains that we should operate *"under obedience to the Spirit."* His promptings will feel like a gentle check, a subtle restraint, or a still, small voice. Learning to be led by the Holy Spirit is much like a baby learning to walk. You will likely fall down at times and are bound to make a few mistakes. But He will always help you get back up and on the right track.

Led by the Spirit

How do you practice this? You practice it daily, hourly, and moment-by-moment. You don't proceed to do *anything* until you surrender your own agenda and ask Him about it. As you enter your closet in the morning to get dressed, ask Him what He would like you to wear that day. Seek His counsel about which errands to run and what time they should be accomplished. As you're driving, seek His advice about which route to take. Ask Him what is best for you to eat and drink that day. Stop and ask Him before you accept a new work assignment. When shopping, ask Him what you should purchase. Instead of automatically sitting in the same seat on Sunday morning at church, ask Him where you should sit.

Why? So that you are always in the right place at the right time for His divine appointments (or interruptions). He can have you exactly where He needs you at all times. You may be prompted to pray with someone in line at the grocery store. You might hear the Holy Spirit urge you to bring an extra coat along that day because you will find someone that needs it. You may take a road you don't normally travel only to find someone that needs help. You may have the exact amount of money in your pocket that you need to share with someone else. You will miss out if you don't listen carefully!

I recently invited Him to decorate my house. Why wouldn't He enjoy it? This is the same One who created beautiful flowers, trees, and animals all around us! I trusted that He could do a much better job than me. And when I was listening carefully, I would be led to a specific store where I would happen to find the perfect chair, in the perfect color, in the perfect shape, at the perfect price (on sale). I also recently invited him to choose a new pet for us. And, of course, we now have the perfect dog! As trivial as these examples might seem, I think He enjoys it when we ask for His help.

For most Christians, this will seem like a foreign way to live. We typically seek His help in the "big" decisions of life – who to marry or what job to take. But most people are not accustomed to such *constant* dependence on Him. That seems… needy. Many will not humble themselves to admit that level of need. But the sooner you admit that *"apart from Him you can do nothing,"*[31] the better off you are.

Surrender is *continually* submitting your own will to the will of God. Get into the habit of continually seeking His counsel on everything, instead of making your own decision and then asking Him to bless it. He wants to instruct you in even the smallest details of life. It is a prideful, arrogant person who thinks they know what to do in every situation. Jesus maintained an inner vigilance to submit His Spirit continually to the Father. You also have the responsibility to keep your spirit in agreement with His Spirit. You must depend on Him for everything – literally *everything*.

The Only Way to Truly Live

This way of life brings you to a turning point – a decision about whether you will continue to go your own way or abandon yourself and see what He has planned for your life. You call Him your "Teacher and Lord,"[32] but *is* He?

Remember that He always prefaced discipleship with *'If,'* meaning, "you do not need to do this unless you want to." *"If anyone desires to come after Me, let him deny himself."*[33] Jesus is not talking about your eternal salvation, but the depth of your relationship in this life, here and now. In other words, to become a beloved disciple, you give up your right to yourself. If you love Him, you will do what He asks without hesitation. If you hesitate, it is because you love something more that you have placed in competition with Him. He doesn't want you picking and choosing the ways and places you're willing to follow Him. He wants full access to your life.

God will not demand your surrender or force you into submission. He will not push

His way into your life or your daily affairs. He will not insist on having authority over you. He will stress very definitely what you *ought* to do, but He will never *force* you to do it. He wants you to want to surrender. He waits to be wanted. He will leave you free to choose.

He didn't beg and plead the rich young ruler to follow Him. He simply said, *"Sell all you have and come..."*[34] The man went away discouraged because he knew exactly what Jesus meant. He had come to Jesus on fire – with such enthusiasm and determination. But the strict command froze him in his tracks. That was asking too much. Jesus did not chase after him but let him go. He won't try to force you either. He will simply repeat His words, saying, "If you really want to be My disciple, these are the conditions."

When Fear Gets in the Way

I remember feeling afraid at the thought of total surrender. *What exactly will He ask? What will have to change in my life?* It felt like jumping off a cliff. I liked my independence. I liked my own ideas and plans. I liked my relationships just as they were. God would be making all the choices now – what if I didn't like some of them? Giving up control was going to be out of my comfort zone. I wavered. I had to **decide** to trust Him.

For most of us, it is frightening to feel out of control and in the hands of another. When you truly start to surrender, expect some uncertainty, instability, and insecurity. Some things may even be painful. At times, the fear may be so intense it feels like it will cripple you and you will wonder if you can continue. But His perfect love casts out fear.[35] The more you understand how much He loves you; the easier surrender will become. Remember, He *"first"* loved you.[36] When you become convinced that God really loves you, then it is "safe" to allow Him to lead.

There is a risk that He may ask something of you that will be very difficult. You can't see the better things He has in store, so you shrink back and your courage dissolves. Push through the fear. Keep going anyway. Do it afraid. The risk of *not* surrendering would be disappointing Him and missing out on His blessings for you. At the end of your life, don't you want to be sure that you gave Him your *all?*

He is Trustworthy

You can trust the One who died for you. He is good. You are committing yourself to the omnipotent Maker of heaven and earth. He is good. He is both a compassionate Father and Mighty Warrior. He is good. He is the Way, the Truth, and the Life. He is what you need. He is the Good Shepherd. The same God of Abraham, Isaac, Jacob, Moses, David, Mary, John, and Paul is now your Lord. And He is just as holy, powerful, and present today as He was then. Start trusting Him! *"The one who trusts in Him will never be put to shame."*[37]

One of the biggest mistakes of your life would be to choose your own way and miss His plans for you. When you choose to walk with God, you will find His perfect will for your life. *"I will give your life to you as a prize…in all places, wherever you go."*[38] You can trust Him to lead you in the path that is the very best for you. Psalm 32:8 says, *"I will guide you along the best pathway for your life. I will advise you and watch over you."* He has plans to give you *"hope and a future."*[39] Yes, God calls you to surrender your own will, but Romans 12:2 points out that God's will is good, pleasing, and perfectly suited for you.

There have been many times I have had two options in front of me. One of those options made more sense to me, logically. It was easier, safer, and in my "comfort zone." But I just knew that He was asking me to take the other option. Initially there was nothing about that path that looked attractive to me. But I would start down it, with faltering steps and a million questions. Of course, when all was said and done, it turned out to be the better choice.

He always provides reassurance along the way. He knows how frail we are and wants to comfort us. It's no accident that He chose to call us sheep – one of the most skittish, timid, and helpless animals on the planet. He wants to prove Himself faithful and uphold His reputation as the Good Shepherd. As you begin to bravely place your life in His hands, He will reassure you in a unique and personal way. I have heard people describe their forms of reassurance as "God-winks," "kisses from heaven," or "sweet signs and wonders." Each one builds your faith and provides a much-needed reminder that He is in control.

During a difficult transition in my life where I was being asked to surrender some significant things, He gave me butterflies. Literally, everywhere! I would see butterfly products in every store I entered. I would see butterfly displays on every wall. I would go outside, and butterflies would dance around me. It had never been like that before and hasn't been since. Throughout that summer, He revealed to me that I would no longer be anchored to this world (like a caterpillar), I would be leaving the safety of my cocoon, and something more beautiful was on its way. During that season, I needed that personal and constant confirmation.

In John 14:21, Jesus promised that He would **reveal Himself** to those who love Him. He does this to prove Himself, increase our faith, and encourage future belief. Don't look for Him to come in a certain way but *do look for Him.* Let Him decide what sweet signs and wonders will be unique to you. When they come, you will know that it is reassurance from Him, and no one will be able to convince you otherwise.

———————◆———————

It Takes Faith

The surrendered life is a life of faith. Having already believed in Christ, you now begin to trust Him for everything. *"So then, just as you received Christ Jesus as Lord, **continue to live in Him**, rooted and built up in Him, **strengthened in the faith** as you were taught."*[40]

Hebrews 11:1 says that faith is *"being sure of what we hope for and certain of what we do not see."* Abraham followed God without knowing *where* he was going. He was told he would become a father without knowing *when*. Mary believed she would give birth to a Savior without knowing *how*. Joseph trusted in God without knowing *why* circumstances unfolded as they did. The Israelites marched around Jericho seven times without knowing *how* the walls would come down.

Surrender means you refuse yourself the luxury of asking questions. In fact, John 16:23 says, *"In that day you will ask Me nothing."* You come to the point of total reliance on Him and are confident that He will reveal things to you as needed. Whatever is happening in your life, you are sure He is orchestrating it and permitting it. You rely on Him to work out all the details instead of forcing your own agenda and trying to manipulate the situation. People who truly live a surrendered life don't really care what happens – they trust He will work all things for good.

Despite Your Circumstances

There will be times when you're tempted to think He has deserted you, let you down, or failed to come through for you. Maybe you've been waiting for a first child and the treatments aren't working. Maybe you have been waiting for that perfect job or promotion and got passed over. Maybe you've been waiting for someone to spend the rest of your life with, but another promising relationship just withered away. Maybe you are drowning in debt that feels inescapable. Maybe you've been diagnosed with a devastating illness. Maybe you have lost someone you love so much you don't know how you will go on without them. Practicing faith does not mean that you will always get the outcomes you want.

Hebrews 11 is known as the "Hall of Faith" chapter in the Bible. There are certainly many examples of positive outcomes where faithful servants conquered kingdoms, won great victories, and gained what was promised. But in that same chapter, there are also many faithful servants who were tortured, imprisoned, and died a martyr's death without seeing deliverance on earth.

Were some more faithful than others? No. They were all *"commended for their faith."*[41] Their faith was not dependent on how their circumstances appeared at the time. They all lived *"by faith, not by sight."*[42] Worldly success does not always indicate faith, and outward appearance of failure does not indicate lack of faith.

God's wonderful plan may not appear wonderful to you initially. It didn't feel wonderful for Joseph to be sold by his brothers, live as a slave, then be falsely accused and thrown in prison. It didn't feel wonderful for Daniel to be in a hungry lion's den all night. It didn't feel wonderful for Job to lose his family and possessions. It didn't feel wonderful for Saul to be blinded on the road to Damascus. But in hindsight, it was all necessary for them to become living testimonies of God's power and faithfulness.

It takes faith to believe that a difficult situation will ultimately bring about good, even when it looks like it might cause pain in the moment. Total surrender means submitting to even painful circumstances if they are needed to fulfill His purposes or bring Him glory. That level of sacrifice doesn't come easily. Even Jesus agonized over God's plan in the Garden of Gethsemane. I have personally experienced tremendous loss and trauma while still believing God is good. Have you come to the point where God can withdraw His blessings without your trust in Him being affected?

Growing in Faith

God is pleased when you choose to believe Him over what you see and feel. *"Without faith it is impossible to please God."*[43] Every time you believe God, it is credited to you as righteousness.[44]

There are degrees of faith. You are told to *"examine yourself to see whether you are in the faith."*[45] At first, you may feel like you cannot trust unless you have some sign of His presence. You put out your fleece, like Gideon, and only then are you willing to trust. The Israelites doubted when they got to the Red Sea – they only believed when He parted the water, led them across, and drowned their enemies. Thomas only believed when he saw Jesus with his own eyes. But Jesus said, *"Blessed are those who have not seen, and yet believed."*[46]

Abraham *"grew strong in faith."*[47] Over time, you will also grow in your faith. It will develop and grow as you walk out challenging situations with God. You start to truly believe He knows best, and to trust His choices for you. As you mature, you will come to fully believe that:

- It's possible to do anything that God asks you to do
- God can change anyone and any circumstance at any time
- God can work good out of any mistake that's been made
- Your life is in His hands.

Lift Your Life Up

Real life begins when you surrender yourself completely to Jesus Christ. The length of time it takes to fully surrender depends on you – not God. But don't rush this first step. You will eventually discover that the greatest stumbling block is your own pride. You cannot fulfill God's purposes for your life when you are focused on your own agenda. Any effort to hang onto the least bit of your own power will only diminish the life of Jesus in you.

I have discovered that while receiving Jesus as my personal Savior was instantaneous, allowing Him to become LORD of my life was a process. I let Him have more and more of my life as I went along, but each time I thought I had given Him my *all*, I discovered I had only given all I could at the time. While surrendering is the first step of becoming a beloved disciple, it is not just a one-time event. Paul said, *"I die every day."*[48] Jesus told us, *"If people want to follow Me, they must give up the things they want. They must be willing to give up their lives daily to follow Me."*[49] This will take conscious practice over time. You may have to deny your own self-interest a hundred times a day at first! I slip back into my old ways sometimes and make a hasty decision without consulting Him first. I just keep practicing.

There are some who will always avoid things that require self-denial or sacrifice. Many will refuse His claim of ownership. This is the chance He took in creating each one of us. Jesus is looking for disciples whose hearts will be set completely on Him. The first disciples gave up everything to follow Him. Now He is waiting for someone who will be more fully devoted to Him than anyone else who has ever lived.

Choose to surrender once and for all, without reservation, and without turning back. Make it as tangible a transaction as possible. Visualize your heart being laid on the altar – saying, "Take this, Shepherd, and do with it as You please." To become a beloved disciple, you must pass this first stage of surrendered faith. He needs you "all in" now so that you don't "back out" later when the going gets tough. How fully you surrender will determine how meaningful the rest of this study will be for you.

Once you decide to live a totally surrendered life, that decision will be tested. It will mean laying down some of the things you care about most…which brings us to Step #2. Are you ready to press on?

"The world has yet to see what God will do with and for and through and in and by the man fully and wholly consecrated to Him."[50]

Prayer

Jesus, I surrender. I give You my life. I lay it all on the altar. I give You my family. I give You my friends. I give You my possessions. I give You my work. My dreams, my plans…Lord take all of it; take all of me. I don't want to resist or hold anything back. I want to let go of everything and everyone that is keeping me from more of You. I want You more than anything! Help me where I can't surrender completely yet.

I am the clay, not the Potter. I am the disciple, not the Rabbi. I am the sheep, not the Shepherd. I am the servant, not the Master. I am the pupil, not the Teacher. I am the branch, not the Vine. I will adjust myself to Your choices for me. I will receive and accept whatever You want me to have. I choose not to grab and hold anything on my own. What You want is more important than what I want. I will adapt to Your leading – whether I am comfortable or not. Take over every room in the house. Take the driver's seat. I place my will under Your throne. I want to do life with You as my Guide. You have answers that I lack. I will follow in obedience.

Lord, I want to be in step with You. I want to be moving in the direction You are moving. I place my past, present, and future in Your hands. I want to be an empty vessel for Your purposes. I'm not going to do it my way or on my own anymore. I am sorry for living as though You are not enough for me. I repent for living as though I am not accountable to You. Reveal to me the extent of Your love and the price that You paid for me so that I can sincerely acknowledge it. I am sorry for leaning on my own understanding instead of first asking You what I should do.

I trust that You are for me, not against me. I will not let fear hinder me from experiencing all You have planned for me. Bring Your perfect love and cast out my fear. Help me to see that You are good and that you have good plans for my life. Give me faith to live one day at a time, not looking too far ahead. Teach me how to be happy and content whether home or away, married or alone, in sickness or in health, in prosperity or adversity. I trust You will work all things together for my good. My hope is in You alone. I have heard You calling my name. You are calling me deeper. Help me see how You are shaping my life. I trust You to supply, not everything I want, but everything I need.

STUDY

1. Read the following verses and record your thoughts about being purchased by the blood of Jesus Christ:

1 Corinthians 6:19-20

1 Corinthians 7:23

Revelation 5:9

2. Because your life belongs to Him, Jesus is interested in your *complete* surrender. Until you are ready to make any adjustment necessary to obey Him, you will be of little use to Him. Which areas of your life are you willing to adjust if asked?

☐ job/business   ☐ finances   ☐ home/location

☐ family   ☐ friends   ☐ traditions

☐ prejudices   ☐ plans/methods   ☐ ministry/service

3. Saying that you are willing is the easy part. The harder part is *taking action* that demonstrates your surrender when asked to make these kinds of adjustments. Describe at least one major adjustment that God has already asked you to make. What was your response?

4. What fears arise when you think of surrendering your *whole life* to Christ?

5. What are you risking if you decide to completely surrender your life to Jesus? What are you risking if you don't?

Who is in Control?

6. In Luke 9:23 Jesus said, *"If anyone would come after me, he must deny himself and take up his cross daily and follow me."* Practically speaking, what does it mean to "deny yourself?"

7. Do your daily actions acknowledge Jesus as LORD of your life? How? If not, what do you want to change?

8. Is there something God is asking of you now that you're not doing? Why are you hesitating?

9. Describe in your own words the difference between a:

Self-centered Life   God-centered Life

_____	_____
_____	_____
_____	_____
_____	_____
_____	_____

Divine Dependence

10. Read John 14:15-17, 26 and John 16:13-14. How will you know if Jesus is asking for a life adjustment?

He may ask you to adjust your life in small ways initially. He wants you to begin to experience how He works and get to know His voice. Until you are faithful with these small assignments, He cannot give you larger ones.

"His master replied, 'Well done, good and faithful servant! You have been faithful with a few things; I will put you in charge of many things. Come and share your master's happiness!'"

Matthew 25:21

---

11. How would your life look different if it were completely controlled by the Holy Spirit?

He is Trustworthy

12. Sometimes God may ask you to do something that doesn't make sense to you, logically. Record what was asked in the following examples:

Joshua 6:1-5

Judges 7:1-8

Genesis 12:1

Matthew 4:18-22

13. According to 1 Peter 1:7 what has greater worth or value than gold?

14. What is the opposite of faith?

15. Trusting an invisible God doesn't come naturally or easily to every believer. Your relationship will only grow by stepping out in faith and making the choice to trust Him. Identify some life experiences that have helped grow your faith in God.

16. Have some life experiences hindered your faith? A loss or perceived betrayal can deeply handicap your faith. If you believe that God has been unfaithful, is it possible that you misinterpreted a promise, missed the answer, or gave up before God's timing? How has your distrust/disbelief kept you from experiencing the life He wants for you?

It Takes Faith

17. What does Hebrews 11:6 say about the importance of faith?

18. According to Isaiah 7:9, what is the danger of a lack of faith?

19. Describe a circumstance in your life that required faith and you responded.

20. Based on these Scriptures, in what ways can you increase your faith?

Luke 17:5

Romans 10:17

Galatians 5:22-23

SPIRITUAL MARKER

faith

WORSHIP

Already All I Need [Christy Nockels]

The Potter's Hand [Darlene Zschech]

You Can Have Me [Sidewalk Prophets]

Alabaster Heart [Bethel Music featuring kalley]

Spirit Lead Me [Influence Music featuring Michael Ketterer]

Give Me Faith [Elevation Worship]

Finally, I Surrender [Misty Edwards]

I Surrender [Hillsong Live]

Keep Making Me [Sidewalk Prophets]

Lift My Life Up [Unspoken]

The Unmaking [Nichole Nordeman]

Have It All [Bethel Music featuring Brian Johnson]

Control [Tenth Avenue North]

Lord I Need You [Matt Maher]

Take Over [Shane and Shane]

I WILL WALK BY FAITH
EVEN WHEN I CAN'T SEE

2 CORINTHIANS 5:1

LAY YOUR ISAAC DOWN

I n Step #1, you surrendered your life to Jesus. He wants you to love Him with *all* your heart, *all* your soul, *all* your mind, and *all* your strength.[1] In Step #2, He is going to ask you to **prove** that love. Are you really committed to becoming a beloved disciple? He will not be satisfied with half-hearted devotion, partial obedience, and the leftovers of your life.

This chapter is about undivided loyalty and commitment. He wants strong and sure disciples. When the going gets tough, He needs you to be sure of who He is and who you are in Him. Your faith may be real – but is it permanent? Is there *anything* that could ever make you turn away from Him – grief, pain, sickness, financial setback, persecution, or significant loss?

Jesus does not want naïve commitment. *"Suppose one of you wants to build a tower. Will you not first sit down and estimate the cost to see if you have enough money to complete it?"*[2] He wants you to consider the cost of discipleship up front – you need to be aware of what Jesus expects of His followers. You must determine that nothing is more important to you than your constant connection with Jesus. You will have to trust Him even if your world falls apart.

"If it is necessary that I lose everything for your sake, then let me lose it. I will not ask what the price is. I only ask that I may be all I ought to be as a disciple of Jesus Christ."

A.W. Tozer

---◆---

Sacrificing Isaac

God is seeking a very definite sacrifice – your Isaac. God tested Abraham this way. He said, *"Take your dear son Isaac whom you love and go to the land of Moriah. Sacrifice him there as a burnt offering."*[3] Scripture tells us that Abraham got up early in the morning and set out for the place God had directed. He built an altar and laid out the wood. Then he tied up Isaac and laid him on the wood. Abraham reached out and took the knife to kill his son.

What a horrible scene. It sounds so brutal. How could a loving Father ask that of a loving father? God had promised Abraham that his descendants would outnumber the stars in the sky. How would that happen if he slaughtered his only son?

Fortunately, this story has a happy ending. God intervened at the last second and said, *"Don't lay a hand on the boy! Now I know how fearlessly you fear God; you didn't hesitate to place your son, your dear son, on the altar for Me. Because you have gone through with this, and have not refused to give Me your son, your dear, dear son, I'll bless you – oh, how I'll bless you!"* Then God provided a ram to sacrifice as a burnt offering instead of Isaac.

Similarly, God will also ask you to **relinquish control** over something or someone you cherish. That treasure of your heart must be laid on the altar. As a result of "laying your Isaac down," something will be gone, or at least changed, in your life. Maybe it's a specific plan or vision you have for your life – such as a desire to be married or to have children. Perhaps it's a person or relationship. Or a sinful habit. He is asking for something specific and difficult. Your faith may be challenged to the breaking point.

A *sacrifice* is defined as "the surrender of something for the sake of something else; something given up; something offered in worship." A true heart sacrifice will mean that you:

- give up something precious to you (your Isaac), even if you don't understand why
- exchange it for God's love
- let go of control over the outcome as an act of worship
- rest in the promise of a hope and a future despite what the circumstances may look like.

> *"Now Abraham was a man wholly surrendered, a man utterly obedient,*
> *a man who possessed nothing. He became a man marked out by the Lord*
> *for special treatment, a friend and favorite of the Most High."*
>
> A.W. Tozer

A Test of Faith

Laying Isaac down was a faith test for Abraham. Earlier in his life, he had failed some major faith tests (e.g., lied about his wife to protect himself *twice*, had a child with his wife's servant) and he was determined not to fail this one. He was willing to surrender what he deeply loved without being able to see the end result.

As horrific as it sounds, God is the one who requested Abraham kill his own son. God didn't demand it – He requested it. He is going to test your faith through some difficult circumstances too. He will ask you to lay down your claim to something specific in complete trust and submission. The high degree of attachment you have to your Isaac is what makes the sacrifice so painful. You don't know ahead of time if you'll get your Isaac back. Sometimes He will provide a replacement ram, other times He will not. Will your faith and hope prevail?

Relinquishing your right to keep your precious Isaac is the most difficult thing you will ever do. In Abraham's example, I am amazed at his ability to "let go" and lay his Isaac down. I have an advanced degree in psychology and consider myself a rational person. And I had a very hard time doing what I'm describing in this chapter myself. Laying my Isaac(s) down involved many sleepless nights, internal (and occasionally external) tantrums, panic and fear that was anything but rational. I had to keep *choosing* my relationship with God over anything and everything else. I wanted to pass the test. I wanted to be found faithful in the end. I knew that anything I suffered here was temporary.

When Your World Falls Apart

Suffering does play an undeniable role in life. A significant sacrifice can feel crippling. Hopes, dreams, relationships, health, and comfort may be shattered. When a replacement ram is not provided (and it may not be), you go through the motions of living while you feel like you are dying inside. I know that "moving on" and "letting go" can take years. And even then, things never quite return to how they used to be. You simply must accept a "new normal."

In writing this difficult chapter, I don't like to walk back through my own pain nor remind you of yours. I don't wish to frighten those who have not yet had their own "Isaac experience." I do want to encourage you not to lose hope. *"Against all hope, Abraham in hope believed..."*[4] The important truth for believers is that our suffering is never in vain. Everything you experience is for a meaningful purpose. I have found this to be true.

At 17 years of age, I was enjoying a pretty perfect and peaceful world in a small, rural Mennonite community in the Midwest. As teenagers often do, I felt strong, invincible, and successful. And I had enjoyed some success at a very young age – having won a national science fair competition, I traveled to Japan to represent the U.S. at an international one. I had a 4.0 GPA in school and was good at sports. I believed there was nothing I "couldn't handle." But my perfect world was soon shattered, and I realized how fragile and temporary it all was.

Just weeks into my senior year of high school, my younger sister was molested and murdered in our home...by a teenage boy my parents had adopted into our family. We found out later that he had been planning to kill all of us and had been sleeping with his pre-ordered list under his pillow at night. Suddenly, my faith in humanity and innocence was gone. And the questions started...How could he do this to us? How could we have been so naïve? Where was our God?

The world became a frightening place. The beautiful 100-year-old farmhouse where my father had been born and raised was tarnished. It happened upstairs, right next to my own bedroom, so I couldn't sleep there anymore. I spent the rest of my senior year sleeping on the floor downstairs, outside my parents' room. I walked through the rest of that year in a daze. I couldn't think clearly. I hated walking into a room with all heads turning to stare. I lost all my confidence. I could barely speak in public – something as simple as returning an item to a store felt traumatic. I couldn't wait to move away and go to college. But the unresolved emotional "baggage" followed me there.

More than 35 years have passed since that horrific tragedy. Thankfully, a lot of healing has taken place in that time. And I have realized I am not alone in experiencing terrible trials. One precious friend lost her brother and father in the same year, both under tragic circumstances. Another dear friend lost her baby after enjoying him less than 3 months. Another cherished friend lost her 47-year-old husband to a heart attack while playing a hockey game. And cancer has affected many – leaving behind motherless and fatherless children. Oh, the suffering...

Suffering is a reality of the human experience. We can't say that God made a mistake in allowing it. We also can't avoid the topic and refuse to address it as part of the process of becoming a beloved disciple. It reveals our humanness, our need for a Savior, and shows us who we are at our very core.

Two Types of Trials

There are two different types of heart sacrifices, or "Isaac experiences," that can occur in your life. If you have lived long enough, you have probably experienced both.

Sometimes a painful crisis is thrust into your life without warning, as in the cases I just described. Other times you may be an accomplice in your own misery, creating a painful mess by your less-than-wise choices. While there can be some overlap between the two types of suffering, I will try to distinguish them here:

Personal Strongholds	Fiery Furnace
Strongholds can result from personal choices you have made in your own life. You are given the option to **voluntarily** sacrifice these on the altar (like Abraham). You will be asked to "let them go" – trusting Him to provide a way.	These trials are part of living in a fallen world. You are not given an option here; this kind of suffering is an **involuntary** sacrifice that is forced upon you. You will be asked to "walk it through" – trusting Him to provide a way.
Examples: • addictions • a sinful habit • co-dependent relationships, soul ties • over-reliance on money, status, fame, beauty, power, or intelligence • a mindset of fear, insecurity, people-pleasing, self-pity, or control • demands for your life to look a certain way – to be married, have a child, live in a specific place, have a certain job, or have a particular friend	**Examples:** • death of a loved one • accidents • natural disasters • health problems, illness • loss of job, finances, or reputation through outside factors • victim of violent crime • child abuse • an unfaithful spouse • betrayal of a friend • religious persecution

Eventually everyone faces the daunting challenge of laying an "Isaac" down – whether by choice or by circumstance. We are each called into this posture of obedience: hands upward and open for whatever is asked. Why does it feel overwhelming? Fear is your reaction to uncertainty; the unknown. When something doesn't look exactly how you want it to look, you feel out of control. This can lead to feelings of rejection, anxiety, and depression. The lesson to be learned in both types of trials is **giving up control** over the situation. You committed to a life of surrender in Step #1. This is the next step. Whether breaking your strongholds or facing the fiery furnace, you must find your certainty in Him alone.

Breaking Strongholds

In the Bible, a *stronghold* is a "mighty fortress that is difficult to penetrate."[5] It is also used to describe something "exalted or lifted high." God wants to be your only stronghold.[6] David said he was not afraid when the Lord was the stronghold of his life,[7] and consider the enemies he faced – lions and bears, Goliath, Saul's army, and more!

Unfortunately, our human nature often tempts us to rely on strongholds other than God Himself. Satanic strongholds invade your life whenever you allow something to become bigger than God. These false ideas and deceptions steal your focus. They become all-consuming; draining your mental and emotional energy so your spiritual life becomes ineffective. In 2 Corinthians 10:5, you are warned to *"cast down every high thing that exalts itself against the knowledge of God."*

Your First Love

A stronghold is anything that causes you to lose your "first love" for God. 1 John 2:15-16 says, *"Do not love the world or anything in the world. If anyone loves the world, the love of the Father is not in him. For everything in the world – the cravings of sinful man, the lust of his eyes, and the boasting of what he has and does – comes not from the Father but from the world."*

You can become enslaved to anything – fears, insecurities, addictions, compulsive behavior, or unhealthy relationships. It's not His best for your life. You want what feels good to your body; God wants you to have what is best for your soul. Isaiah said, *"My deluded heart misleads me...Is not this thing in my right hand a lie?"*[8] You may be holding tight to a relationship that is draining you of resources and preventing you from moving forward. You may be letting fear rule your life and refusing to step out of your comfort zone into a new calling. You may be addicted to a substance that you believe is helping you "get through the day," but in reality, it is holding you back from new opportunities.

You don't want to be mastered by anything but the Master Himself. *"You were shown these things so that you might know that the Lord is God; besides Him there is no other."*[9] He will not allow you to keep a tight grip on things that are not good for you. He wants to see if you're willing to give up what you love to Him who loves you more. He loves you more than you love your Isaac – more than any benefit you are getting from your stronghold. Solomon had everything anyone could possibly want on this earth, and he called it all *"meaningless…like chasing after the wind!"*[10] In contrast, King David said that God's love was *"better than life."*[11]

God loves to give you good gifts and means for you to enjoy them.[12] He doesn't refuse you the right to possess anything. But He doesn't want your possessions to possess you. *"Salt is excellent. But if the salt goes flat, it's useless, good for nothing."*[13] In other words, good things can sometimes turn bad – they are no longer helpful to you and must be thrown out. God needs your desires to be purely for more of Him. He wants first place in your life with *"no other gods before"* Him.[14] Anything you try to put in the place of Jesus to meet your needs is an idol.

Turning from Idols

The Bible clearly cautions, *"Keep yourselves from idols – false gods – from anything and everything that would occupy the place in your heart due to God, from any sort of substitute for Him that would take first place in your life."*[15] Over and over again, God asks us to remove things to put Himself in their place. Admit where you have yielded yourself to something that now controls or dominates you. I have yet to meet a person with no dysfunctional attachments. You might think, "Oh, I can give that up anytime I feel like it." But it's not that easy.

Do you have even the slightest reliance on anything or anyone other than God? It doesn't mean you aren't saved; it just means you aren't *entirely His.* If you have to have anything in your life other than Jesus to be satisfied, the devil will use that against you. Beware if you catch yourself saying any of the following:

- I need this drug to feel good.
- If I just had a child, I know I would be satisfied.
- I can't live without this friendship.

- If only my spouse loved me right, I could be happy.
- I would enjoy life more if I just had more money…or a better job.
- I could never move away – all my friends and family are here.

When you are dependent on certain circumstances more than God, you are on the wrong track. You believe that material things, power, or people will make you happy. When you seek satisfaction in the wrong places, you are going to be disappointed and frustrated. God never intended anything else to fill your deepest needs. A crucial part of "laying down" your strongholds is allowing Him to fill the empty places. He is the only thing that will make you feel *"complete."*[16]

You are designed to thirst for more of God.[17] Isaiah 55:1-2 says, *"Come, all you who are thirsty; come to the waters…Why spend money on what is not bread, and your labor on what does not satisfy? Listen to Me and eat what is good, and your soul will delight in the richest of fare."* If you don't rely on Him to be filled, you can easily be misled. The enemy will tempt you with various idols, saying "this will satisfy you," just as he did with Adam and Eve. But God said, *"Whoever drinks of the water that I will give him will never be thirsty again. The water that I will give him will become in him a spring of water welling up to eternal life."*[18] If you keep your focus on Jesus, giving Him first priority in your life, you won't be so easily misled.

Breaking Free

God is love and His love will pursue you until you are completely captivated by Him alone! He will begin to show you things you didn't see before to help you become all He wants you to be. God is not looking for ways to make you uncomfortable. He just wants to be Lord of your life. He will press His thumb right on those places where you have refused Him Lordship.

With a stronghold, He won't *take* it from you – He wants you to *willingly give it up*. Recognize that God is the One asking; He is involved in the situation. He is moving you forward. His desire is for your very best even if you can't see what that looks like at the time. Any adjustment He asks you to make is for your own good in the long run. But for you to be free, He must be allowed to hurt whatever may be in the way.

In laying your Isaac down, you can expect to experience similar stages as in grieving a death:

- **Denial** – you deny that you are enslaved by the stronghold; you stay busy and try not to think about it; you try harder to control it, in your own strength
- **Bargaining** – you make deals with God; you feel it slipping through your fingers

and try to hang on for dear life; you come up with your own "bright ideas" to fix it; you try pouting, controlling and manipulating; you keep wishing it looked like before

- **Anger** – you panic; you get frustrated and have tantrums; you argue; you follow, but "kicking and screaming;" you're mad at yourself for getting that invested in the first place
- **Depression** – your sleeping and eating habits are disrupted; you withdraw from others; you make wrong assumptions; you feel embarrassment, shame, and discouragement for not handling it better; you're afraid "I'll never get this together"
- **Acceptance** – you let go and let God have complete control over the situation; you wouldn't even want to go back to how "things used to be;" you've moved on

I know how difficult it is – I have been through this process myself. I have idolized my career, home, and finances. I have gotten my self-worth from my performance and position. I have held some relationships in a virtual death grip before God revealed to me that what I held in my hand was a lie. At this point, I want *everything* He wants me to have and *nothing* that He does not want me to have. Don't settle for anything else!

Demolishing Strongholds

The very nature of a "stronghold" implies that it has a powerful hold on you. You can't just wish it away. Fortunately, 2 Corinthians 10:4 says that *"The weapons we fight with are not the weapons of the world. On the contrary, they have **divine power to demolish strongholds.**"* What are these divine weapons? Ephesians 6 tells us that prayer and the Word of God assist us in our spiritual battles. Prayer keeps you in constant communion with God while His Word refreshes you with truth to transform your mind.[19] You demolish strongholds when you make your mind captive to Christ.[20] Ultimately, your mind is retrained to exalt God instead of your idols.

Sometimes the power of a stronghold can be broken instantly through prayer. Other times, it is a difficult process of slowly renewing your mind and learning to depend solely on God to maintain your freedom. Some of the idols in your life can take a long time to remove. They have been in place for years and only the power of God can get them to budge. Remember that the battle *"belongs to the Lord."*[21] Begin by confessing your idols and admitting their inability to satisfy you completely. Ask for His help. Practice, practice, practice operating in the Spirit instead of your flesh. Make different choices, one at a time. You can do all things through Him – hold on to that truth.[22]

Some things in your life may just need a slight adjustment. But it can be hard to maintain your balance on a slippery slope, so other things need to be completely stopped, ended, and finished. There are some activities, relationships, and substances that are so toxic that moderation won't work. There may be some things that seem perfectly legitimate to others, but if you are going to be a beloved disciple, you can't have them. Break it off before it breaks you. Jesus said, *"If your right hand causes you to sin, cut it off..."*[23] Your right hand is obviously very helpful, but Jesus said "cut if off" if it hinders your relationship with Him. He is asking you to eliminate things that may seem good but, in reality, are holding you back.

Don't tiptoe around it. Don't evade with the excuse, "I'm not quite ready." Abraham *"rose early in the morning."*[24] A sacrifice is to be made; full obedience is expected. He wants you to recognize any part of you that is still demanding rights to yourself. Abraham did not choose what the sacrifice was to be. Don't leave any place where the enemy can smugly say it was too much, too hard, or impossible. Get help. Establish some accountability with a support group or counselor.

God needs you to make room, move over, and loosen your grip. The thing you're holding may be great, but He is better! Trust Him. He wants to bring you out pure, spotless, and undefiled. He has good plans to redeem any loss. Joel 2:25 says, *"I will restore to you the years the swarming locust have eaten."*

It *is* from the Lord, let Him do what seems best.[25] Trust me – with the loss of this *one* thing will come *so many* other good things. 1 Corinthians 2:9 tells us that we cannot even conceive of the things that God has prepared for those who love Him!

Facing the Fiery Furnace

You are given a voluntary choice to surrender strongholds (one type of trial). In contrast, facing the "fiery furnace" is not optional (the second type of trial). Here, God doesn't ask our permission. He doesn't say, "Would you like to go through this loss of a loved one, this struggle, or defeat?" Jesus told us to expect problems in this world.[26] Peter warned us that trials and suffering would be a normal part of life, saying, *"Dear friends, do not be surprised at the painful trial you are suffering, as though something strange were happening to you."*[27]

Jesus *"learned obedience"* and was *"made perfect"* through suffering.[28] Because beloved disciples are to be made like Jesus, He will take you through the same experiences. That means you will encounter stress, rejection, hardship, and trials over time. *"Indeed, we share in His sufferings in order that we may also share in His glory."*[29]

Expecting a Storm

In Matthew 8:23-27, Jesus knew about the storm ahead and sent His disciples straight into it anyway. He seemed to be asleep while the storm was raging, and the boat was sinking. The disciples thought He didn't care – remember how mistaken they were. He rebuked them saying, *"Where is your faith?"*

Don't be surprised when God allows storms in your life. Pain initiates change. And under intense pain, you are motivated to change in ways that you normally wouldn't be while in your "comfort zone." There is no growth without change; there is no change without loss; and there is no loss without pain.

Sometimes you can't recognize true security until everything else proves false. David said, *"When I felt secure, I thought I would never be shaken."*[30] In other words, when life was good, he felt nothing could ever move him. God will often allow your world to be "shaken" so that you no longer depend on earthly securities to sustain you. Hebrews 12:26-29 explains that He sometimes shakes things up so only that which cannot be shaken (His foundation) remains. Until your world is shattered, you have no idea what will last. God isn't trying to destroy you – He's trying to keep you from destroying yourself.

These trials can be God's way of opening your eyes to see things about your character or patterns of behavior that need to be changed. These problems are not punishment; they are wake-up calls from a loving Father. He will do whatever it takes to bring you into alignment with Him. *"For our light and momentary troubles are **achieving for us an eternal glory** that far outweighs them all."*[31]

By His Permission

You can take comfort in knowing that nothing happens to you without God's permission. Everything that a beloved disciple experiences is filtered through the Father first. He is intimately involved in every detail of your life, saying *"this is My doing."*[32]

God could have kept Daniel out of the lion's den. God could have prevented Job from devastating loss. God could have kept my sister unharmed. But He didn't – in any of these cases and many more throughout the Bible. According to this pattern, you will also be tested through senseless tragedies, undeserved criticism, and unanswered prayers. But nothing is random. In God's eyes, there are no "accidents" – everything that you experience has spiritual significance.

There is a Master plan and purpose. Joseph told his brothers, *"You intended to harm me, but God intended it for good."*[33] Romans 8:28-29 explains, *"We know that **God causes everything to work together** for the good of those who love Him and are called according to His purpose."* He doesn't promise that everything will work out as you would like. He doesn't promise that living in this world will always feel good. He *does* promise that everything will eventually fit together as part of His plan to make you more like Him. He will bring good out of the situation. And if you've walked with God long enough, I am sure you can personally testify to a time when He used a negative circumstance to achieve a positive result.

It Won't Feel Fair

In the moment, it might not feel fair or make sense. The Bible tells us that, James, the brother of John (the beloved), was the first disciple to be arrested and killed in Jerusalem.[34] Peter was arrested next. But he was miraculously led out of jail by an angel of the Lord. While we normally celebrate this amazing deliverance, think about it from John's perspective for a moment. His brother dies…Peter is given a "get out of jail free" card. Do you suppose he wondered why?

In Acts 19:11-12 we are told that God did many extraordinary miracles through Paul, so that even handkerchiefs that touched him were taken to the sick and they were healed. But in 2 Timothy 4:20, we read about Paul's regret that he had to "leave a sick friend behind." If Paul was able to heal so many others, why couldn't his own friend be healed? It is difficult to explain the difference. We don't know why God heals some and not others.

Jesus also said there was *"no one greater than John the Baptist."*[35] John the Baptist had given his entire life preparing the way for the Lord. But then he was imprisoned for two years. Jesus had the power to save him but chose not to. Did John feel abandoned? It does seem he began to have some doubts (Matthew 11:1-6). He wanted reassurance, asking *"Are you really God or not?"* Jesus responded with a list of all the miracles He had performed for others. He continued to tell the crowds of John's greatness. John was still beheaded. The last word Jesus sent to John was *"Blessed is the one who is not offended by me"* (v 6). Essentially, He was saying to John, "I understand my choice will not make sense to you. The reward is great if you won't hold it against me."

Even though He loves you as His beloved disciple, He will still ask hard, difficult things of you. Many of you have pleaded with God to save the life of a loved one. He understands your confusion, disappointment, and pain when the answer you want doesn't come. Perhaps you lost a job with no possibilities on the horizon. Maybe you feel betrayed by a friend you thought was trustworthy. The list of disappointments big and small is endless. We've all experienced our share of things not turning out how we thought they would. But there is a larger plan, a bigger picture, even if you can't see it right away. You won't have all the answers in advance. This is an important test - **will you be offended by Him?**

Shadrach, Meshach, and Abednego seemed to have the right approach in their fiery furnace. They believed God *could* save them, but they were fine with dying if He didn't. *"Our God whom we serve is able to deliver us…**But if not…**"*[36] But if not, they would not love Him less, change their minds, or defect. And Job said, *"Though He slay me, yet I will trust Him."*[37]

Blessed are those who don't fall away when they don't understand, when He doesn't act, when there are obstacles, and when they feel deserted. Blessed are those who don't give up when things keep going wrong. Blessed are those who don't pout when answers are delayed. Blessed are those who keep on believing when the night is long and black. Morning will come.

The Purpose of It All

The purpose of trials and suffering is to draw you closer to Himself.[38] Desperately close. Psalm 34:18 says, *"The Lord is close to the brokenhearted; He rescues those who are crushed in spirit."* During trials, I believe you remain in God's "intensive care unit." When my dad had open heart surgery, he received very close 1:1 attention in the ICU for the first 24 hours. In a similar way, Jesus draws near to those who desperately seek Him through the pain. Psalm 91:15 says, *"I will be with him in trouble."* He will demonstrate that His concern for you is even deeper than when things are "normal."

When your heart is broken and you run out of all other options, you typically turn to God. Looking back over my life, I know that I have prayed most intensely during times of difficulty. When life is easy, you tend to coast along and assume your faith is intact. Trials make you gut-level honest and authentic with the Lord of the universe. You will seize His promises with a tighter grip. Problems also force you to depend on God instead of yourself. Paul testified that *"I was crushed and completely overwhelmed…I thought I would never live through it. But that was to make me rely not on myself, but on God."*[39]

If you are never in trouble, how will you ever testify to His delivering power? Paul tells us that in the midst of his trials, *"the Lord stood by me and strengthened me."*[40] Let

Him prove that He is a Redeemer. Let Him prove that He is Savior. He does indeed exchange *"beauty for ashes, the oil of joy for mourning, and the garment of praise for the spirit of heaviness."*[41]

Until you are able to confront the deepest, darkest difficulties of life without damaging your view of God's character, you don't truly know Him yet. Every circumstance that you endure has a lesson meant to teach you some valuable piece of truth about His character or to change your own. As a beloved disciple, you must be willing to place your Isaac on the altar. It means a time of testing, refining, purification, and separation for only one purpose – the elimination of every affection not of God.

"The greatest lesson a soul has to learn is that God, and God alone, is enough for all its needs. This is the lesson that all God's dealings with us are meant to teach, and this is the crowning discovery of our entire Christian life."

Hannah Whitall Smith

A Time of Testing

Deuteronomy 8:16 says, *"He might **test** you, to do you good in the end."* We know that God tested Abraham by asking him to sacrifice his son Isaac. We also know that Job was tested.[42] Satan wanted to destroy him, and God allowed it (to a point), to test his faith. There was tremendous devastation – Job lost all his children and all his possessions in one day! That is hard to digest. Yet Job acknowledged the *"hand of the Lord has done this."*[43]

This is not cruel punishment; it is tender preparation for the future. God assures us that *"He keeps His promise, and He will not allow you to be tested beyond your power to remain firm; at the time you are put to the test, He will give you the strength to endure, and so provide you with a way out."*[44] James says, *"Blessed are those who endure when they are tested. When they pass the test, they will receive the crown of life that God has promised to those who love Him."*[45] Every time you pass a test, God is planning a reward for you in heaven.

Your character is being revealed and refined by these tests. *"Suffering produces perseverance; perseverance, character; and character, hope."*[46] He is more interested in developing your character than your comfort. He purposely permits difficult situations that allow you to demonstrate your faith, obedience, and loyalty. Why do you think He put a restricted fruit tree right in the center of the Garden of Eden? He wanted to see how Adam and Eve would respond to the test. Now He is watching to see how you respond to your tests. Will you take matters into your own hands or try to force your own way? Will you rationalize your behavior and pretend that nothing is wrong? Will you hide and turn your back on Him because things aren't going your way?

Many people never "pass the test," so they spend their entire life going around in circles in the desert (like the Israelites). I believe God will continue to bring you back to the same tests over and over again until you pass them. Instead of asking "Why me, Lord?" ask "What do you want me to learn here, Lord?" Many times, we pray for relief, healing, or deliverance from trials, but if your problem, pain, or circumstance is necessary to fulfill His purpose, do you really want Him to take it away?

The Refiner's Fire

Most disciples want to enjoy a relationship with Jesus, but few are willing to be refined in His fire. *"For our God is indeed a consuming fire."*[47] And His fire is essential to advancing to a deeper level of intimacy with Him.

Peter said, *"…you have been grieved by various trials so that the genuineness of your faith, being much **more precious than gold**, though it is tested by fire, may be found worthy…"*[48] Refined gold is pure. Gold that has other metals mixed in, such as copper, iron, or nickel, is harder and more corrosive. To refine gold, it must be exposed to intense heat. The impurities (or *dross*) are slowly drawn to the surface and skimmed off. When all the impurities have been removed, the gold becomes softer and more pliable.

In the same way, your heart can become hardened with the impurities of sin.[49] God purifies and refines us through trials. *"Behold I have refined you; I have tested you in the furnace of affliction."*[50] Everyone must go through the *"refiner's fire."*[51] He needs to burn away everything in your life that does not bring Him glory. Sin and deception can easily hide in your life when there is no intense crisis. Under the heat of trials, however, unforgiveness, bitterness, and envy can surface. In times of difficulty and stress, we can become manipulative, controlling, fearful, and angry. James said, *"Under pressure, your faith-life is forced into the open and shows its true colors."*[52] The fire brings these impurities to the surface to be removed.

Getting rid of selfishness and pride takes a lot of fire. He will use all kinds of circumstances to teach you to walk in love and humility. *"So don't try to get out of anything prematurely. Let the process continue until you become mature and well-developed, not deficient in any way."*[53] Those who willingly go through the fire instead of running from it will bring the greatest glory to God. Eventually you will welcome His fire, saying "Refine me, Lord, I don't want to stay the way I was." And when He has tried you, you *"shall come forth as gold."*[54]

A Pruning Process

Just as fire is a method of purifying, so is pruning – cutting away dead parts or things that are going in the wrong direction. John 15:2 says, *"Any branch in me that does not bear fruit He cuts away; and He cleanses and repeatedly prunes every branch that continues to bear fruit, to make it bear more and richer and more excellent fruit."*

Pruning *seems* to be destroying the vine – the gardener appears to be cutting everything away. The plant looks disfigured and bare. But the gardener sees the future and knows that the end result will be a greater abundance of fruit, a hundred times better. Remember you are in the hands of the Master Gardener. He makes no mistakes. And there are blessings you can never have unless you are ready to pay the price of painful pruning.

He is not trying to take things away from you – He actually wants you to have more! To those who are not following Christ, it will seem like torture. But those who have chosen to become beloved disciples will welcome this pruning because they know that a holy thing is taking place. They are being shaped for a higher purpose and calling. A gardener only stops pruning after he expects nothing more from the vine. So freedom from this painful work would mean you're no longer useful. Do you really want Him to leave you alone?

Life from Death

God can work much more effectively with a broken spirit than one that is prideful, confident, and self-sufficient.[55] Jesus said, *"Listen carefully: Unless a grain of wheat is buried in the ground, dead to the world, it is never any more than a grain of wheat. But if it is buried, it sprouts and reproduces itself many times over."*[56] As a "seed," you must be willing to be buried in the earth (and to die temporarily) and trust that God will bring forth a crop when the time is right.

To produce a harvest, the change must go deeper than the surface. Soil must be plowed. Grains must be planted, harvested, and then crushed to produce bread for a hungry world. Trust that He can powerfully transform your life for a future purpose. *"If you continue to be faithful, sowing even through tears, you will return with songs of joy – carrying armloads of grain!"*[57] He can cause you to be *"fruitful in the land of your suffering."*[58] Remember that God always has your best interests at heart. He is *"doing what is best for us, training us to live God's holy best."*[59] He has good plans for you – plans to *"prosper you and not to harm you, plans to give you hope and a future."*[60]

Our God is not a cruel God. He allows the heating, shaping, pruning, and testing in our lives for a reason. They are purifying us so we will reflect Him. Is it an easy process?

No. But is having a life that points others to Him worth the discomfort? I truly believe so. I am grateful to know that nothing God allows us to go through is pointless or wasted. Even in the midst of hurt, He will work things out for our good and for His glory.

As a result of suffering, you can become a wise counselor and valuable comforter.[61] It takes sorrow to deepen a soul. Your scars and suffering will save others. Your brokenness will lead to higher levels of compassion. It will melt your pride. You will find a patience and gentleness you didn't have before.[62] Jesus said, *"Behold I make all things new."* This is the reason that Christians can look back over a long life shaped by tragedy, cruelty, setbacks, suffering, disappointment, and depression – and still see a road of blessing through it.

"Only when you minister out of brokenness is it true ministry."

John Kilpatrick

Hope for Eternity

While enduring trials, wait in hope. Refuse to despair. There will be days when you cope poorly. Countless times you will have to give control back to God as you pick it up again. Fear may sometimes cloud your ability to see and think clearly. Don't try to look too far ahead – take "one day at a time." Seek Him in the morning, hang on to Him through noon, cling to His presence in the evening, count on His restoration in the night, and be renewed by His strength again the next morning. Through it all, you will feel carried by a power not your own.

David said, *"I would have despaired unless I had believed that I would see the goodness of the Lord in the land of the living. Wait for the Lord; be strong, and let your heart take courage; yes, wait for the Lord."*[63] God does not hide Himself in your times of desperation. He is *"your refuge and strength; a very present help in trouble."*[64] He is everything He claims to be. Get to Him and find your strength and comfort there. *"Do not lose heart. Though outwardly we are wasting away, yet inwardly we are being renewed day by day...So we fix our eyes not on what is seen, but on what is unseen. For what is seen is temporary, but what is unseen is eternal."*[65]

> *"A vertical perspective prevents horizontal panic."*
>
> Charles Swindoll

The Enemy's Plan

The enemy would like to keep you focused on your pain and problems. It is easy to fall prey to doubt, discouragement, and worry. You will be tempted to dwell on how unfair it is or whose fault it is. He wants you tied up in knots of fear and insecurity. He will encourage you to disengage and withdraw from others. Satan may tell you that if God really loved you, He would have protected you from this, or that if you had been a "better Christian" this wouldn't have happened. These are all lies.

Decide not to wallow in self-pity and uncertainty. Don't let your circumstances make you doubt God's love for you. The One who is asking for your sacrifice has gone through pain and suffering Himself. He can't have you interpreting how much He loves you based on how "blessed" your circumstances are at the moment. Settle it now, in these early stages of beloved discipleship (this is only Step #2), that His love will never change no matter how your circumstances may change.

He Will Make a Way

Isaiah 43:1-3 says, *"When you pass through the waters, I will be with you…When you walk through the fire, you will not be burned; the flames will not set you ablaze. For I am the Lord, your God, the Holy One of Israel, your Savior."* He didn't say there would never be floods or fires; He only promised that you would not be destroyed by them. He will not give you more than you can bear. Paul said, *"We are hard pressed on every side,* **but not crushed;** *perplexed,* **but not in despair;** *persecuted,* **but not abandoned;** *struck down,* **but not destroyed."**[66] If you can stay calm, faithful, and committed in the midst of turmoil, the purpose of God will be accomplished in you.

Many people live in fear, believing "I could never survive if that happened to me." But those who *did* experience it and *did* survive found their God to be faithful. Record in a journal where you see evidence of Him moving in your life despite your circumstances – write down how you have grown and what you have learned. Recognize His small but steady blessings. Choose hope in light of eternity.

The Source of All Hope

Hope gives you the desire to go on living because you believe something better is coming. Your hope cannot come from financial security, success, health, or people. The only constant hope is the Source of all hope:

- *"I wait quietly before God, for my **hope** is in Him. He alone is my rock and my salvation, my fortress where I will not be shaken. My salvation and my honor come from God alone. He is my refuge, a rock where no enemy can reach me."*[67]
- *"Those who **hope** in the Lord will renew their strength. They will soar on wings like eagles; they will run and not grow weary; they will walk and not faint."*[68]
- *"For everything that was written in the past was written to teach us, so that through endurance and the encouragement of the Scriptures we might have **hope**."*[69]
- *"Blessed is he whose **hope** is in the LORD his God."*[70]

Hebrews 12 tells us to lay aside everything that entangles us and run the race that is set before us. Remember this is a long-distance race…don't give up! What would you think of a runner who threw himself on the ground in despair at the first hurdle? You need to be patient, steady, and persistent. Keep your eyes on Jesus! Remember how He did it – He never lost sight of where He was headed, so He could endure anything. The difficulties you find yourself in are not punishment, it is part of your training. Submit, endure, and don't lose heart. God is doing what is best for you – His holy best. It pays off! The well-trained find themselves mature in their relationship with God. It never feels good at the time; it is painful. Don't be shortsighted. Don't trade away your eternal rights for some temporary short-term desire. God is actively cleaning house, burning away all that is not of Him, and He won't quit until all is cleansed.[71]

He is waiting at the finish line! Keep your focus on eternity. Moses endured because *"he was looking ahead to his reward."*[72] Romans 8:17-18 says that *"If we are to share His glory, we must also share His suffering. But what we suffer now is nothing compared to the glory He will give us later."*

Is It Well with Your Soul?

He won't allow a beloved disciple to be satisfied with anything else but Him. So, in this discipleship process, He will walk into your heart and empty it of everything but Him.

You will no doubt wrestle with God through this step. You can turn back and decide the cost is too great. At this very point, *"many of His disciples turned back and no longer followed Him."*[73] Jesus then turned to the rest of the disciples He had chosen and asked, *"Do you also want to leave?"* Peter answered, *"We've already committed ourselves, confident that you are the Holy One of God."*

Only disciples who show great promise are singled out for rigorous training. He needs disciplined disciples! Will you *"refuse the cup of suffering?"*[74] You have asked to be set apart – sold out no matter the cost. His dealings with you now are for deepest spiritual gain. Make the most of it.

Trials are only for a season. Keep in mind that storms are part of life, but they are not *all* of life. Suffering is one means to draw closer to God, but not the only way. There is peace, joy, and rest still to come in your walk as a beloved disciple. But let's get one last bit of surrender out of the way in Step #3 – forgiveness. Are you ready to press on?

Prayer

Jesus, I come trembling, but I do come. I want to know You more, but my fearful heart does not want to give up my toys. Please root from my heart all those things which I have cherished so long, so that You can dwell there without a rival. I don't understand why You are asking this of me, but I need Your comforting touch right now. I open my hands and give You my Isaac. Fill the hole in my heart. I hate this process, but I want more of You. Hold me close to You. I know You hear the cry of the broken. I submit myself into Your care. I am grateful, Lord, that this is creating a fresh dependence on You. I do want more of You.

I'm tired of being enslaved by fear. I'm tired of trying to control my own circumstances and outcomes. I surrender to Your will, Your way, and Your plans. Even though I may not know the plans, You do. I relinquish control, even if it seems I can only do so for five minutes. I want to get to the point of complete surrender. Just hold my hand and get me through this.

Oh God, other gods besides You have ruled over me, but You alone are the one I want to honor. My Lord and my Creator, I confess that I'm weak in my natural self. I have been enslaved to sin. I need Your absolute intervention. I've learned the hard way that nothing good lives in me, that is, in my sinful nature. For I desire to do good, but I cannot carry it out. You have the power that I need. Thank you, Father, that no matter how I've been enslaved, You can set me free! God, I desperately need Your discernment when something may be permissible for me but not necessarily beneficial. Please empower me to resist things that are not beneficial so that I will not be mastered by anything. I thank you in advance that I'm going to be set free from every idol. I seek you first first first.

Father, forgive me for every way that I have given other people and things Your place in my life. Where they have usurped Your power and authority over me, it has only weakened me. Cover me with Your blood and wash me clean. I want to be free of everything and everyone that has hindered my walk with You. Align my heart, mind, and soul with Your truth. I break every curse, assignment, and attachment that the enemy hoped to use against me as a result of my sin. Holy Spirit fill me, renew my hope, and help me trust in Your faithfulness that You are completing a good work in me.

Free me from the anxiety that comes from too much dependence on my earthly circumstances. Only with Your help is this possible. I thank you and boldly claim that the weapons with which I fight these strongholds are not the weapons of the world. I choose to take every thought captive and make it obedient to Christ. Don't ever let me forget that I have a very real enemy who wants to keep me in bondage. Help me to discern his schemes and take my stand against him in the power of Your Spirit. Father, this process of breaking free is hard work! Please remind me often that it is also very good work. Help me to know without a doubt that any effort You require of me will have effect. Please help me to never give up, no matter how long it takes. Father, Your incomparably great power is available to those who believe. If you can raise Jesus from the dead, You can deliver me from any stronghold.

Your Word says that knowing You is so wonderful that I can consider everything a loss compared to Your surpassing greatness. Help me to consider everything else worthless that I must lay down to gain more knowledge and a more abiding presence of You. I trust there is something more You are trying to teach me. Father, Your Word promises that we can know that in all things You work for the good of those who love You, who are called according to Your purpose. You can and will work this situation for good if I will cooperate with You.

You have seen every tear I've cried. God, please don't waste this suffering. Turn my circumstance into something that will give You glory and further Your kingdom. Your Word tells me to humble myself under Your mighty hand; that You may lift me up in due time. Help me to see beyond this moment here. Father, give me the spirit of wisdom and revelation so that I may know You better. I pray also that the eyes of my heart may be enlightened in order that I may know the hope to which You have called me, the riches of your glorious inheritance.

Father I pray for those that you have put in my path to restore me. I pray for their protection as well as my own. I also pray that I will know when I'm strong enough to help others. At the proper time, I will reap a harvest if I do not give up! You always lead me in triumphal procession in Christ. You only lead to victory. If I keep following You, I'll get there.

STUDY

1. Review Hebrews 11:32-38. Describe some of the possible outcomes of a faithful life:

"Good" results	"Bad" results
_____	_____
_____	_____
_____	_____
_____	_____

What does this reveal about using outcomes to determine our attitude toward God?

Your First Love

2. Psalm 86:11 says, *"Teach me your way, O LORD, and I will walk in your truth; give me an undivided heart, that I may fear your name."* What does it mean to have a <u>divided</u> heart?

3. Read 1 John 2:15-16. Which of these things threaten your "first love?"

☐ yourself   ☐ spouse   ☐ children
☐ your friends   ☐ career   ☐ home
☐ money   ☐ material things   ☐ parents
☐ ambition   ☐ food or other substance   ☐ technology/devices
☐ church activities   ☐ sports of physical fitness   ☐ fun, pleasure
☐ ministry   ☐ appearance, image   ☐ popularity
☐ hobbies   ☐ knowledge   ☐ reputation

4. Is there anything in your life that has a stronger hold on you than Jesus? What have you been attached to that could keep you from living *completely* for God's purposes? Have you been holding on to anything so tightly that it has caused you to lose your balance?

5. If Jesus asked you to "Let _____ go," would you? Will you loosen your grip on *anything* and *anyone* as a prerequisite for following Him?   YES   NO

6. Some pleasures only become sinful when you let them get out of hand. How do you keep this from happening?

7. A stronghold is anything that exalts itself in your mind, making itself bigger or more important than God. You demolish strongholds when you fix your eyes on Jesus and make your mind captive to Christ. Your mind is retrained and renewed when you choose to think His thoughts about a situation instead of your own and those influenced by the enemy. This takes time and diligent effort on your part. What do you think it means to *"take every thought captive"* and make it obedient to Christ (see 2 Corinthians 10:5)?

8. Why is it so difficult to break strongholds in your own strength? Why can't you just "decide you're not going to do that anymore?"

9. What are some things you have tried to use in the past to satisfy you, but you remained unfulfilled?

10. What does a truly satisfied person look like? Does that describe you?

11. Read Philippians 3:8. How did Paul feel about his relationship with Jesus?

"I consider everything a loss compared to the surpassing greatness of knowing Christ Jesus my Lord, for whose sake I have lost all things. I consider them rubbish, that I may gain Christ."

Philippians 3:8

12. What would it take to put Jesus at the center of your life? How would your priorities and actions have to change?

Facing the Fiery Furnace

13. List some people of faith you have known that have suffered a disease, tragedy, or death. Did you ever question 'why'?

14. What do you do when you can't explain what God is doing – like when He doesn't stop a tragedy or ease suffering? From our earthly point of view, God appears either mean or weak in these situations. How do you resolve this? Have you been able to come up with an answer that is satisfying to you?

15. In Psalm 30:6 David wrote, *"When I felt secure, I said, 'I will never be shaken.'"* Why does God allow things in our world to be "shaken" at times?

16. Have you ever been disappointed with God? What restored your trust in Him?

17. Read Daniel 3:16-18. How did Shadrach, Meshach, and Abednego demonstrate a faith that is hard to offend?

18. In Psalm 119:28 David said, *"My soul is weary with sorrow; strengthen me according to your Word."* How can God's Word strengthen you?

The Purpose of It All

19. Do you find yourself more dependent on Jesus when in "a storm?" What tends to happen when things are quiet and more at ease?

20. According to 2 Corinthians 1:8-11, what are some reasons that God might allow suffering or difficulty in our lives?

21. Circle all the ways that you have personally experienced Jesus during times of difficulty:

Comforter	Advocate	Counselor
Deliverer	Bread of Life	Friend
Hiding Place	Great High Priest	Father
Prince of Peace	Refuge and Strength	Savior
Shepherd	Redeemer	Stronghold

22. John 15:2 says that God prunes every fruitful branch so that it may bear more fruit. What are some ways that God prunes us?

23. What kind of cooperation is required of you during the "pruning process" or "refiner's fire?"

24. No one likes tests, but teachers know they get your attention and promote understanding. What have you learned from the tests God has allowed you to go through? Has He used life and circumstances to correct something in you?

25. List any good things that have resulted from a bad situation in your past.

26. Explain how this moment of time in your life is like looking at only a single puzzle piece. How does this change your perspective? How would you describe God's "big picture" for you?

27. Why is it crucial that our hope is stored up in heaven (see Colossians 1:5)?

28. Read Psalm 73:25-28 as a personal prayer.

SPIRITUAL MARKER

hope

WORSHIP

Before the Morning [Josh Wilson]

Even If [Mercy Me]

Thy Will Be Done [Hillary Scott]

Scars [I Am They]

Fall Apart [Josh Wilson]

Held [Natalie Grant]

It Is Well [Bethel Music featuring Kristene DiMarco]

No Matter What [Kerrie Roberts]

Praise You in This Storm [Casting Crowns]

Though You Slay Me [Shane & Shane featuring John Piper]

Once and For All [Lauren Daigle]

Trust in You [Lauren Daigle]

New Wine [Hillsong]

Another in the Fire [Hillsong United]

Be Still My Soul [Kari Jobe]

TRUST IN THE LORD
WITH ALL YOUR HEART

PROVERBS 3:5

FORGIVE 70 X 7

Growing up in a small Mennonite community in rural Nebraska (population 1,000) was a beautiful, sheltered life – until the day my sister was murdered. The town prided itself on perfect churches, perfect lawns, and a perfectly pure 'no drinking-no dancing' policy. To my knowledge, no one had a drug problem, no one had an eating disorder, and no one would consider cutting their own wrists. We didn't even know that most of these things existed. But now our situation was messy; far from perfect.

Most people didn't know what to say or do, so they did nothing.

There was a trial, and then another one years later because of a legal loophole. All our testimonies had to be repeated. It provided scandalous headlines for eight long and frustrating years. I had several supportive friends, but most of the community kept their distance, embarrassed by all the negative publicity. And the senior pastor of our church said it would be too dangerous (spiritually) for him to pray with us.

There would be much to forgive.

Someday, I thought.

Having been saved at an early age, I wish that I could say that as a "good Christian" it was simple and easy for me to forgive. But it wasn't. In fact, when my best friend raised the issue 10 years after the tragedy, I was annoyed. She simply didn't understand what our family had been through.

But God couldn't let me stay where I was… and it was time.

Until now, I haven't shared this part of my life story with many people. I am quite a private person, so why share such details now? Because I want you to clearly understand that I clearly understand the concept of forgiveness. It's the next step of surrender in this journey.

Maybe your situation is not as bad as mine; maybe it's worse. No matter what your circumstance, forgiving is not beyond your capability with the help of the Holy Spirit. With access to your fully surrendered heart, He will continue to press in this area until you resolve it. It's the only way to advance in your relationship with Jesus.

Because He Said So

The importance of this topic cannot be underestimated. We see many examples in the Old Testament that model the behavior: Joseph forgave his brothers for selling him as a slave,[1] Esau forgave Jacob for stealing his birthright,[2] God continually forgave the Israelites for their grumbling in the desert,[3] and David forgave Saul for trying to kill him, even going so far as to show favor to Saul's descendants.[4]

But forgiveness takes on even greater significance in the New Testament:

- **It is part of the Lord's Prayer** – and the only phrase in that prayer with a condition attached… *"Forgive us our trespasses, as we forgive those who trespass against us."*[5]
- **It is a requirement before you pray.** *"And when you stand praying, if you hold anything against anyone, forgive them, so that your Father in heaven may forgive you your sins."*[6]
- **It is mentioned in connection with receiving the Holy Spirit.** *Immediately* after Jesus breathed on the disciples and they received the Holy Spirit, He talked to them about forgiveness.[7] He said that if they forgive the sins of anyone, they are forgiven; if they retain the sins of anyone, they are retained. If this was the first duty assigned to the disciples upon receiving the Holy Spirit, it should be a priority for us as well.
- **It was included in Jesus' dying words.** Of the few things spoken from the Cross (when every word must have been agonizingly painful), He chose to address forgiveness.[8]

There's no getting around it and no way to avoid it. God cannot complete His work in you amid an atmosphere of bitterness and resentment. An unforgiving heart will hinder your spiritual growth and relationship with Jesus. If you don't feel your connection with Jesus growing, it may be because you are withholding forgiveness in some area. Become unrelenting in your pursuit of healing!

Jesus said it is impossible to live this life and not have the opportunity to be hurt or offended.[9] He also said one of the signs of the end times would be that *"many will be offended, will betray one another, and will hate one another."*[10] Notice He didn't say a few, but *many*. It is imperative that we learn exactly how Jesus wants us to handle these offenses in the proper way. Your willingness to do the hard thing is what will set you apart as a beloved disciple of Christ.

His Wonderful, Merciful Plan

To be able to forgive others, you must first fully grasp how He has forgiven you. Eternal forgiveness was the primary purpose of Jesus' earthly ministry. The Cross was not something that "just happened" to Jesus – He came to die; the Cross was His purpose. *"But He was pierced for our transgressions, He was crushed for our iniquities; the punishment that brought us peace was on Him, and by His wounds we are healed."*[11]

Jesus endured the Cross because there had to be an atoning payment for our sin. The spotless, innocent lamb paid the debt of the guilty. *"He made Him who knew no sin to be sin for us, that we might become the righteousness of God."*[12] Because of what Jesus went through, every human being has been provided with a way into the presence of God. You can *"draw near with a sincere heart in full assurance of faith…sprinkled clean from an evil conscience and washed with pure water…for He who promised is faithful."*[13]

It is Finished

The debt has been paid. The blood of Jesus Christ "cleanses us from all sin."[14] It is just as though you never sinned! *"For I will forgive their iniquity, and I will remember their sin no more."*[15] Once you have confessed your sin and asked for God's forgiveness, don't continue to bring it up to Him. You will only be reminding Him of something He promised to forget; something He removed from you *"as far as the east is from the west."*[16] Micah 7:19 says that God casts our sin to the depths of the ocean floor.

So many people harbor feelings of guilt for things they have done in the past. Once you have repented of your sin, anything else that remains is false guilt, one of Satan's favorite weapons. His voice will try to accuse, belittle, and shame you, telling you that you've gone too far, you're beyond grace, and that you need to make yourself right before you can turn back to God. But 2 Corinthians 7:10 says, *"Godly sorrow brings repentance that leads to salvation and **leaves no regret**, but worldly sorrow brings death."* Debilitating, hopeless sorrow and shame over past failures is from the devil. You can despise the sin, but do not despise yourself. If something is still tormenting you after you have confessed it, you need to fight against it. That's not what Jesus intends for you. The Bible tells us, *"There is now no condemnation for those who are in Christ Jesus."*[17] Stop punishing yourself for something that no longer exists. You are a new creation, the old has passed away, and the new has come![18]

Peter intended to be brave and strong for Jesus. When he failed by denying his Master three times, shame and remorse overwhelmed him. But look how gently and lovingly Jesus restored him! He simply asked Peter if he loved Him – three times. Would you calmly ask a friend, *"Do you love me?"* after they betrayed you? Peter had to first grasp this level of compassion and forgiveness before he could become the leader of the church. Once he experienced Jesus' love and restoration, he could truly speak of Jesus as his Savior.

Even if you have stumbled in this life, you too can press on to greatness. Do not let past failures paralyze your heart. Give yourself a fresh start. To do otherwise implies the Cross has had no effect on your life. You must accept and receive the forgiveness God gives you. You cannot become a beloved disciple if you are filled with guilt and condemnation.

The Hardest Thing to Give Away

Once you realize your own debt of sin has been forgiven, you can turn your attention to the process of forgiving others. Not an easy task.

On the cross, Jesus prayed to forgive the men who tortured and crucified Him. He said, *"Father, forgive them, for they know not what they do."*[19] He did not wait for them to say, "Oh sorry, we made a mistake." He released them unconditionally, and in doing so, He became the perfect example of God's unconditional love and forgiveness.

Infinite Grace

Peter was hoping to impress Jesus when he asked, *"Lord, how often should my brother sin against me and I forgive him? Up to seven times?"*[20] In Hebrew, the number 7 represents perfection. Peter was sure he had come up with the perfect solution. But Jesus told him to multiply that by 70. Actually, the Lord had an infinite number in mind. God's forgiveness toward us is limitless and He expects us to extend the same forgiveness to others. According to this perspective, there should never be a time when you harbor unforgiveness.

Jesus then told a shocking parable to emphasize His point:[21]

"The kingdom of heaven is like a certain king who wanted to settle accounts with his servants. And when he had begun to settle the accounts, one was brought to him who owed him 10,000 talents."

In those days, a talent was a unit of measure for something precious, such as gold. One talent was equivalent to approximately 75 pounds. Ten thousand talents would be approximately 750,000 pounds, so this servant owed the king an *impossible* debt. Jesus was emphasizing that this servant owed a debt he could never repay.

Because he was not able to pay, the king demanded that he be sold as a slave, along with his wife and children and all that he had, for some payment to be made. The servant fell before him, saying, *"Master, have patience with me, and I will pay you all."* The king was *"moved with compassion, released him, and forgave him the debt."*

The king represents God, who forgave a debt impossible for us to pay. The Bible says, *"He canceled the record of debt that stood against us with its legal demands. This He set aside, nailing it to the cross."*[22] There is no way we could ever repay God what we owe him. God gave us salvation and forgiveness as a free gift.

But the story continues…that servant went out and found one of his fellow servants who owed him a hundred denarii; *"and he laid hands on him and took him by the throat, saying, "Pay me what you owe!"* His fellow servant fell at his feet and begged him, *"Have patience with me, and I will pay you all."* But he would not show compassion – he threw him into prison until the debt could be paid.

The fellow servant owed a sizable sum of money, but it was nothing compared to what the servant owed the king. When the other servants saw what happened, they were angry, and went to tell the king. Then the king said to him, *"You wicked servant! I forgave you all that debt because you begged me. Should you not also have had compassion on your fellow servant, just as I had pity on you?"* The king was furious and delivered him *"to the torturers until he should pay all that was due to him."*

Webster's dictionary defines *torture* as "the infliction of intense pain to punish." From God's perspective, the instigators of this torture and pain are demonic spirits. God will allow demons to inflict pain on your mind and body if you withhold forgiveness from your fellow servants. *"So My heavenly Father also will do to you if each of you, from his heart, does not forgive his brother his trespasses."*

You want mercy for yourself, but justice for others. You can't have it both ways. If you demand justice because someone hurt you, then you cannot ask for mercy for yourself. That is what the wicked servant did. You have been released from your debt; the least you can do is forgive your fellow servants. It is the merciful who obtain mercy.[23]

Mandatory Mercy

In almost every other parable in the Bible, Jesus did not offer an interpretation unless asked. In this example, however, He wanted no mistaking the severity of consequences for those who refuse to forgive. You are not punished for your sins in the way you deserve. Instead, Jesus was punished in your place. Jesus has forgiven every sin you have committed or ever will commit, and His love requires that you do the same for others.

You may have done nothing wrong. Jesus asks you to forgive even when the situation is not your fault. You extend forgiveness even though the other person may not deserve or ask for it. You must choose to forgive whether they feel remorseful or not. Sometimes the person who has caused the trauma does not even realize what he or she has done.

When you don't forgive, quite simply, you are telling Jesus that you refuse to give to others what He has so freely given to you. Jesus meant it when He said, *"But if you do not forgive, neither will your Father in heaven forgive you."*[24] He does not just say this once, but many times. He wanted to emphasize the importance of this warning. The Bible Knowledge Commentary clarifies that although you don't earn your own salvation by forgiving others, your ability to forgive is based on recognizing what you have been forgiven. The parable was teaching that because you have been forgiven all, you should in turn forgive all.

◆

Clear the Bitterness Away

The depth of your relationship with Jesus will be affected if you refuse to forgive others. Besides affecting your relationship with Jesus, unforgiveness comes with other unpleasant consequences. A bitter heart is one of them.

Before leading the Israelites out of Egypt, the Lord told them to prepare a Passover meal which included bitter herbs. This was to serve as a reminder of the bitterness they had experienced in bondage. Bitterness and bondage go together. It is believed that those bitter herbs tasted something like horseradish. You know that taking a big bite of horseradish can cause some serious consequences! Bitterness can cause the same consequences in us spiritually. Not only does it make us uncomfortable, but it also holds us in spiritual bondage.

When you sow seeds of criticism, condemnation, and unforgiveness, bitterness will take root in your life. The Bible says, *"Look diligently and make sure that **no root of bitterness** shoots forth and causes trouble and many become contaminated by it."*[25] This root can't be easily seen as it grows deep under the ground. You are told to "look carefully."

If the root of bitterness is watered, fed, and given your attention, it will increase in strength. Soon it will become very hard to pull out. Your emotional reaction to the hurt will intensify. Instead of the fruit of peace being produced in your life, you will see a harvest of anger, resentment, jealousy, hatred, strife, and discord.[26] Bitterness will eventually contaminate you and everyone around you. The longer you ignore it, the stronger it will become, and the harder your heart will grow.

You Can't Be the Jury and the Judge

You can't hide a bitter heart. It's going to come out one way or another. The Bible says, *"Above all else, guard your heart, for everything you do flows from it."*[27] And then *"the mouth speaks what the heart is full of."*[28] When you have a bitter heart, it often shows up in your critical words.

The instructions are clear about judging others – *don't*. Nothing good is accomplished by it. *"Do not judge, or you too will be judged. For in the same way you judge others, you will be judged, and with the measure you use, it will be measured to you."*[29] The way you treat people is the way you will be treated. You must understand this spiritual law. And it should make you want to be the most forgiving, loving, and understanding person on earth! Would you dare to stand before God and say, "Please judge me as I have judged others?"

When God first started addressing this issue in me, He would bring up 10 instances of judgment a day! Once I was sitting in church, and before the service even started, I noticed that I had several critical thoughts about the people around me – "Her hair is a mess…That dress is too tight…It's too cold in here!" Ugh. I felt the Holy Spirit tapping me on the shoulder as if to say, "You're missing the point of being here, aren't you?" It is impossible to enter the presence of God when you are in a critical mood.

When you try to correct the wrong done to you, you set yourself up as a judge. But *"Who are you to judge another?"*[30] The Holy Spirit is the only one in the proper position to judge. I have found that trying to take the role of the Holy Spirit in someone else's life is exhausting – we are not meant to be the controlling conscience for anyone else. We tend to be very critical of the shortcomings of others, yet blind to our own. *"How can you say…'Brother, let me remove the speck that is in your eye,' when you yourself do not see the plank in your own eye?"*[31]

Each heart is so complex, only our Maker can understand it. Every individual is different – driven by different motives, controlled by different circumstances, and influenced by different sufferings. It takes time, effort, and supernatural discernment to look beyond the surface of any human being…what the Bible calls the *"hidden man of the heart."*[32] There is always something more that we don't understand about every person's situation.

Try to see the one who offended you not as they currently are, but as they *could be* when fully surrendered to Jesus.

Begin to pray for the person who has hurt you. In your quiet times alone with God, He can provide the insight you need to understand what and why it happened. Trust in God's justice and release your own bitterness and anger. It doesn't mean you minimize, mitigate, or excuse what happened. It does not mean that you can't pursue justice here on earth through the appropriate legal avenues. It simply means you release your own personal wrath and desire for vengeance; trusting that God will eventually bring justice, whether in heaven or on earth.

In my situation, God helped me to see that the person that killed my sister was wounded himself. He had been severely abused as a child before coming to live in our home. He became angry and took out his frustration with life on us. I realized he did not know how to properly deal with his own fear, anxiety, and disappointment. While that's no excuse for his poor choices, recognizing this helped me to better understand his actions.

The Prisoner Set Free is You

Showing mercy, compassion, and forgiveness is the only way to be set free from the burden of bitterness and judgment. However, the process of forgiving will probably be one of the most exhausting struggles you will face. This is because the battle will involve your mind, will, and emotions. Maybe you have been mentally replaying the event for days, months, or even years. As a result, you repeatedly experience the same intense fear, anxiety, anger, and frustration. These are among the most toxic emotions a person can have, draining your energy and resources. Your heart cannot rest in this state, and you suffer physical and emotional problems.

Medical professionals agree that many of our long-term illnesses are the result of bitterness, unforgiveness, and emotional stress. Pent-up hostility can produce depression and anxiety along with a host of physical problems. Nearly 20 years of research on the Forgiveness Project at the University of Wisconsin showed that people who forgave had better psychological health. The studies revealed significant improvements in depression, anxiety, post-traumatic stress, self-esteem, and coping skills among those who were able to forgive.[33]

Bottom line…unforgiveness will make you sick. *"That is why many among you are weak and sick, and a number of you have fallen asleep. But if we were more discerning with regard to ourselves, we would not come under such judgment."*[34]

Get the Target Off Your Back

Satan will try to taunt you with feelings of resentment. He would love to keep you feeling sorry for yourself. This makes your reaction to the situation sinful. Satan will then go to God and demand his right to use the principle of sowing and reaping against you:

"Do not judge, and you will not be judged. Do not condemn, and you will not be condemned. Forgive, and you will be forgiven. Give, and it will be given to you. A good measure, pressed down, shaken together and running over, will be poured into your lap. For with the measure you use, it will be measured to you."[35]

We often reference this Scripture of sowing and reaping in relation to financial blessings. But notice the first three statements are about judgment, condemnation, and forgiveness, rather than financial blessings.

Satan loves to take advantage of this spiritual law. When you make judgments about others, it gives him the legal right to operate in that area in your own life. Whenever you hold a grudge, condemn others, or harbor bitterness and resentment, *you invite attack against yourself* in that same area. Whatever you are most angry about may keep manifesting in your life.

When you refuse to forgive, you essentially put a target on your back for the enemy to take aim. If you don't forgive a controlling mother, you will attract those around you that continue to manipulate and control you. If you don't forgive an abusive father, you will be surprised how frequently the enemy brings a similar situation to your attention, constantly making you relive the experience. If you leave a relationship resentful and bitter, you will enter the next relationship inviting similar problems to follow you. Statistics show that the vast majority of divorced people end up getting divorced again. Their inability to forgive their first spouse hinders their relationship with the second one.

This is a spiritual law, and you are only damaging yourself when you operate on the wrong side of it. Where you demand justice, you are stepping back into a legalistic system where the enemy has power to demand justice and payment for your sins as well. If the enemy can get you to sow judgment and condemnation, then he will be legally entitled to bring into your life all the punishment that you deserve. That is the enemy's plan. The only safe response is mercy.

Second Corinthians 2:11 warns us to forgive so that Satan might not *"outwit us."*

The Amplified version says, ***"to keep Satan from getting the advantage over us."*** Satan will take tremendous advantage of any unforgiveness in your life. I believe the enemy is trying to keep this truth hidden from the body of Christ. The Bible says, *"My people are destroyed from lack of knowledge."*[36] But the Lord has provided a way to set the captives free, to heal the brokenhearted, and to open the prison doors.[37] The path of forgiveness is the only way to healing and freedom.

See Through Eyes of Grace

Forgiveness requires surrender – laying down your rights and your version of justice in the situation. Each time you forgive, you essentially "re-enact" the Cross by surrendering your anger, laying down your judgment, and releasing those who harmed you. The enemy hates anything resembling the Cross, so he will work very hard to prevent you from growing in this area.

The Greek word most often translated "forgiveness" is *aphiemi,* meaning "to send away, let go from oneself" or to "let it drop." The *opposite* of that word means "to bind together, unite together, or bring into bondage." Essentially, you must make a choice to separate yourself from the hurt or be in bondage to it. Harboring unforgiveness will unite you to the other person and allow them to maintain a form of control over you. In spiritual terms, picture yourself being continually chained together in the unseen realm. You can break that chain.

You may feel that you have a right to be mad. You may feel that withholding forgiveness is the only way you can punish that person. But surrendering means you let go or drop your right to get even. That doesn't mean that what happened to you is acceptable. And it doesn't mean God will let that person off the hook. You are simply choosing to cooperate with God in surrender, forgiving another as Christ forgave you. And keep in mind, forgiveness doesn't make the other person right, it makes you free.

Counselor, Comforter, Keeper

The Bible says, *"Never take your own revenge, beloved, but leave room for the wrath of God. For it is written, 'Vengeance is mine, I will repay,' says the Lord."*[38] No matter how badly you have been hurt in the past, leave the consequences to God. He is faithful. He will plead your case and take up your cause, but only after you stop defending yourself in the matter. Notice that if you try to pay people back, you close the door for God to do it. *Leave room for Him to do it His way.* What a liberating way to live! You don't have to try to manipulate the situation to your own advantage.

When David had the opportunity to kill Saul, his response was, *"Do not destroy him; for who can stretch out his hand against the Lord's anointed, and be guiltless? ...the Lord shall strike him, or his day shall come to die, or he shall go out to battle and perish. The Lord forbid that I should stretch out my hand against the Lord's anointed."*[39] Though he was encouraged by others to do it, David would not avenge himself. He left the outcome of Saul's life in the hands of God. Eventually, Saul did die in battle against the Philistines. But even after the news of his death reached David, he did not rejoice.

You may never see God's retribution on your behalf. You may never see the other person get what you think they deserve. That is not the point. Keep in mind, Jesus does not give you what you deserve either. The band of brothers who treated Joseph so badly all became the patriarchs of Israel! Joseph eventually forgave his brothers, and the plan of God was fulfilled in all their lives.

It Takes Everything You Have

Not only should you not avenge yourself, but Jesus suggests that you should be willing to open yourself to the possibility of being hurt again. He says, *"If anyone slaps you on the right cheek, turn to them the other cheek also. And if anyone wants to sue you and take your shirt, hand over your coat as well. If anyone forces you to go one mile, go with them two miles."*[40]

This implies it is not enough just to forgive your enemies, but you are instructed to go further and bless **them.** *"Love your enemies and pray for those who persecute you."*[41] This does not mean you pray for them to make more money or have more possessions; you are praying for spiritual blessings. You can ask the Holy Spirit to work in their life, bringing truth and revelation so that they can repent of their sins and experience God's plan for them.

I also want to clarify that this does not mean that you tolerate an abusive relationship. Don't confuse forgiveness with trust. Forgiveness must be freely given; trust must be earned through *trustworthy* behavior over time. Forgiveness does not mean you are a doormat. After forgiving, ask the Holy Spirit to clearly direct whether you should repair, restore, or remain in a particular relationship.

He Makes All Things New

God is aware of every painful experience you have encountered. The conversation that stunned you. The divorce. The wrongful death. The day your friend walked away. That marked moment in time where you now define life before the hurt and after the hurt.

I truly understand this kind of defining devastation in a personal way. And God understands that you need to grieve, heal, and be restored from the hurt you have experienced. Psychologists and medical doctors do not have the adequate tools to repair your broken heart and shattered trust. Only Jesus can reach deep into your soul and heal this type of damage. Once your heart becomes hard, it is nearly impossible to fix it on your own. It requires a supernatural working of the Holy Spirit. He alone can restore you to the joy and peace you felt prior to the injury.

The healing process takes time. By forgiving the other person, you "clean and disinfect the wound." But you cannot heal it. Jesus is the Healer. Let Him tend it properly. Sometimes a deep physical wound appears to be healed on the outside but is still painful on the inside. It's the same with emotional wounds. Wait for Him to heal your tender feelings at a deeper level.

Healer of Your Heart

One of the most tragic consequences of unforgiveness is an inability to give and receive love. If you can't risk being hurt again, you can't love unconditionally. Unconditional love demands that you give others the *right to hurt you.*

Those who harbor unforgiveness have not fully and completely opened their hearts to Jesus. They build up walls to protect themselves and prevent any future injury. They carefully guard their relationships, letting very few people "in." Without realizing it, those walls of protection become a prison. Wounded people only feel safe in the controlled environment they set up for themselves. But the life of an unforgiving person can soon become stagnant, like the Dead Sea in Israel. The Dead Sea receives water in but does not release any water out. As a result, there are no living plants or fish in it. Life cannot be sustained if hoarded – it must flow freely.

You may need to *pour out* some of the negative contents in your heart – like hurt, anger, despair, bitterness, unforgiveness, and confusion – before the Lord can *pour in* His fresh, living water. Be honest and tell Him exactly how you feel about what happened. David, Job, Hannah, Abraham, and Moses all poured out their frustrations to Him. You can too!

Do the Impossible

If unforgiveness controls your life, you cannot become the person God created you to be or enjoy an intimate relationship with Jesus. You won't be able to pray effectively, worship effectively, or experience His love fully without forgiving others. In other words, you can't become a beloved disciple until you take this next step. This means giving up your resentment and desire to retaliate, no matter what that person has done.

We live in a broken and fallen world. Spouses, parents, friends, pastors, teachers, coworkers, and bosses aren't perfect. We are incapable of walking in perfect harmony all the time. You are going to get some battle wounds as you journey through life. And the closer the relationship, the more severe the wound!

Sometimes our disappointments are the result of unrealistic expectations for another human being. We demand total perfection from the other person. We want them to take care of us, meet all our needs, and never hurt us. But some of these needs can only be met by God. When you expect a person to meet a need that only God can fill, you are setting yourself up for disappointment. *"What causes fights and quarrels among you? You cannot get what you want, so you quarrel and fight. You do not have because you do not ask God."*[42]

Who is He asking you to forgive – A parent? Your spouse? Your boss? Someone who bullied you? The "other woman"? It's not going to be easy, but which do you prefer – more of your own bitterness or more of Him? That person has already caused enough pain. There's been enough damage done. You don't have to be held hostage by it. You get to decide how you'll move forward.

In His Hands

Some of you have lost a loved one due to a mistake by another person. You may need to forgive a negligent doctor. Or a reckless drunk driver. Or a murderer. But allow me to remind you that your loved one did not go home "early" because of their actions. I know it feels like they took your loved one's life. You are hurt and want someone to blame. But God knows exactly when and how each of us will draw our final breath.

Someone I know recently died of cancer. The doctor missed the diagnosis until it was too late. It was frustrating and painful to us, to say the least. But God was not sitting in heaven saying, "Ooops, the doctor missed that…so I guess she's coming home sooner than I planned. And I don't have her room ready!" *No.* The Bible tells us that every hair on our heads is numbered.[43] He knows our going out and our coming in.[44] He is preparing a place for each of us.[45] Far in advance, He has each room ready.

No one can change the will of God. Nothing comes against us without God's knowledge of it before it happens. *Who sent Joseph to Egypt?* His brothers or God? *Who sent David to serve Saul?* We know that it was God. Both men had favor dangled in front of their eyes only to experience horrific trials for many years. This was a perfect opportunity for Joseph and David to be offended – by people and by God. Resist the temptation to question God's plan.

Let it Go and Be Amazed

Let me assure you: forgiveness is possible. And it is good. Forgiveness is a necessary step you must take to heal and move on. When bitter feelings from your past take center stage in your life, you will miss God's favor. God wants you to forgive those who have hurt you so that you can experience the blessings He has in store for you. Unless you let go of the old, God cannot bring in the new. If you let Him work, He will bring good out of the situation.

Many people get off track and wonder why their lives are not going the way they had hoped. Whenever you stay angry with others and refuse to forgive, you are not fully surrendered. You are still controlling your own life. Jesus will test your attitude to see if you are fully devoted to trusting Him with every trial and heartache. And He will give you plenty of opportunities to practice!

If I had refused to do what I knew God was instructing me to do, I would have missed a tremendous blessing and an opportunity to minister to others. Most likely I would not have written this chapter if I could not surrender my rights and forgive. I chose forgiveness because I did not want to step away from His will or be hindered from reaching my full potential. I didn't want to weaken His ability to use me. I didn't want to make myself sick. I didn't want to have a bitter heart for the rest of my life. I didn't want to be a target for the enemy. I didn't want to miss any blessings God might have in store for me.

The Bible says that *after* Job had prayed for the friends who had ridiculed him, the Lord made him prosperous again… blessing the latter part of Job's life more than the first.[46] You cannot imagine how He will use you and bless you if you will surrender all your hurts to Him.

New Life Begins

Forgiveness is an attitude and action that you must choose to learn. It takes practice! Paul compared it to exercising – *"and herein do I exercise myself, to always have a conscience void of offense toward God and toward men."*[47] You will need to practice strengthening your heart, mind, and emotions to be less prone to future injury. Take the following steps:

- ☐ Get quiet and still. Ask the Holy Spirit to bring to mind anyone you need to forgive.
- ☐ Verbally confess, out loud, your desire to forgive them (one at a time).
- ☐ Repent of judging the other person and release them for God to be their Judge.
- ☐ Ask God to break every curse, assignment, and attachment that the enemy might use against you because of your sin of judgment. Ask God to break all unholy soul ties between you and the other person. Ask for a cleansing covering of the blood of Jesus over it all.
- ☐ Verbally renounce (reject) your participation with anger, offense, unforgiveness, fear, bitterness, hate, self-pity, depression, or jealousy (or anything else the Holy Spirit brings to mind). Take authority and kick out the demonic spirits associated with these things in the name of Jesus (Luke 10:19).
- ☐ Ask Him to wash away all negative memories, emotions, and associations from your mind, body, soul, and spirit. Ask God to bring a deep healing to these areas.
- ☐ Ask the Holy Spirit to come in and fill every void (don't leave your soul empty now). Ask Him to bring in the joy of the Lord, the presence of God, the mind of Christ, His will, and His plans and purposes for your life. Thank Him for doing this.

Practice casting down thoughts as soon as you start to revisit the hurt. Remind yourself of the command to forgive and *why* it's important. Be aware of the consequences of unforgiveness (physical, emotional, and spiritual). Healing is a *process,* and you won't feel better overnight. After you choose to forgive, there is still a deeper work in your heart that God must complete over time. When negative feelings resurface, recognize that God may want to take you to a new level of deliverance. He began the work, and He will keep perfecting it. If He shows you a new piece of the puzzle that requires further forgiveness, respond in obedience quickly.

The Bible says, *"Let all bitterness and wrath and anger and clamor and slander be put away from you, along with all malice. Be kind to one another, tenderhearted, forgiving each other, just as God in Christ also has forgiven you."*[48] Ask Him to help you avoid being drawn back into unforgiveness. Satan will try to bait you, even through fellow believers, and re-ignite your anger. When someone tries to bait you into talking about the problem again, steer the conversation in a different direction. Simply say, "I did have an issue with that for a while, but God is working everything out now." When painful memories resurface, it doesn't mean you're still holding a grudge. Remind yourself that you've chosen to forgive that person and move on.

Maturity in forgiveness does not come easily. If it did, everyone would be a beloved disciple by now. Few reach this level of surrender because of the internal resistance they face. They stubbornly hold on to their selfish point of view and refuse to humble themselves enough to forgive.

Don't wait another day. Don't set this chapter aside until you have addressed the issue. This is a test you will have to pass if you want to deepen your relationship with Jesus. He is determined to have His beloved disciples as pure, clean, and white as snow. Many will turn back at this point because they are unwilling to look at things from God's perspective. You will feel some tension and resistance as you are asked to move a little farther in your faith. But it is only through full surrender that your heart will be prepared to move on to the next phase of becoming a beloved disciple in prayer (Step #4), thanksgiving (Step #5), and worship (Step #6).

Prayer

Jesus, I welcome the conviction and truth of Your Holy Spirit. Please provide the grace and strength to carry out what You are asking of me. Lord, help me to work through this. Make me willing to be willing. I give You permission, Holy Spirit, to bring up whatever issues You need to so that I can forgive and repent in order to be free. Your word is clear that if I do not forgive others, You will not forgive my sins. I am not without sin. I do not want to be deceived in this matter. Give me the honesty and courage to take the plank out of my own eye before I try to remove the speck from another person's eye. Help me to see the monumental price of unforgiveness. I do not want to be enslaved or suffer repercussions if I refuse to forgive. Help me to be aware of the devil's schemes, that he might not outwit me.

I know I have grieved the Holy Spirit by criticizing others. I have judged others in bitterness and anger. Forgive me for not forgiving those who have offended me. Forgive me for attributing malicious motives to people when I don't fully understand what motivates them. Father, forgive me for dishonoring my parents, my spouse, my pastor, my friends, my coworkers. It was my own pride that demanded justice. I now choose mercy over judgment. I choose to forgive those who have hurt me. I want to defeat the enemy and take away his legal rights to harm me. I place the cross of Jesus Christ between me and everything I was due to reap from the spiritual law of sowing and reaping with regards to unforgiveness. I break every curse, assignment, and consequence that the enemy planned to use against me as a result of my sin. I bring all the wrongs done to me to the feet of Jesus. I release it all into Your capable hands. Father, blot all past failures (my own and others) completely out of my heart and mind.

Lord, I give you permission to move powerfully in my life. Help me not to be overcome by evil but to overcome evil with good. Help me not to take revenge but leave room for your wrath. You will take up my case; You will redeem my life. I will wait for you, Lord, and trust that You will deliver me. Help me to lay this burden down and let You carry it instead. I humble myself that You may lift me up in due time. As far as it depends on me, I want to live at peace with everyone. Lord, take away my tendency to feel sorry for myself so I will be less easily offended in the future. Help me get rid of all bitterness, anger, slander, along with every form of malice. I want to be kind and compassionate and forgiving, just like You. I ask that You bless those who harmed me and lead them into a closer relationship with You. I trust You to redeem it all and turn it into something good.

STUDY

1. What do the following Scriptures say about who you are in Christ?

2 Corinthians 5:21

Colossians 1:22

Hebrews 10:14

2. Have you completely accepted Christ's death on the cross as the *total* payment for your sin? If you repent of sin but still let the enemy convince you that you are guilty, what are you implying about Jesus?

3. In what ways can God tangibly give grace to a person? How, specifically, has He extended grace to you?

See Through Eyes of Grace

4. Leviticus 19:16 says, *"Do not go about spreading slander among your people."* Do you think you can you go a full week without saying <u>anything</u> negative about someone else?

5. What do the following verses have to say about judging others?

Matthew 7:1-5

Luke 6:36-37

Romans 2:1-2

Romans 14:10-13

6. Where does Philippians 4:8 tell us to keep our focus?

Clear the Bitterness Away

7. How would you answer the following questions: <u>circle your response</u>

I have high expectations of others.	yes	no
I am easily disappointed in others.	yes	no
I tend to love conditionally.	yes	no
I don't like to be vulnerable with others.	yes	no
I am selective about my relationships.	yes	no
I have walled others out to avoid getting hurt.	yes	no

8. What inevitably happens when you attempt to get all your needs met by another person (spouse, children, friends, etc)?

9. Where would you rate yourself on the following scale:

I am easily, and often, offended   I am rarely offended

10. Which of these feelings have you experienced when offended in the past?

☐ hurt   ☐ jealousy   ☐ anger

☐ bitterness   ☐ resentment   ☐ hatred

11. How are these impurities in your heart impacting your life?

12. Which of these reasons have you used to hold on to unforgiveness?

☐ the offense was too great   ☐ they won't accept responsibility

☐ they aren't truly sorry   ☐ they never asked to be forgiven

☐ they will do it again   ☐ they did it again

☐ they did it deliberately   ☐ someone has to punish them

☐ I don't feel like forgiving yet   ☐ if I forgive, I'll have to be nice to the offender

In His Hands

13. Briefly review the story of Joseph (see Genesis 37-48). If you had been Joseph, how do you think you would have responded?

14. Review Psalm 105:16-22. Why did God send Joseph through those trials?

15. Think about a time you took matters into your own hands to avenge a wrong and did not wait upon the Lord. Describe the consequences.

Do the Impossible

16. When someone rejects or offends me, God wants me to...

17. List all the people who have offended you in the past:

_____   _____

_____   _____

_____   _____

_____   _____

_____   _____

18. The only way to be healed is to forgive. Your spiritual maturity depends on your willingness to forgive past offenses. A lack of compassion and a hardened heart result from an unwillingness to forgive others. For each person listed above, take the following steps to freedom through forgiveness:

I have been hurt by _____

Lord, I confess that I was offended when _____

Jesus, I understand that You desire for me to _____

Jesus, I choose to forgive _____

Lord, I surrender my right to be right in this situation. I repent of judging the other person and release them for You, God, to be their Judge and hold them accountable. I also repent for participating with anger, offense, unforgiveness, fear, bitterness, hate, self-pity, depression, and jealousy (or anything else the Holy Spirit brings to mind). I ask You Lord to take these negative emotions away from me. I kick out any demonic spirits associate with these things in the name of Jesus Christ.

I break all unholy soul ties between me and _____.

I now break every curse and assignment that the enemy hoped to use against me as a result of my unforgiveness in the past.

I ask You, Father, to wash away all negative memories and associations from my mind, body, soul, and spirit. Bring a deep healing to these areas. I choose to receive the joy of the Lord, the presence of God, the mind of Christ, Your will, and Your plans and purposes for my life. Thank You Jesus.

> # SPIRITUAL MARKER
>
> ## mercy

WORSHIP

Forgiveness [Matthew West]

Wonderful, Merciful Savior [Selah]

Your Grace Still Amazes Me [Phillips, Craig, and Dean]

Forgiven [Sanctus Real]

East to West [Casting Crowns]

Tell Your Heart to Beat Again [Danny Gokey]

All Things New [Elevation Worship]

Gone [Elevation Worship]

His Mercy is More [Shane and Shane]

Clean [Natalie Grant]

Mighty Cross [Elevation Worship]

Only Grace [Matthew West]

BLESSED ARE THE MERCIFUL FOR THEY WILL BE SHOWN MERCY

MATTHEW 5:6

WAIT UPON HIM

If you have made it this far, I am impressed by your courage and dedication to become a beloved disciple! Those first three steps were difficult and intense. You have been in the "refining fire." Now He will pour His soothing oil over you to refresh and restore you.

Have you ever taken off in an airplane on a cloudy, rainy day? If so, you know the process of climbing up through the clouds can be a turbulent ride. But once you break through, it's bright and sunny. It's as if the storm doesn't even exist down below. You, beloved disciple, have passed through some storms in the previous steps. And yet you desire to climb higher still. Let's continue the journey. You will now enter a phase of gentle growth – also known as "waiting."

- *"The LORD longs to be gracious to you…Blessed are all who **wait** for Him!"*[1]
- God *"acts on behalf of those who **wait** for Him."*[2]
- *"**Wait** for the LORD; be strong and take heart and **wait** for the LORD."*[3]
- *"Those that **wait** upon the Lord shall renew their strength…"*[4]

If you don't learn to wait on the Lord, you will never gain the strength of the Lord. The word *wait* means "to remain stationary in readiness or expectation," "to look forward expectantly," or "to be ready and available." One of the Hebrew translations for *wait* (qavah) means "to be braided together with." Picture a trellis where a vine can weave and intertwine itself into the supporting structure. The trellis provides security to the fragile vine so it can handle the weight of future fruit. This is the next phase in your discipleship – becoming completely intertwined with Him!

Every beloved disciple in the Bible experienced a period of waiting on the

Lord. Moses waited forty years in the desert before his burning bush assignment. David hid in caves for years before receiving his promised position in the palace. Abraham and Sarah waited until "old age" to bear the much-anticipated son. Joseph waited in a dungeon before ruling a nation. Even Jesus spent thirty years in privacy before He began His work.

Waiting is often God's preparation for a great mission. But it is not wasted time! God is the Master Builder – and the best buildings (the ones that stand the test of time) require firm foundations. He is shaping His precious vessels on the Potter's wheel. He is slowly transforming the caterpillar into a butterfly in ways that can't be seen. He is carefully tending the soil so that the newly planted seed can sprout successfully.

There is a wonderful plan ahead that you could not fully receive before you chose this path of discipleship. But **wait**…God is not in a hurry. He spends the greatest amount of time with those He expects to greatly use. Don't rush off, running ahead. Wait patiently. Give God this time to speak to you and reveal His will for your future. Let Him train you for higher service and develop qualities that will fit you for the future.

In the first three steps you surrendered your life to Him, now He will transform you – teaching you to think of Him, look to Him, and talk with Him. God wants you to *"grow up,"* into your full maturity, even to the *"fullness of Christ."*[5] But you will only grow as fast as He allows. It's not possible to become spiritually mature all at once. You will gradually be given new knowledge through the Holy Spirit; wisdom not found in textbooks. God alone can make Himself known as He really is.

The next three steps will mature you in the spiritual disciplines of: prayer (Step #4), thanksgiving (Step #5), and worship (Step #6). As you draw closer to Jesus, these new habits will unite in ceaseless praise as your spirit becomes intertwined with God's presence.

PRAY WITHOUT CEASING

Every beloved disciple before us knew the power of prayer. Abraham prayed. Isaac prayed. Jacob prayed. Moses prayed. Joshua prayed. David prayed. Elijah prayed. Job prayed. Hannah prayed. Samuel prayed. Daniel prayed. Mary prayed. John prayed. Peter prayed. Paul prayed. Even Jesus placed a high priority on prayer. Clearly prayer is important in the life of a beloved disciple!

"Prayer is to the spiritual life what the beating of the pulse and the drawing of breath are to the life of the body."

John Henry Newman

Before you can bear fruit in the future, God must first teach you to pray. For Him to use you greatly, He will need you to pray greatly. The Bible is a book of prayer. God said His temple was to be a *"house of prayer."*[1] Where is His temple now? In you![2] *You* are called to be a house of prayer.

In this chapter, I address the "who, what, why, when, where, and how" of prayer, but only to present the many varieties and options that are available to you. One method is not better than another; the only important thing is that you *pray*. And prayer is simply finding your way to Jesus.

Coming to Jesus

Many years ago, a missionary doctor from Africa spoke at our church. He described a day when he was summoned to treat the king of Chad. To approach the king, he had to follow a very specific protocol. Upon entering the court, he could only take one step at a time. If the king nodded in approval, he could take an additional step forward. One false move could result in dismissal. One step. Wait for approval. Another step forward. Wait for approval. Depending on the king's mood, this tedious process could take hours. But the purpose of his story wasn't to describe the demanding royal practice. Just as the doctor had made it halfway down the aisle, the doors behind him flew open. The young son of the king came whizzing by him and leaped right into the king's lap! Clearly the arduous protocol did not apply to this intimate relationship.

The missionary asked each of us to consider how we approach Jesus. Some approach with fear and trepidation, waiting for each nod of approval. Others come flying in with shouts of joy, jumping right into their Savior's lap. There is no right or wrong way to come to Jesus. He certainly is worthy of our reverence. But, as beloved disciples, you want to enjoy all the privileges that come with being His child. Our merciful King does not require such regal etiquette that a small misstep will get you dismissed from His court.

Who: In the Name of Jesus

Prayer is meant to bring divine comfort and help whenever you need it. Attaining this help is as simple as calling on the name of the Lord. God said, *"Call upon Me in the day of trouble; I will deliver you."*[3] Job tells you to *"Pray to the Lord and He will hear you… The light of heaven will shine on your ways."*[4]

Whoever calls on the name of Jesus will be saved.[5] Not on the name of all the other gods in the world's many religions. Not on a saint, living or dead. Not on idols: *"They have eyes but cannot see. They have ears but cannot hear."*[6] Call upon the living God revealed in the Bible:

- El Shaddai – The Almighty God[7]
- Jehovah Jireh – Our Provider[8]
- Jehovah Rapha – Our Healer[9]
- Jehovah Tsidkenu – Our Righteousness[10]
- Jehovah Nissi – Our Mighty Warrior[11]
- Jehovah Shalom – Our Peace[12]
- Jehovah Shammah – The Ever Present One[13]
- Jehovah Sabaoth – The Lord of Hosts[14]
- Jehovah Rohi – The Good Shepherd[15]

John tells us that when you pray in the name of Jesus, His authority cloaks your prayers.[16] He stands at the right hand of the Father, interceding as your High Priest.[17] He is always praying with you and for you. The prayer that He presents to the Father on your behalf is perfect. His stamp of approval makes it happen. Jesus promised that *"My Father will give you whatever you ask in My name."*[16]

When you pray in the name of Jesus, His honor is now attached. Many beloved disciples have used this to their advantage. Moses and Joshua both argued mightily with God, saying, *"What will You do for Your Great Name?"*[18] This is a legitimate strategy to use in requesting His intervention, for *"God is not a man, that He should lie, nor a son of man, that He should change His mind. Does He speak and then not act? Does He promise and not fulfill?"*[19] It's not that you are using His name as a magic wand, but you are trusting in the honor and integrity of His very nature. What a privilege to be lifted into this level of relationship – to pray in His name!

What: The Divine Purpose of Prayer

Purposeful, intimate fellowship with Jesus is the only way to get the power and strength you need to live as a beloved disciple. James 5:16 says that the earnest prayers of the righteous *"availeth much."* The word *avail* means "to be helpful, of use or advantage" and "to bring success in achieving something." Through your prayers, He will provide all that you need to accomplish all that He calls you to do.

> *"No one can believe how powerful prayer is, and what it is able to effect, but those who have learned it by experience."*
>
> Martin Luther

Building a Relationship

Prayer is a conversational dialogue between you and Jesus. It's about building a relationship – a close, trusted, and intimate friendship. This is more than a master-servant relationship. Friends are meant to enjoy direct access and share confidential information.

He told His followers, *"I no longer call you servants, because a servant does not know His master's business. Instead, I have called you friends..."*[20]

Just because God knows everything doesn't mean you don't need to bother to talk to Him about it. It's true that He does already know, but in the telling, you experience the fellowship of a friend. You pray so that He can adjust your thoughts, reveal His purposes, and strengthen you. You pray not just for answers, but for companionship. You seek God to find *Him*.

Friendship is built by sharing all of life together, not just a Sunday morning church service. He wants to be included in every part of your day – your thoughts, your feelings, your frustrations, your problems, and your joys. Long, fancy speeches are unnecessary. Stop using memorized prayers. In fact, stop using complete sentences! Just present your heart to Him.

He wants to hear your honest heart – your true feelings, not what you think you should say in a "proper" prayer. Express your hurts and disappointments – even toward Him if necessary. He would rather have *real* than *ritual*. Melt your pride. Stumble over your words. Your cries are sweet incense to Him.[21]

Prayer is pouring out your heart to Him. Hannah, the mother of Samuel, said *"I have poured out my soul before the Lord."*[22] Her prayers were so intense the priest accused her of being drunk! And David, described as *"a man after God's own heart,"*[23] filled pages of the Bible with all kinds of doubts and fears mixed right in with praise and thanksgiving. Every possible emotion is poured out in the Psalms, which is why they are so comforting to us today. God doesn't want you to hold anything back either.

Quiet Meditation

Sometimes you will pour out your heart in prayer, while other times you may sit in quiet meditation. In this world of busy schedules, noisy offices, and invasive technology, people are hungry for the peace that meditative prayer can bring. But meditation has become associated with a mystical ritual practiced by eastern religions, so most Christians have removed the word from their vocabulary. The word is used quite frequently in the Bible:

- David said, *"Oh how I love your law! I **meditate** on it all day long," "I **meditate** on all Your works,"* and *"I **meditate** on You in the night."*[24] He was also concerned about the quality of his meditation, saying, *"Let the words of my mouth and the **meditation** of my heart be pleasing in Your sight."*[25]
- Joshua encouraged the Israelites to **meditate** on the Book of the Law all day long for it would bring them prosperity and success.[26]

- Paul told the Philippian church to **meditate** on whatever is true, noble, just, pure, lovely, and praiseworthy.[27]

Biblical meditation is reflecting on God's Word. It involves calling to mind, thinking over, and dwelling on the ways of God. Meditation is defined as focused thinking – a skill obviously useful in prayer. It is a means to let His truth have a full and proper impact on your heart. Psalm 119:97-100 lists some of the benefits of meditation including guidance, wisdom, discernment, insight, and heightened obedience. Exactly what we need today! When meditating on the Lord, He can lift your burdens, change your perspective, and enlighten your mind on a particular matter. In fact, David declared, *"In Your light, we see light."*[28]

Proper meditation involves *filling* your mind with God's truth, rather than *emptying* your mind as in Eastern practice. Eastern-style meditation involves repeating a *mantra,* which Webster's dictionary defines as "a mystical formula of invocation or incantation (as in Hinduism)." The goal in Eastern meditation is to move into a trance-like state and progress to the point where "spirit guides" appear to lead and instruct you. Hmmm… that's a problem. There is only one Holy Spirit you should be seeking, not multiple spirit guides. You only want the true Holy Spirit speaking into and over your life; anything else is going to lead you astray.

Satan has always tried to imitate the power of the Holy Spirit by offering deceptive alternatives. But the Bible says, *"Beloved, do not believe every spirit, but test the spirits, whether they are from God…Every spirit that confesses that Jesus Christ has come in the flesh is of God, and every spirit that does not confess that Jesus Christ has come in the flesh is not of God."*[29] When you open up your spirit for guidance and direction, make sure it is only to the Spirit of God, not a counterfeit.

Why: Doesn't God Already Know?

We have just discussed *who* we pray to and *what* prayer provides. Now we're going to talk about *why* it's important to pray. We pray to bring the Father our petitions, intercession, and confession. Yes, God already knows what He wants to do, but He waits to be asked. *"Your Father knows what you need before you ask Him."*[30] The reason for asking is to draw closer to Him. Psalm 31:19 says He has *"great things stored up for those who take refuge in Him."* These things are stored up by God but released through prayer.

> *"Through prayer, God is inviting man into full partnership with Him, not in making divine decisions, but in implementing those decisions in the affairs of humankind."*
>
> Paul Bilheimer

Bold Petition

Does the God of the universe really care about your problems? Scripture provides innumerable examples of a God that is closely involved in the lives of His beloved. He has invited and encouraged you to come boldly to the throne. David clearly did this as he said, *"I cry aloud to the LORD; I lift up my voice to the LORD for mercy. I pour out my complaint before Him; before Him I tell my trouble."*[31] Jesus promised that *"If you believe, you will receive whatever you ask for in prayer."*[32] Come then – urgently, persistently, and fervently with your plea, *"I am poor and needy; come quickly to me, O God."*[33]

It is a spiritual law to *"ask and you shall receive."*[34] It is a rule not even altered for Jesus! We know that while on this earth Jesus regularly brought His prayers and petitions before the Father. Jesus asked the Father for permission to raise Lazarus from the dead.[35] And in the Garden of Gethsemane, Jesus asked the Father if the *"cup might pass from Him."*[36] Psalm 2:7-8 suggests that Jesus even had to ask the Father for His own inheritance. If Jesus was not exempt from asking to receive from the Father, you and I must expect to ask as well.

Ask for strength, ask for direction, ask for wisdom, ask for comfort. Be specific about your present and most critical needs – *"in everything by prayer and supplication, **let your requests be made known to God.**"*[37] He wants you to plead with Him and to *"bring forth your strong reasons."*[38] This is more for your benefit than His; it helps you to consider the importance of what you are seeking. Take time to reflect on your motives – is it a *want* or a *need?* If you were to receive everything you wanted without asking, would you really appreciate it as much?

All of heaven lies within your grasp – if you would only ask! *"All things are yours... and you are Christ's."*[39] We have a very rich Father and expect too little. Through earnest and persistent petition, wrestle from Him the treasures of His Kingdom. He longs to give! The promises of God are rich and inexhaustible. Claim big, really big, things. He longs to provide more than you can ask or imagine.

Selfless Intercession

As you grow in discipleship, God will eventually mature you beyond simply receiving His gifts. If you have only come so far as to ask God for things, you haven't come to a full understanding of surrender. The foundation of the relationship is still based on your needs. When beloved disciples truly begin to pray, He can align their hearts with His intentions. Soon He will start to ask you to intercede on behalf of others. Are you prepared to disregard yourself and launch out into the real work of prayer? And it is *work* – intercession will require a great deal of your time and energy.

Interceding for others takes the focus off yourself and turns your attention to the needs of others. You are encouraged in James 5:16 to *"pray for one another."* You carry someone else's burden to the Cross of Christ.[40] Intercession releases the power of the Holy Spirit into the lives of others. I have personally seen God drastically change medical reports for loved ones, suddenly bring substantial financial resources to those in urgent need, miraculously bring justice to an unjust situation, and provide peace that surpasses all understanding to those under tremendous strain.

You are asking God to work in a way that He might not otherwise work in the life of another. Several times Moses pleaded with God to change how He was going to deal with the Israelites. Abraham pleaded with God to save Sodom if he could find at least ten faithful ones there.[41] People who don't realize the error of their ways need your prayers. People who are sick need your prayers. Your own loved ones, neighbors, and coworkers need your prayers. The church, the government, and those in authority need your prayers. You are even encouraged to pray for your enemies.[42]

True intercession involves bringing the person, and their circumstance, before God. You seek the mind of God and His perspective on the situation.[43] It doesn't mean you personally step in and take control of the situation (playing God's role). Intercession simply involves taking hold of God's will and refusing to let go until it comes to pass. To be certain you are praying His will, here are some things you can confidently ask for in the life of another: direction, courage, deliverance, open eyes/ears, favor, abundant life, good health, the mind of Christ, protection, provision, strength, success, wisdom, peace, faith, hope, joy, and love.

Some people have a deep burden to pray for others; intercession is their spiritual gift. But the Bible is clear that all believers are called to be intercessors. It is not a privilege limited to an elite group of super-Christians. In fact, Samuel believed it was a sin not to pray for others saying, *"As for me, far be it from me that I should sin against the LORD by failing to pray for you."*[44] God will intentionally bring you to certain places, people, and circumstances so that you can bring them to His throne. In this way, He will use you to touch the world.

Humble Confession

Along with petition and intercession, another important purpose of prayer is confessing sin in your life. Proverbs 28:13 declares, *"He who conceals his sins does not prosper, but whoever confesses and renounces them finds mercy."* Lay your soul completely open before God. David was quick to repent when God convicted him, saying, *"Against you, you only, have I sinned..."*[45]

Let the Holy Spirit expose any weakness in your life. He will shine His light on any area that needs correction. He will put His finger on areas of your life that are misguided, whether intentional or unintentional. Keep in mind that the Lord is doing this out of love for you. His reproach will bring gentle conviction, not harsh condemnation. Even the most tender father expects a child to humble himself and admit wrongdoing. Don't make excuses or rationalize your behavior. Don't trivialize the sin – remember that Jesus had to die to free you from it.

Where: In the Secret Place

If prayer is coming to Jesus with petition, intercession, and confession, where is the best place to find Him? Trying to decide which place of prayer is better (public or private) is like asking which hand is more important. You need both! While there are many examples of corporate prayer throughout the Bible, there are also clear instructions to pray privately. *"When you pray, go into your room, and when you have shut your door, pray to your Father who is in the **secret place.**"*[46]

It is clearly important to spend time alone with God. Joshua, Jacob, Gideon, Elijah, and Moses were all commissioned while alone with God. Cornelius and Peter received their instructions to meet while praying alone with God. John, the beloved disciple, received the Revelation of Jesus Christ while alone with God. Even Jesus often withdrew from the crowds to pray alone. God cannot guide, direct, and establish you unless you provide Him the opportunity.

It will be impossible to become a beloved disciple without some time of secret prayer. When you pray alone, there is less temptation to pray with false motives and you can give Him your undivided attention. Quiet the clamoring of other voices, questions, duties, distractions, obligations, and your to-do list. Get your list on paper first, turn off your cell phone, and lock the door if necessary. One mother with seven children used to flip her apron over her head to pray – the kids knew that was her "quiet time" for a few minutes a day. You must also find a way to lift up your soul and let Him work for *"in quietness and trust, you find your strength."*[47]

When: Finding Time to Pray

I like to start my day with prayer. For the last several years, I have rarely set an alarm clock. I let Him decide when I need to wake up to pray. If He wakes me early, I assume I need to pray more that day. If He wakes me at 3 am, I trust there is a reason I need to pray right then. Sometimes I might wake very early for several weeks in a row because there is a more intense urgency for prayer during that particular "season."

Jesus never commanded us to have a regular time with Him each day. Rather, He simply tells us in Matthew 22:37-38 to *"love the Lord your God with all your heart and with all your soul and with all your mind."* When we love Him, we naturally run to Him – frequently and zealously. The result is time spent in intimate prayer. And our motivation changes from guilt to love.

Setting a Time

Some people need structured times to pray, while others prefer more of a free flow. You will, with the Spirit's leading, find a pattern that is just right for you. What works for me may not work for you. A pattern that works when you have young children may not be the same pattern when you're retired. What works during a season of spiritual dryness may not be as useful during a season of abundance. It's all about discerning what draws you closer to Jesus and keeps you attentive to the God who loves you. Nothing is set in stone.

David proclaimed, *"Seven times a day do I praise thee."*[48] This sounds like he had specific times set aside to meet with God. We also know that Daniel prayed three times a day.[49] These "set times" likely corresponded to the temple sacrifices provided in the morning, afternoon, and evening. After the temple was destroyed, the Jewish people offered prayers in place of the sacrifices that could no longer be provided there.

Setting specific times of the day to pray might work well for you. This may not work for an exhausted mom with a newborn. Don't stress; find whatever time you can to connect with Him, even if it's only a few minutes for a squeeze of His hand. The important thing is that you don't get into a monotonous routine. In that state of mind, you tend to watch the clock more than the face of Jesus. Don't get more devoted to your *practice* of prayer than to the *presence* of God.

God simply wants prayer to be a priority in your life. You can't watch television for three hours then pray for three minutes and expect to become a beloved disciple. The lasting impact of your public service to Him will be measured by the depth of your personal prayer life. Take time to pray, no matter how busy your life gets.

"The men who have done the most for God in this world have been early on their knees. If God is not first in our thoughts in the morning, He will likely be in last place the remainder of the day."

E.M. Bounds

Measuring the Time

There is no prescribed amount of time you are instructed to pray. Paul simply said, *"Devote yourself to prayer."*[50] Dr. Moody Stuart's only rule was *"pray till you pray."* God doesn't listen to your longer prayers more because they are somehow better. He is just interested in your sincerity. Charles Spurgeon said, *"Prayer is not measured by the yard or weighed by the pound. It is the might and force of it, the truth and reality of it, the energy and intensity of it."* To some, 15 minutes of prayer seems like a long time. To others, it is insufficient.

Many years ago, I went on a mission trip to distribute Jesus videos and Bibles to travelers between Europe and North Africa. I knew before arriving that we would be working 8 hour shifts each day. I soon discovered that those 8 hours were laid out as follows: 2 hours prayer, 2 hours distributing, 2 hours prayer, 2 hours distributing. I initially thought, "I will be wasting so much time! I came all this way to distribute materials (i.e., to *work*), not to pray!"

But, oh, the wisdom of the mission leaders…they had already discovered it was a spiritual battleground out there. We *needed* that much prayer interspersed with our work to get anything accomplished! And it certainly wasn't wasted time in terms of my spiritual growth – that is where I learned to love to pray for extended periods of time. In fact, those times of prayer became my favorite periods of the day and much anticipated on my return trips to the region.

Praying All the Time

The Bible says to *"pray continually"*[51] and to *"always pray, without giving up."*[52] The secret to "ceaseless prayer" is recognizing that He dwells within you, in the center of your being. Very few fully grasp this. You can carry on a continuous conversation with Him all throughout the day, sharing every experience moment-by-moment. Just keep your soul resting in God as you go about your daily activities.

You may not be on bended knee or speaking aloud, but your spirit is continually in the act of prayer. You remain constantly aware of God throughout the day. Stop your work from time to time and adore Him in your spirit. It is just a slight turn of attention. Give Him a look of confident faith. Squeeze His hand and take hold of His security. Few realize that these are all "prayers." Get in the habit of turning to Him continually. Then, when a crisis comes, you will instinctively turn to Him – the habit is already formed. This should become as deeply ingrained as breathing. Prayer is then no longer an "event," but your entire life.

Brother Lawrence described this as *"practicing the presence of God."*[53] It means keeping your soul's attention on God, inviting Him to be involved in all your activities. Throughout the day, you can pray simple phrases such as "Lord, help me with this," or "I belong to You Lord," or "Use me however You want to Father." When you are feeling afraid, quickly say, "Lord, surround me, protect me." When you need to resist a temptation, remind Him, "Lord, keep me from evil." When you recognize His divine intervention say, "Thank you Jesus."

You can pray always and often this way. These short, continuous prayers keep you in constant communion with God – much as He originally intended in the Garden of Eden. They remind you of your dependence on God. In the times we are living in, I am more convinced than ever that you can't make it through life without constant, abiding, fervent, ongoing prayer. Don't question whether you can skip a day of praying – you simply cannot.

"He who prays well is so absorbed with God that he does not know he is praying."

Francis de Sales

How: Fixed on Jesus

We have covered who, what, when, where, and why to pray. In addressing *how* to pray, I'm not going to give you a manual to follow in which you pray through a list in a specific order. Personally, I have found those methods only produce feelings of guilt that I am somehow not doing it right. The Bible contains prayers of all shapes and sizes. You lose your spontaneity with Jesus when you follow memorized and mechanical prayers. I am just going to give you some important "tools in your toolbox" of prayer, each one helping you to pray the Father's will in your life.

To effectively pray God's will, the most important thing is that you first surrender your own. Understand that if your heart is not completely surrendered, you are capable of misunderstanding God. We tend to approach God with such strong desires for things to go our own way, it becomes very easy to confuse our will with His. We believe He is saying "yes" because we want something so badly; we couldn't hear a "no" if He were yelling it! Then when things don't turn out as we expected (e.g., we don't get that job, we don't get pregnant, etc.), we are angry with God. Lay down your own agenda every time you come to God in prayer.

The Lord's Example

If you are just starting to develop your prayer life, a good place to start is with the Lord's example. When the disciples found Jesus praying alone one day, they asked Him to teach them how to pray.[54] He gave them a few key phrases that can still guide your prayers today:

Our Father	Let the full meaning of that word touch your heart. You are His child. Never doubt God's deep love for you. He loves you as much as He loves His own son, Jesus.
Who art in heaven	He is infinitely greater than you are. You are on earth; He is enthroned in heaven.
Hallowed be Thy Name	He is to be regarded as Holy, Holy, Holy. Give Him the reverence and honor He is due.

Thy Kingdom Come	Call upon the King of Glory to take His rightful place. Acknowledge His right to rule over all the earth.
Thy will be done on earth as it is in heaven	Tell Him that whatever He wants is ultimately what you want. No matter how you may need to adjust your own plans and desires. Let Him do with your heart as He pleases. If you mistakenly ask anything that is not in His will, allow Him to deny you.
Give us our daily bread	Ask Him to provide for *all* your needs. Trust that He will.
Forgive us our trespasses as we forgive those who trespass against us	Repent *daily* for any judgment you hold against others in your heart. Keep yourself free of bitterness and resentment. Thank Him for the blood of Jesus that covers your sins. Thank Him for enduring the Cross to make that possible.
Deliver us from evil	Ask Him for both physical protection from the enemy, as well as protection from any temptation to do evil. In other words, you need His protection both inside and outside.
For thine is the Kingdom, thy power, and the glory...Forever and ever. Amen.	He is coming again. He is going to reign. He is worthy of all the glory and honor and praise. Forever. Can you imagine how great that will be?

Pray His Word

After getting comfortable with the Lord's Prayer, you can advance to praying through the Bible itself. It is the heart of God in print. *"All Scripture is God-breathed and is useful for teaching, rebuking, correcting, and training in righteousness."*[55] His Word truly is a *"lamp to your feet"* (showing you the very next step) and a *"light for your path"* (allowing you to see into the distance).[56]

A variety of books give examples of how to personalize Scripture and pray their promised truth over your life. Grab hold of a favorite verse and claim it. David boldly said, *"O Sovereign LORD, you are God! Your words are trustworthy, and you have promised these good things to your servant."*[57] You can turn any portion of Scripture that touches you into a personal prayer. Nothing could be more beautiful, strong, or safe. His eternal promises are unalterable and irrevocable. You can be *"absolutely certain that whatever promise He is bound by; He is able to make good."*[58]

To become a beloved disciple, you will need to abide in His Word. Jesus said, *"If you abide in My Word, then you are truly disciples of Mine."*[59] The words in the Bible promise to develop your faith, dispel fear, bring healing, impart joy, release power, renew your mind, make the devil flee, establish victory, and make all things new. You are encouraged to *"feed on"* those words.[60] Throughout the Bible, the Word is referred to as milk, bread, solid food, and sweet dessert.[61] Everything you could possibly need to nourish your body and soul! No other method can more powerfully transform your life than praying His Word.

Soak in His Presence

The Lord's Prayer and praying through the Bible both require talking. In the early stages of my prayer life, I was full of requests to God. But then I started to just *soak* in Him. "Soaking" is my now favorite form of prayer! Someone described it to me like a pickle, soaking in its flavorful juice. The longer it soaks, the more flavor. The pickle isn't responsible to do anything – it just soaks. I have also heard this form of prayer described as a sponge. When you put a dry sponge in water, the water slowly permeates the sponge. When you soak in Him, you allow His presence to saturate you completely.

In this type of prayer, you simply position yourself with Him, soaking in His presence. There is nothing to *do,* just *be.* No passionate appeals. You are not seeking anything from the Lord. Most of all, you just want to abide in His presence. Only very good friends can sit in comfortable silence together.

Try to envision yourself in His presence. Oswald Chambers said that one of the reasons for our "futility in prayer" is that we have lost the power to visualize. We can't imagine putting ourselves deliberately in the presence of God. But clearly David did this as he said he loved to *"to gaze upon the beauty of the LORD and to seek Him in His temple."*[62] Ask Him for a sanctified imagination. Ask Him to help you envision walking on the beach with Him, strolling in the lush garden with Him, dancing with Him, resting in the meadow of flowers with Him, sitting by the glassy sea with Him. Ask Him to help you picture His glory filling the temple…the sparkling gold particles dancing in the air. Dr. Joseph Parker once said, *"If we do not get back to visions, peeps into heaven, consciousness of the higher glory and the larger life, we shall lose our religion."*

In the presence of the Lord, you are being taught, you are absorbing an atmosphere, and you are being changed – whether you feel it or not. You may worry that your soaking time is unfruitful because you don't see any immediate change or benefit. But anytime He is invited, He deposits more of Himself. His life is simply breathed into the soul that rests near Him.

Be Still and Know

The greatest difficulty in prayer (particularly with soaking) is keeping your mind focused on Jesus. Your mind has a very strong tendency to wander around wherever it pleases. So how do you quiet your busy mind?

In Psalm 46:10 you are instructed to *"Be still and know…"* The words *be still* actually mean "to cease striving; to let go and relax." Come to a place of rest. When you set aside time to be with the Lord, turn your attention to Him. The key is where you set your focus – on God or on the cares of this world. I usually keep pen and paper near me. If I think of something that I need to remember, but that isn't related to my prayer, I'll quickly jot it down so my mind can "let it go" and move on. I also like to keep music on as it helps me focus my mind on worship.

Try to hold your heart in His presence. When your mind begins to wander, just turn your attention back again to His presence. At first, you may only be able to remain quiet and still for 30 seconds. Gradually you will build up to longer periods of time where you can maintain your focus. You are slowly training and disciplining your mind – the process will get easier over time. Don't get discouraged. When you get frustrated, you only stir yourself up more. Instead, just keep gently turning your focus to the Lord's presence. He will give you abundant grace in the early stages so that you will grow hungry for more!

Pray in the Spirit

Sometimes you may find you don't know what to pray, especially when interceding for others. At these times, the Holy Spirit *"helps us in our weakness"* and *"intercedes for us with groans that words cannot express."*[63] When the Holy Spirit prays for you, He prays in agreement with the will of God. Praying in tongues is a way to pray accurately when you *"don't know what we ought to pray for."*

When you pray in tongues, you pray in a language understood only by God. *"Those who speak in strange tongues do not speak to others but to God, because no one understands them. They are speaking secret truths by the power of the Spirit."*[64] Your mind may not understand what you're saying, but that doesn't mean the prayer is unfruitful. Jude verse 20 says that when you pray in the Spirit, you *"edify yourself and build yourself up."*

I first started praying in tongues as a teenager. Then I promptly ignored it for the next ten years because none of my friends seemed to be doing it. And it certainly wasn't talked about in our church. Satan tried to get me to believe I was making it up. But God brought me repeatedly back to the beautiful prayer language. Now I pray in tongues regularly. Despite not understanding the words, I usually have a general impression of what or who I am praying about. Through it all, I believe I am praying the perfect prayer that needs to be prayed at that time.

I understand that praying in tongues is a controversial topic and many do not understand the need for it. Some believe it is a spiritual gift given to a few, but not everyone. Many churches teach that believers no longer need to speak in tongues at all. Other believers are afraid to speak in tongues because of the stigma attached to it. There are plenty of books out there that debate this issue, so I do not plan to do so here. But it is odd that such a fuss has been made over this one particular gift. Perhaps the enemy has worked so hard to disrupt it because of its value. While you don't need to pray in tongues to get to heaven (or even to be a beloved disciple), you can certainly desire every tool in the toolbox while living on this earth!

Fast and Pray

The final tool in your toolbox of prayer involves fasting. In her book, *The Power of Prayer and Fasting*, Marilyn Hickey says that prayer and fasting go together like conjoined twins that cannot be divided. There are numerous scriptures in both the Old and New Testaments that teach us to fast and pray. It involves a humbling of both body and spirit. Andrew Murray said, *"Fasting helps express, deepen, and confirm the resolution that we are ready to sacrifice anything, even ourselves, to attain what we seek for the Kingdom of God."* To become a beloved disciple, both prayer and fasting should be a part of your spiritual life.

Most people feel compelled to initiate a fast when they are unable to gain victory in some area through prayer alone. You may sense that you need to do something more, something different, to get results. The early disciples were casting out demons all over Galilee, so they were puzzled one day when they were unable to heal a young boy. Jesus explained that there are certain kinds of demonic attacks that can only be broken through the additional discipline of fasting.[65]

Fasting can bring greater strength and power to overcome the attacks of the enemy in your own life. It can lead to an emotional breakthrough or change of habit. What hasn't been working can suddenly work. A time of fasting sends a message that you are calling a "time out" and things cannot continue as "business as usual."

The Hebrew translation for *fasting* means "not to eat" while the Greek translation means "no food." So merely fasting from social media or chocolate is not what I'm talking about (though it is fine to sacrifice these at times). I believe fasting is abstaining from food and replacing it with prayer. There are many ways to fast – a fast can be as short as one meal. Some people fast a specific food group, such as meat. Others do a strict water-only fast. It is not a matter of what you do or don't eat. It's just important that you turn your attention away from food and back to God. I'm not saying that is easy! I find fasting very difficult. And the devil uses the same tactics on me that he used with Eve: "Did God really say you can't eat…*anything?* Has God really called you to fast… how does He expect you to survive that way? You're going to get a headache…it's not worth it." It takes firm resolve and determination to proceed with a fast when everything reminds you of food!

While Jesus did teach that His followers should fast, He did not specify how long or how often. He just said *"when you fast…"*[66] That leaves it a private matter between you and God. And "private" is important – you are commanded not to seek sympathy or attention while fasting. You should fast as the Holy Spirit leads you to fast. The method, timing, and purpose of a fast should be of His design.

Every example of fasting in the Bible yielded positive results. God sees this as an important step of faith and promises to reward you. Isaiah 58 contains some of these great promises for those who fulfill His fasts:

"Then your light will break forth like the dawn, and your healing will quickly appear; then your righteousness will go before you, and the glory of the LORD will be your rear guard. Then you will call, and the LORD will answer… The LORD will guide you always; He will satisfy your needs in a sun-scorched land and will strengthen your frame. You will be like a well-watered garden, like a spring whose waters never fail."

What incredible blessings! He wants to move you to a higher level of prayer. Ask the Holy Spirit to confirm His call to fast and what type of fast might be right for you as you deepen your relationship with Jesus.

Are You Listening?

So far, we have talked about your role in prayer, but prayer is meant to be two-way conversation. That includes listening to the Creator of the universe. He can talk. He can communicate. He is the *Word*. And the focus of His attention is on you! If you desire to hear His voice and can get quiet enough to listen, He will begin to speak specifically and personally to you.

Don't let anyone tell you that you can't hear from God. *"He who belongs to God hears what God says."*[67] The whole Bible supports the idea that God is forever speaking to His creation. Not God spoke (in past tense), but *God is speaking.* It is the nature of God to speak. He fills the earth with His speaking voice.

It was always His idea to communicate with us; it is His job to speak clearly enough for us to hear Him. When God spoke to individuals in the Bible, they knew it was God. God has not changed – He still desires to reveal Himself, His plans, and His purposes. In the New Testament, Jesus assured us that we would recognize the voice of our Shepherd.[68]

We all have those times we wish the voice of God would audibly speak so loudly there's no way we could miss it. While it doesn't typically work that way, one of the most important things you can learn as a beloved disciple is how to listen to God. He doesn't want you to wander aimlessly through life. He has promised to guide you continually.[69] Jeremiah 33:3 says, *"Call to Me, and I will answer you, and teach you great and unsearchable things, which you do not know."*

Hearing from God

There is no formula or method for hearing God's voice. God used a burning bush with Moses. He spoke to Job in a whirlwind. In 1 Kings 9:12, God spoke to Elijah in a *"still, small voice."* Based on the Bible, here are some examples of how God might speak to you:

- through angels (some obvious; some disguised as people)
- through visions (mental pictures) or dreams
- through prophets
- miraculous signs
- an impression in the spirit – prompting or restraint
- an audible voice
- through music (song lyrics)
- through nature (e.g., rainbows)
- physical touch
- the Word of God
- the Holy Spirit

As you practice hearing His voice, begin with simple yes-no questions (e.g., Should I spend money on this right now? Should I accept this work assignment? Should I call this person today?) and wait quietly for answers. Keep in mind, God will never tell you to engage in something that contradicts Scripture, impulsively gratifies the flesh, hinders your spiritual growth, or would bring dishonor to His Name. If you are not sure you heard correctly, pause and wait. Your Father will patiently show you again. He would never say, "Sorry, you missed it the first time and that was your only chance!" He's not going to scold you or make you feel stupid when you mess up.

Beware that Satan will try to get you off course. He will bring distractions so that you devote your time and energy to the wrong things. He can even quote Scripture to confuse you. But you will soon learn that his voice is loud, urgent, and insistent to precipitate a crisis. He wants you to act hastily and impulsively. Learn to take authority over the enemy.[70] You can command all other voices not of God to be silent when you need to hear something more clearly.

Obeying God

The most important thing is not *how* He speaks, but *your response* to what He says. You will learn to hear more clearly if you listen and then immediately obey what He says. Jesus said, *"Consider carefully how you listen. Whoever has will be given more; whoever does not have, even what he thinks he has will be taken from him."*[71] If God speaks and you do not respond with obedience, there may come a time when He stops speaking.[72]

There may be times you don't like what you hear and struggle with total obedience. Even Jesus struggled in the Garden of Gethsemane. He clearly knew the Father's will but questioned whether there might be a different way to fulfill it. Even if you must wrestle with God over what He says, try to maintain a submissive attitude so that you can continue to hear correctly in the future. An area where you haven't yet obeyed is an area where you haven't fully surrendered. Procrastinating after He has spoken is an indication you don't truly trust Him.

Possible answers from God	1. Yes, I thought you'd never ask 2. Yes, and there's even more I plan to give you 3. Yes, but it will be different than you expect 4. Yes, but not yet 5. No, I love you too much and have a different plan

Delayed Answers

God answers prayer in the best way every time. But it will be on *His* timetable. There was a delayed response from Jesus when Lazarus died.[73] Daniel had to wait 21 days for an answer to his prayer due to hindrance from Satan.[74] Moses and Joshua waited on the mountain for six days before God finally spoke.[75] In 1 Kings 18, Elijah got an immediate answer to his request for fire from heaven but had to persistently ask seven times for rain.

Clearly these periods of delay were not rejection from God. Don't be discouraged if your prayers are not answered immediately. There are many possibilities why an answer might be delayed:

- It is too soon for you to know – He may be waiting for someone else's choice in the matter before answering.
- He may be waiting for a time when He can intervene more effectively, in a better way, for His ultimate glory.
- A fulfilled answer for you may mean an unfulfilled answer to someone else's equally earnest prayer. It will take longer to reconcile both of your desires.
- God may be testing you – to see if you will truly trust Him, if you will continue to wait until you hear, or if you will become resentful or impatient with His timing.

The hardest part is **waiting.** I understand that. I have waited years for some promises to come to pass. I am still waiting for some others. You may be waiting for your first child and the treatments aren't working. Or you may be waiting for the right person to spend the rest of your life with. Or waiting for that perfect job. As the days turn into weeks and months, it's easy to get discouraged. The repeated disappointments make you want to hide and not put yourself out there again. You wish people would stop asking how it's going. And you start to question what God is doing – or rather, *not doing.*

Don't mistake the slow unfolding of a promise as rejection from God.

Trust that from the moment you placed it in His hands, He began working out a solution for you. Isaiah 65:24 says, *"Before they call, I will answer – while they are still speaking, I will hear."* Thank Him that He will answer in His way and in His timing – this avoids frustration, confusion, and possible resentment if you don't get the answer you want right away.[76] I have come to believe that even the time of waiting is not wasted.

Other times there may be no answer at all. This might be because you are asking for the wrong reasons or asking out of the will of God.[77] Be prepared to examine what it is you want from God and why you want it. James 4:3 says, *"You ask and do not receive because you ask with wrong motives."* God is not as concerned about your happiness right now as He is about your ultimate perfection. He knows the more satisfied you become with life the less you will seek Him, so some of your requests may be delayed or denied.

Silence

Many beloved disciples have experienced an extended period of "silence" from God. For 36 chapters, God said nothing as Job poured out his complaints. David also protested God's lack of intervention, saying, *"Why, O LORD, do you stand far off? Why do you hide yourself in times of trouble?"*[78] Isaiah understood that *"The Lord has **hidden Himself** from His people, but I trust Him and place my hope in Him."*[79]

In your growing relationship with Jesus, you won't always *feel* His presence. He may test the maturity of your relationship by a period of seeming separation. These times have been referred to by others as "the dark night of the soul," "the ministry of absence," and the "ministry of the night."[80] Of course, God never leaves or forsakes anyone, as promised in His Word.[81] But He didn't promise you would always *experience* His presence. In fact, He admits that He intentionally hides His face at times.[82] Job said, *"I go east, but He is not there. I go west, but I cannot find Him. I do not see Him in the north, for **He is hidden**. I turn to the south, but I cannot find Him. But He knows where I am going."*[83] As confusing as the silence may be, trust that you are not alone. God knows where you are.

If you pray and experience an unusual silence, first be sure to confess any sin in your life. Sin will distance you from the Father's heart. If, after that, there is still a silence from God, wait patiently and simply abide in His presence. This period of separation may be a test of faith – will you continue to trust even when you don't feel His presence as you had in the past? He may want to teach you not to depend on those experiential feelings anymore. He is looking for faithful disciples who will remain steadfast even when He withdraws Himself. Just patiently wait.

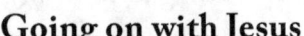

Going on with Jesus

To grow as a beloved disciple, nothing else will do but quiet communion with God. His presence will refresh, encourage, and strengthen you. A few short minutes with your Creator can completely transform your day and renew your mind. If you fail to develop an active prayer life, you will miss out on His very best for you!

> *"Pray for prayer. Pray until you can pray. Pray to be helped to pray,*
> *and do not give up praying because you cannot pray. It is when*
> *you think you cannot pray that you are most praying."*
>
> Charles Spurgeon

The enemy will use many means to stop you. Resist him. Don't let your prayer life be choked by the cares of this world. A mind devoted to prayer is committed, sensitive, and teachable – good soil that will soon yield a fruitful crop. Beloved disciple, use this waiting time of prayer to deepen your relationship with Jesus. Grow in your knowledge of Him. The next step will be thanking Him for all He has done and will continue to do. Let's move up to an even higher level – on to Step #5!

Prayer

Jesus, I want more of You. I come with great expectation. I know You would not make me this hungry or lead me this far if You did not intend to meet with me. I will come and sit at Your feet. I will wait for You. I'm desperate for Your presence. I'm not seeking You for Your benefits – all I want is more of You. Nothing else in this world will satisfy my soul. The world has left me weak and dry. You are what my heart longs for. Let me become more aware of Your presence. Holy Spirit, come and fill me. May Your will be done in my life and on this earth, as it is in heaven.

I need You…oh I need You. Provide what I need for this day, Lord. You are where my help comes from. I look to You and You alone. Give me wisdom. I need Your protection. Surround me. Be a pillar of fire before me and my rear guard. Though the storms rage all around, I will not be moved. I will not be shaken. I will not be overwhelmed. Your Name is a strong and mighty tower. You shelter me. I find my refuge in You. Nothing else has the power to save but Your Name.

Lord, search me. Show me any way that I have grieved Your Holy Spirit. I repent for keeping my Bible closed or reading it without focus. I am sorry for daydreaming instead of fervently praying. Forgive my weaknesses and help me overcome them. Keep me from temptation, guide me with Your strong hand. Deliver me from evil, that I may not cause pain. Wash me and make me clean. Thank You for the blood that makes me free.

Lord, teach me how to pray. Not my own will, my plans, or what I want. I know I have gotten in the way. Show me what You want, Father. You hold my past, present, and future. Give me vision to see things as You do. Give me open ears. Help me to love as You love. Give me the tongue of an instructed disciple so that I can encourage and teach others. Give me a part to play in Your ultimate plan. Help me, Lord, to become a house of prayer for you. For all honor, power and glory are Yours, Lord. Forever and ever. Amen.

STUDY

1. What are some specific things you can do to *"fix your eyes on Jesus"* (see Hebrews 12:2)?

2. With complete honesty, how would you rate the extent that you believe God answers your prayers:

My prayers seem to have no effect   God frequently answers my
                                                      prayers in a powerful way

What recent experiences (positive or negative) have brought you to this conclusion?

Bold Petition

3. Read the following verses and record what you learn about prayer:

2 Chronicles 30:27

Psalm 18:6

Psalm 116:1-2

Isaiah 65:24

James 5:16

4. In what areas of your life do you need God's direction most right now?

5. Read Jesus' specific words to the Father in John 11:41-42 prior to raising Lazarus from the dead. What confidence did Jesus have when He prayed? How would your prayer life be different if you had the same confidence?

"Then Jesus looked up and said, 'Father, I thank you that you have heard me. I know that you always hear me...'"

John 11:41-42

---

6. Read Daniel 2:17-18 (NIV). The Aramaic word translated plead means to "to ask, pray for, look for" with urgency. This word appears 12 times in the Bible, each time in the book of Daniel. What does the repetition of this word *plead* say to us if we want to be like Daniel?

7. Read Psalm 86 out loud as a personal prayer.

A Time to Pray

8. How regularly do you communicate with Jesus?

9. What keeps you from putting more priority on times of prayer?

10. How could you take more time for prayer during the day?

Hearing from God

11. John 8:47 tells us, *"He who belongs to God hears what God says. The reason you do not hear is that you do not belong to God."* How do you personally hear from God?

12. Describe an experience you've had when you were certain that God was speaking to you.

13. How have you learned to distinguish whether a word you receive is from God, your own selfish desires, or from the enemy?

14. How could you cultivate the ability to hear God's voice more?

Obeying God

15. List the benefits of obeying God in the following Scriptures.

Deuteronomy 28:1

Jeremiah 7:23

Luke 6:46-49

16. Describe a command or instruction from God that you have obeyed.

17. Can you recall a time when you ignored the Holy Spirit's guidance? Is there a command that you have not obeyed yet?

18. Where there is disobedience, what do you think is the root cause? What does it tell you about yourself?

19. Is there an issue where God is calling you to prayer *and fasting?*

SPIRITUAL MARKER

patience

WORSHIP

Teach Me How to Pray [Jason Upton]

Waiting Here for You [Passion featuring Christy Nockels]

God, I Look to You [Bethel Music featuring Jenn Johnson]

Find Me at the Feet of Jesus [Christy Nockels]

Walk with Me [Jesus Culture]

Talking to Jesus [Elevation Worship]

Take Courage [Bethel Music featuring Kristene DiMarco]

Hurry [Kim Walker-Smith]

A Little Longer [Brian & Jenn Johnson]

Speak to Me, I'm Listening [Kari Jobe]

Nothing Else [Cody Carnes]

Waymaker [Sinach]

Do It Again [Elevation]

Spirit of the Living God [Vertical Worship]

In Jesus' Name (God of Possible) [Katy Nichole]

I Speak Jesus [Here Be Lions]

PRAY WITHOUT CEASING

1 THESSALONIANS 5:17

COUNT YOUR BLESSINGS

Nothing feels better than to receive genuine praise and appreciation from those we love. The same way we enjoy it, God loves it too! Instead of offering sacrifices as they did in the Old Testament, we now offer God *"the sacrifice of praise"*[1] and the *"sacrifice of thanksgiving."*[2] You are offering a "sacrifice of praise" when you notice His activity, when you obey His Word, when you savor His grace, when you glorify His Name, and when you delight yourself in Him.

In becoming a beloved disciple, you are seeking deeper intimacy with Jesus. Psalm 100:4 says the best way to get there is through praise – ***"Enter His gates with thanksgiving, and His courts with praise."*** So arrive at His feet with thanksgiving on your lips! He finds your praise irresistible.

"A single thankful thought towards heaven is the most perfect of all prayers."

Gotthold Ephraim Lessing

◆

An Attitude of Gratitude

Praise and thanksgiving are the natural outpouring of a grateful heart. Gratitude is derived from the Latin word *gratia,* meaning "grace" or "gratefulness." The source of gratitude is *undeserved merit.* The grateful person acknowledges that a gift was freely given. I trust, as a beloved disciple, that you will not behave as the nine lepers who failed to express appreciation for their miraculous healing. Only one of them returned to give thanks to Jesus.[3] Never forget to say, "thank you Jesus."

We truly have so much to be thankful for! In fact, the Bible says, *"God **generously** gives us everything for our enjoyment."*[4] He has *"blessed us in the heavenly realms with every spiritual blessing in Christ."*[5] He has *"given us every good and perfect gift"*[6] and has *"done great things for us."*[7] Psalm 63:3-4 says, *"Your love is better than life, so my lips will praise You. I will bless You while I live. I will lift up my hands in Your Name."*

It may be hard to find the words to express all that you are grateful for. Have you ever been excited to find a perfect Hallmark® card because it says *exactly* what you wanted to say to someone? First Chronicles 16 does that for us:[8]

Give thanks to the Lord, call upon His Name!
Sing to Him, sing praises to Him, meditate on and tell of all His wondrous works!
Glory in His Holy Name; let the hearts of those who seek the Lord rejoice!
Seek the Lord and His strength; yearn for and seek His face!
Strive to be in His presence continually!
Earnestly remember the marvelous deeds He has done!
Declare His glory among the nation for great is the Lord and greatly to be praised!
He is to be reverently feared above all other gods.
For the gods of the people are lifeless idols, but the Lord made the heavens!
Honor and majesty are found in His presence; strength and joy in His sanctuary!
Ascribe to the Lord the glory due His name!
Bring an offering and come before Him, worship the Lord in the beauty of His holiness!
Tremble and reverently fear before Him!
Let the heavens be glad and let the earth rejoice!
Let men say among the nations, "The Lord reigns!"
Let the sea roar and all that fills it!
Let the fields rejoice and all that is within them!
His mercy and loving-kindness endure forever!

It is important to get into the habit of thanking God for His provision. And to be specific – you wouldn't want someone to thank you with no explanation. Tell God exactly you are grateful for – your clothes, your food, your home, your car, your job, strength to complete your tasks, the way your body functions, the ability to walk and talk, the ocean, the sunrise, a snowflake, gentle rain, flowers budding, a butterfly, every smell, sight, sound, and taste…the list is endless!

Bless the Lord, O My Soul

The Bible often speaks of people "blessing the Lord" as when David said, *"Bless the Lord, O my soul, and all that is within me..."*[9] It is actually a prayer of thanksgiving. The Jewish people have a tradition of offering specific, short prayers throughout their entire day. These short prayers of appreciation are called *berakhah* or *brakha* (bra-KHAH), which means "blessing."[10] To bless the Lord is to thank Him and to acknowledge His provision. The root word *berakah* can also mean "to kneel." So, in that moment, you are mentally and humbly bowing before God, praising Him for His faithfulness.

You are encouraged to extravagantly bless Him – all day long. Scripture says, *"Blessed are those who have learned to acclaim you, who walk in the light of Your presence, Lord. They rejoice in Your name **all day long;** they celebrate Your righteousness."*[11] Sadly, most of us must admit that whatever thanksgiving we have already offered falls far short of what He is due. Let your praise pour forth! Speak even more passionately about His mighty deeds. Talk about His goodness all day long. It does not matter if you repeat yourself. You cannot have too much of a good thing!

You may think that this Jewish tradition of blessing the Lord hundreds of times a day is excessive, but listen to what Paul says about being thankful at all times:

- *"**Always** be giving thanks to God the Father for **everything.**"*[12]
- *"Whatever you do...do it **all** in the name of the Lord Jesus, giving thanks to God the Father."*[13]
- *"Rejoice in the Lord **always.** I will say it again: Rejoice!"*[14]
- *"Let us offer the sacrifice of praise **continually.**"*[1]
- *"Give thanks **in all circumstances,** for this is God's will for you in Christ Jesus."*[15]

Who is speaking here? It is the apostle Paul. Where is he? Likely in a dungeon, beaten and flogged (at least on some of these occasions). His chains are probably clanking together as he writes these beautiful phrases. He humbly requests that we join him in a sacrifice of praise. We are not in prison; we do not have shackles on our feet...I think we can all join him in abundantly praising God!

Your Heart Must Choose

It is easy to thank Him when "all is right with the world" and things are going your way. But how many of us can give thanks and praise when things go wrong? Can you still praise Him when money or food is scarce? Will you still thank Him when your health is failing? What about when He seems a million miles away and you need answers?

When times are tough, it is easy to become negative. And in Lamentations 3:19-20, you see the result of that – *"I remember my affliction and my wandering, the bitterness and the gall. I well remember them, **and my soul is downcast within me.**"* Thinking about your painful circumstances can start a depressing downward spiral of negativity. Excessive focus on bad memories from your past and difficulties in your present will bring destruction to your body and soul. Nothing good can be accomplished in a discouraged frame of mind.

Notice that in 1 Thessalonians 5:18 Paul doesn't say to be thankful *for* all circumstances; just *in* all circumstances. God doesn't expect you to be thankful for evil, suffering, or the sin in this world. However, He does want you to thank Him while He is working on your behalf to bring good out of your circumstances. Similarly, the command in Philippians 4:4 is to *"Rejoice in the Lord always."* You don't have to rejoice over pain and suffering, but you can rejoice in the Lord's provision. You can express your appreciation for His love, power, and faithfulness in the midst of trials – He has *"never forsaken those who seek Him."*[16]

Even if Jesus never did anything else for you, He would still deserve praise for the rest of your life because of what He did on the cross. He died for you! He gave up His life so you could have yours. He has given you a new name and is preparing an eternal place for you. He has given you rights as His heir. He has given you complete forgiveness of your sins. He has given you access to Him. He has tended, planted, pruned, and watered the garden of your heart. He has brought you out of the miry clay and set your feet upon a rock. His precious blood is falling on you, making you clean. He has made you acceptable before the infinite holiness of the Most High God. He has given you a robe of righteousness, and you are already wearing it. He doesn't "owe" you anything else. Can you comprehend all this favor and not praise His Name? You should always be able to praise Him – you are unable to thank Him enough.

Renew Your Mind

A grateful heart is closely linked to a renewed mind. Proverbs 23:7 says, *"For as he **thinks in his heart,** so is he…"* This one Scripture shows you how important it is to keep your mind filled with positive, healthy thoughts. Proverbs 4:23 also warns you to *"Guard your heart above all else, **for it determines the course of your life.**"* What does this mean? It means you are responsible for keeping your heart and mind clear of depression, disappointment, bitterness, self-pity, and anger.

The more you focus on negative memories or circumstances, the more negative you feel. You cannot enjoy life if you're always thinking negative thoughts. It is a battle for your mind! That's why 2 Corinthians 10:3-5 demands that you take *"every thought captive."* God will not bring your thoughts into captivity – you have to do it. And when Romans 12:2 says, *"Renew your mind"* it means you must break the stronghold of negative thinking patterns.

Throughout the Psalms, David felt oppressed by the enemy and forgotten by the Lord. He described *"tears day and night"*[17] and said his only friends were *"the darkness and the grave."*[18] But at the end of each passage, he always shifted his thinking back to praising the Lord. He chose to remember all that God had done in the past and determined to trust Him for the future. In the same way, when Jeremiah's soul was *"downcast within him"* in Lamentations 3, he specifically worked to refocus his mind. In verses 17-25, he says, *"Yet this I call to mind...."* and *"I say to myself, 'The LORD is my portion; therefore, I will wait for Him.'"*

You must decide in your mind not to let adversity rule your thoughts, feelings, and behaviors. Stop dwelling on and talking about your problems. Choose to concentrate on the goodness and faithfulness of God, even when you can't see the big picture. This will not happen on its own. You must deliberately shift your focus moment-by-moment.

Mind Over Matter

Recent discoveries in cognitive science have demonstrated that the thoughts you store in your mind are constantly building new networks – like young trees sprouting up in a forest. Your thoughts occupy physical "property" in your brain. They also influence your genetic code by sending electromagnetic signals to your DNA strands, activating the creation of amino acids and proteins. This then influences your emotions, words, and actions. The expression "mind over matter" really is true!

Dr. Caroline Leaf is a cognitive neuroscientist (and fellow believer) who has studied the mind-body relationship for decades. In her book, *Switch on Your Brain*, she demonstrates how important is to be careful what you think about. What you choose to dwell on in your mind influences your body. You can create life or death within your own mind. This confirms the scripture found in Deuteronomy 30:19 which says, *"I have set before you life and death, blessings and curses. Now choose life..."*

Science is proving what Scripture has said all along. The actual structure and "landscape" of your brain follows your thought patterns. You are capable of controlling your thoughts, rewiring your brain, and changing your mind. God gave you the power to control your own behavior, body, and emotions. This new era of science proves that you truly can *"renew your mind!"*

Choose Life

Your thoughts have consequences. You can *choose* peace. You can *choose* joy. You can replace toxic thoughts with God's truth. Give your circumstances to God and fill your mind with Scriptures that reassure you that He is in complete control. Psalm 34:8 says, *"O taste and see that the Lord is good."* He is GOOD. Trust Him. Instead of thinking, "This is a mess," trust that the "Lord is good." Instead of believing, "I'll never get it right," trust that the "Lord is good." Instead of getting frustrated that things aren't going your way, trust that the "Lord is good." Leave everything in His hands, knowing *only* that He is good. He can bring order out of chaos, good out of evil, peace out of turmoil. He is good.

The outcome of your life is determined by what is in your heart, not your circumstances. A study by the American Medical Association found that stress plays a role in at least 75% of all illness and disease.[19] You must be proactive to keep your heart and mind pure. Matthew 5:8 says, *"Blessed are the pure in heart…"* If you have a habit of thinking negatively, work on changing your thought patterns. Ask the Holy Spirit to help you. The Scripture in Ephesians 5:20 instructing you to be *"thankful for everything"* is closely tied to the Scripture teaching you to be *"ever filled with the Holy Spirit"* (verse 18). God knew that maintaining an attitude of thankfulness no matter what your circumstances look like would require the power of the Holy Spirit.

Tame Your Tongue

Renewing your mind is important, but controlling your tongue is even more critical. God has ordained that your spoken words carry an authority even more powerful than your thoughts. For example, Romans 10:8-10 commands you to confess what you believe *with your mouth* in order to be saved. Matthew 17:20 tells you to *say* to the mountain "move" and it will move. 2 Corinthians 4:2 instructs you to *renounce* sin, in other words, to "speak out against it."

Scripture suggests that how you speak is a significant sign of your Christian maturity. James compared the tongue to a small rudder with sufficient power to steer a large ship.[20] A little while later, he compared the tongue to a fire from hell that can set the whole body ablaze.[21] Clearly a vital step in becoming a beloved disciple is learning to tame your tongue.

The Spoken Word

Your spoken words have an impact. In fact, *"The tongue has the power of life and death."*[22] That is no small power to disregard! I'm sure you can agree that your tongue has the power to destroy relationships, dreams, and even your own self-confidence.

The tongue's ability to create monumental damage is astounding. It also has the potential to bring about remarkable results under the influence of the Holy Spirit. You have been called to share Jesus and give your testimony any time you have the opportunity. You have been called to pray and worship. You've been called to encourage the tired and weary. Malachi 3:16 says that when those who love God speak encouraging words to one another He *"writes it in a scroll and remembers it later."* That's amazing – and I want Him to have something to write about me!

If no part of the body is harder to submit to godly authority than the tongue,[23] you can be assured that Satan is vying for control over your mouth. Remember, Luke 6:45 says, *"For out of the overflow of his heart the mouth speaks."* A corrupt tongue indicates a corrupt heart. Some examples of the misuse of our words include gossip, profanity, unkindness, criticism, lying, complaining, offensive humor, and taking the Lord's name in vain. How many times have you said, "I don't think I'm going to make it..." or "My life is a mess..." or "I'm so sick of this!" The way we speak can be a huge challenge for most of us.

What and *how* you speak indicates your level of faith – *"we believe therefore we speak."*[24] Notice the power of the spoken word when most of the Israelite spies came back with a bad report about the Promised Land. They incited fear, grumbling, and panic among the rest of the group. After the faithless words of the spies had soaked into their minds overnight, the men imagined themselves dead by the sword and the women and children taken as plunder. They begged to return to their slavery in Egypt.[25]

You can drive out panic and fear with spoken words of praise. The Bible says, *"Offer to God the sacrifice of thanksgiving and pay your vows to the Most High;* **then call upon Me in the day of trouble and I will deliver you.**"[26] The divine order is first praise, then deliverance. Notice that in John 11:41 Jesus gave thanks to the Father *before* He raised Lazarus from the dead. Thanksgiving preceded the miracle. Jesus gave thanks for what He was *about to* receive. You should follow His example. Praise is vital preparation for the working of miracles in your life.

Break Every Curse

With the tongue we praise our Lord and Father and *"with the same tongue we curse men, who have been made in God's likeness. My brothers, this should not be."*[27] With your words you can speak life or death. Your words can tear down or build up. Your words can encourage or discourage.

Hurtful words can penetrate and take root in a soul. I strongly encourage you to take some time to repent and renounce any negative words you have spoken over the lives of others. Also forgive anyone who has spoken harsh words into your own life and renounce any hold they might retain in your heart and mind. Some examples include:

- You'll never be good enough.
- You're hopeless.
- It's too late now – you missed your chance.
- No one cares about you.
- You'll never accomplish anything.
- God can't use you now.
- You're just like your…father, mother, etc.
- You're not attractive. You're too fat, too short…
- You're a loser.

Take away the power of those harmful words by renouncing them now. Repent of every way that you have participated in agreement with them. Confess that you are covered by the blood of Jesus Christ – and you are fearfully and wonderfully made in His image. Ask God to remove each memory of the hurtful words and realign you with His truth.

Speak the Truth

Make sure that everything you speak over yourself and others is in alignment with the truth of God's Word. Take a few minutes and confess these truths *out loud* regarding your identity in Christ Jesus (and trust me, there's a difference between speaking these out loud and merely reading them quietly!):

- Because I am in Christ, I am a new creation. The old has gone, the new has come![28]
- God has chosen me.[29]
- I am engraved on the palms of His hands.[30]
- He goes before me and makes the rough places smooth. He calls me by my name.[31]
- I have been established, anointed, and sealed by God.[32]
- I am confident that the good work that God has begun in me will be perfected.[33]
- I have not been given a spirit of fear but of power, love, and a sound mind.[34]

- I have the mind of Christ.[35]
- I am God's handiwork. I have been created in Christ Jesus to do good works, which He prepared in advance for me to do.[36]
- I cannot be separated from the love of God.[37]

Great is His Faithfulness

You can strengthen your identity in Christ by remembering His faithfulness in the past. Over and over in Scripture, God's people are told to intentionally recall His miracles and mighty works. Psalm 77:11-12 says, *"I will **remember** the deeds of the Lord; yes, I will **remember** your miracles of long ago. I will **meditate** on all your works and **consider** all your mighty deeds."* Deuteronomy 8:10 teaches, *"When you have eaten and are satisfied, you should bless the Lord your God for the good land which He has given you."* This passage goes on to warn that once you get established, you may be tempted to forget the Lord, thinking that your own hard work produced your prosperity (verse 14).

Wandering and rebellious hearts are often the result of forgetting what He has provided. The Israelites were guilty of this up-and-down roller coaster of faith and failure:

1. *"We have sinned and acted wickedly. When our fathers were in Egypt, they gave no thought to Your miracles; they did not remember Your many kindnesses, and they rebelled."*[38]
2. *"Then they believed His promises and sang His praise."*[39]
3. *"But they soon forgot what He had done and did not wait for His plan to unfold. They put God to the test."*[39]

In Psalm 145:7, you are encouraged to *"abundantly utter **the memory** of His great goodness."* I know that my memory is much improved when I write things down. If you want to remember His goodness, you must let it make an impression on you and make note of it. The more you notice and think about it, the more likely you will be able to recall it later. You cannot abundantly praise unless your memory supplies the materials. You must *"stir up your mind by way of remembrance."*[40] If you don't keep your own journal of His signs and wonders, rely on the Bible – there's plenty recorded in there! David went from the sheep fields to the palace. Joseph went from the dungeon to the throne. The disciples went from fisherman to "fishers of men" – all by the marvelous hand of God.

Recognize His Activity

Taking time to appreciate God's provision is a part of the process of building faith for the future. Romans 4:20 says Abraham *"grew strong in faith **as he gave praise and glory to God."*** The recognition of God's activity in your life will bring a sense of gratitude, hope, and joy.

Throughout your life, the Lord has always been there. First Samuel 7:12 says, *"Hitherto the Lord has helped us."* This directs your focus to the *past*. He has undoubtedly been faithful over your lifetime. Psalm 139:13-16 reminds you that you are *"fearfully and wonderfully made."* He created your inmost being and *"knit you together in your mother's womb."* All the days ordained for you were *"written in His book before one of them came to be."* Acts 17:26 says that He has *"determined the times set for you;"* even the *"exact places"* where you would live. Trust that He has been there all along, even before you knew Him as your Savior.

Take a moment now to consider how God has worked throughout your life. Ask the Holy Spirit to show you His activity as you were growing up. Spend time in prayer over the coming week with the goal of remembering how God has moved in your life. He has always been at work, whether you noticed or not. Trace back the countless instances that a "coincidence" was actually His loving hand. Recognize His intervention as David did in Psalm 52:9, saying, *"I will praise you forever for what You have done."* The more you actively remember His faithfulness, the more you will be willing to trust Him with your future.

As you grow in your walk as a beloved disciple, He will reward you with fresh signs and wonders and more of Himself. Since I started seeking Him more seriously, I can testify that I have seen more of His divine activity. As He begins to reveal Himself to you, don't forget what you have seen. If you don't fully appreciate the revelations He does provide, it's less likely you will continue receiving them in the future. Don't follow the pattern of the Israelites who, shortly after witnessing incredible miracles, turned to whining and complaining that He never did anything for them. Be mindful and grateful of every touch He pours into your life. He wants to be remembered.

Eternally Grateful

Martin Luther referred to gratitude as "the basic Christian attitude" and it is still considered "the heart of the gospel."[41] Cicero, in *Oratio Pro Cnoeo Plancio* (XXXIII) deemed it *"not only the greatest of the virtues, but the parent of all others."*

Even the field of psychology has begun to acknowledge the importance of gratitude for producing abundant life. For the first 100 years, psychology focused its efforts on psychological problems and how to remedy them. Those efforts resulted in great strides in the treatment of psychological disorders. But the consequence of this sole focus on problems was that psychology had little to say about how to enjoy life. After being mired for a century in the study of dysfunction, a new field called Positive Psychology is rapidly emerging as the direction for the future.

Instead of trying to bring people at *-5 to 0,* Positive Psychology shifts the focus to getting people from *0 to +5.* This new branch of psychology studies positive emotions, strengths-based character, ethical behavior, and energizing relationships. It is a science that seeks to understand the factors that allow people to flourish. This is not simply the power of positive thinking, a self-help movement, or a passing fad. It is the fastest growing area of psychology.

With the advent of the Positive Psychology movement, gratitude has become a mainstream focus of psychological research. In a recent book entitled *Positive Organizational Scholarship,* studies on gratitude fill an entire chapter![42] This new body of research suggests that gratitude is the key to living life well. Grateful people are happier, less depressed, less stressed, and more satisfied with their lives and social relationships.[43] Grateful people have higher levels of personal growth, purpose in life, and self-acceptance.[44] Grateful people have more positive ways of coping with the difficulties they experience in life and rely less on dysfunctional strategies, such as avoiding or denying the problem, blaming themselves, or coping through substance abuse.[45] Grateful people even sleep better![46]

Count Your Blessings

Given that gratitude appears to be a strong determinant of our well-being, several psychological interventions have been developed to increase gratitude. Clinicians practicing principles of Positive Psychology suggest that their clients keep a daily "gratitude journal" of *Three Blessings.* The task is simple enough. At the end of your day, you think of at least three things that you are most happy about and why you believe they happened.

The outcome of this exercise is astonishing. It has been shown to have a powerful effect on reducing symptoms of depression and anxiety, while simultaneously increasing a sense of joy and well-being. In a recent study, participants completing this task for *one week* experienced those positive outcomes for *six months!*[47] That is not a misprint. One week of doing this simple activity had a lasting effect for six months. The exercise was so successful that although participants were only asked to journal for a week, many participants continued to keep the journal long after the study was over.

William Penn understood that *"the secret to happiness is to* **count your blessings** *while others are adding up their troubles."* And a hymn writer obviously knew this secret a century ago (Johnson Oatman, 1897). Do you remember his words, *"Count your blessings, name them one by one. Count your many blessings and see what God has done"?*[48] If you haven't counted your blessings lately, try it. It really works!

<hr />

Cultivate Joy

When you express appreciation for all God has done for you, it brings Him joy. At the same time, it also increases your joy. He has JOY waiting for you! The Father loves to see His children happy. One of the fruits of the Spirit is joy.[49] In God's presence is *"fullness of joy."*[50] You have been *"anointed with the oil of joy."*[51] Isaiah 61:7 says, *"everlasting joy will be theirs."* Joy is not a requirement of Christian discipleship; it is a consequence. Joy is not what we work up; it is what God gives. Joy is your inheritance. Joy is the climate of heaven. It's up to you to receive your full portion now.

Don't let the enemy steal your joy! Recognize *what* steals it and become a fierce warrior against it – things like resentment, bitterness, unforgiveness, worry, doubt, and depression. Choose to appreciate what you already have. Choose to trust Him; believe that He is in control. Cultivate a grateful heart and joy will *"overtake you."*[52]

If you want to become a beloved disciple, you're going to have to get rid of grumbling, negativity, and faithless talk. Despite any sorrows and troubles in life, there are blessings too numerous to count. *"Great is the Lord and most worthy to be praised!"*[53] Acknowledge His greatness, love, and grace. It should not be difficult for a beloved disciple's heart to be filled with admiration and praise of the Lord Jesus Christ.

As you progress in discipleship, your responsibility to raise your level of gratitude will also grow. If God is greater to you now than He was a year ago, let your praise be greater! This is a necessary step in your relationship with Jesus. It is not so for everyone, but it is true for those who are asking to serve Him well and do much for Him. Begin the work for which you were created and called. Spend today, tomorrow, and the rest of your life praising God!

Your tongue will become an instrument of divine power and praise. Psalm 7:17 says, *"I will **give thanks** to the Lord because of His righteousness and will **sing praise** to the Name of the Lord Most High."* Beloved disciple, in the next step, we are going to advance from "giving thanks" (Step #5) to "singing praise" (Step #6)!

Prayer

Jesus, I long to draw closer to You. Help me now to bless Your heart. I repent for neglecting to thank You for so many answered prayers and blessings. I pause to remember Your greatness now. Your mercy never ceases. My name is engraved in the palm of Your hand. It is unspeakable grace that even allows me to know You. Thank You for setting me apart for all eternity. I rejoice in knowing I am Yours forever!

Precious Lord Jesus, You gave Your life for mine. You ransomed me with Your heart's own blood. Thank You that my sin is nailed to the Cross, and I no longer bear its penalty or guilt. You are worthy to receive all power, honor, glory, and praise. The angels adore You and bring everlasting hallelujahs to Your feet. O my Savior, accept this praise that comes from a heart that loves You. I proclaim Your great faithfulness to me.

Enable me to rise above the cares of this world to bring You my thanks and praise. Take away everything that hinders me from delighting completely in You. Help me to reject discouragement, resentment, bitterness, and self-pity. When my soul is downcast, I will remember Your faithfulness and loving-kindness. Your steadfast love endures forever.

I will not be conformed to this world but choose to renew my mind with Your truth. I take every thought captive and make it obedient to You, my Lord. My faith embraces all You have promised. I believe I have been given power, love, and a sound mind. I lay aside every other attraction and distraction. I choose to meditate on only those things that are noble, worthy of reverence, honorable, just, pure, lovely, excellent, and praiseworthy. I want to be captivated by You, and only You. I will keep my eyes fixed on You.

Lord, teach me how to talk wisely. May the words of my mouth and the meditation of my heart be pleasing in Your sight. Keep me from sinning with my mouth. Guard my tongue against evil that I would not speak hurtfully with my lips or participate in anger with my words. Give me greater watchfulness over my speech, so that I can tame my tongue and thus control my whole body. Give me the privilege of speaking Your truth. Teach me to better express the message of Your Cross. Increase my joy and peace, the fruits of Your Spirit. Saturate my heart in Your love and compassion so that I can accomplish all Your plans and purposes for me.

STUDY

1. Paul mentions thankfulness six times in his letter to the Colossians – 1:3 and 12; 2:7; 3:15 and 17; and 4:2. Why is thankfulness so important for Christians?

2. While beaten and in prison, Paul can't seem to thank God enough. Think of someone you know who always seems to be *"overflowing with thankfulness."* What kinds of hardships has that person been through? How can you imitate his or her attitude?

3. Read through 1 Chronicles 16:23-34, meditating on one phrase at a time.

Renew Your Mind

4. Proverbs 23:7 says, *"As a man thinks within himself, so he is."* What are some of the things you think about most frequently? Talk about most?

5. Do you spend a lot of time thinking about your weaknesses and failures? Do you tend to focus more on what you *don't* have rather than what you *do* have? How can you change that?

6. Read Lamentations 3:17-20. Describe what negative memories can do to you if you let them.

7. In Lamentations 3, how does Jeremiah refocus his mind in verses 21-25?

8. How do you think a person sets his/her mind *"on things above"* (see Colossians 3:1-2)?

9. What does Hebrews 12:2 say about how to "endure?"

Speak Life

10. What does James 3:2-12 have to say about the importance of your tongue?

11. In which of the following areas does your tongue tend to struggle most?

☐ gossip or slander   ☐ lying

☐ cursing/swearing   ☐ rudeness/unkindness

☐ inappropriate humor   ☐ criticism/judgment

12. Read Malachi 3:16. How does God respond when we speak good words about Him?

13. What are some positive prophecies that have been spoken over your life? Have they come to pass?

14. Have there been any negative words spoken over your life that have a limiting influence on you today?

15. In a time of private prayer, try to recall every statement contrary to God's Word that has been spoken over your life. Tell God how much the words hurt and any power you feel they have had over your life. In Jesus' name, renounce every statement one by one, along with any effect it has had on you. Ask Him to replace all the hurtful words with words of healing. Ask Him to empower you to forgive those who spoke them over you.

Great is His Faithfulness

16. What has God done recently that caused you to rejoice? What are some specific blessings you have received from God in the past year or so?

17. Can you recall an occasion when God did *not* give you what you asked for and you are thankful for that now? Have you ever experienced what initially seemed like a setback that you were grateful for later?

18. Consider starting (if you haven't already) a prayer/gratitude journal. Try to become intentional about remembering every answer to prayer. **Every day for one week, identify three things you are grateful for.**

19. For those that already keep a diary/journal, why is it important to you?

20. According to Psalm 77:11-12, what kinds of things did the writer want to remember?

21. Psalm 106 is unparalleled in outlining the pattern of remembering and forgetting God's goodness. Read the entire Psalm carefully. Note the key words *remember* and *forget*. What invariably happened when the Israelites forgot God's mighty acts on their behalf?

22. Think about Paul and his view of the trials in his life. Read 2 Corinthians 4:17 and describe what Paul believed in faith.

> *"For our light and momentary troubles are achieving for us*
> *an eternal glory that far outweighs them all."*
>
> 2 Corinthians 4:17

SPIRITUAL MARKER

joy

WORSHIP

10,000 Reasons [Matt Redman]

Forever [Chris Tomlin]

I Desire Jesus [Darlene Zschech]

Blessed Be Your Name [Newsboys]

Speak Life [tobyMac]

Great is Thy Faithfulness [Various Artists]

God You're So Good [Passion]

Good Good Father [Chris Tomlin]

Goodness of God [Bethel Music featuring Jenn Johnson]

Great Things [Phil Wickham]

Praise Before My Breakthrough [Brian & Katie Torwalt]

Breathe [Influence Music featuring Matt Gillham]

Gratitude [Brandon Lake]

BE JOYFUL ALWAYS

1 THESSALONIANS 5:16

WORSHIP IN SPIRIT AND TRUTH

In the process of becoming a beloved disciple, prayer is good (Step #4), thanksgiving is better (Step #5), and worship is best (Step #6)! Charles Spurgeon pointed out that prayer is important, but it is a lower form of worship in that it is often "selfish."[1] Prayer is an outpouring of your own needs, petitions, and requests to God. Praise is superior because it elevates God. In *Come Away My Beloved*, Francis J. Roberts said, *"Doors are opened by prayer and faith, but by praise and worship, great dynamos of power are set in motion. Praying for specifics is like requesting light for individual houses in scattered places, while worshipping floods the whole area with available current."*

When you *praise* God, you are thanking Him for what He has done in your life. When you *worship* God, you exalt who He is – the King of Kings, the Great I AM. A. W. Tozer said, *"We begin to grow up when our worship passes from thanksgiving to admiration."* The dictionary defines admiration as "wondering esteem accompanied by pleasure and delight." You are growing in discipleship - do you admire Jesus this way?

Worship is far more than music; it is an attitude of the heart. It is about falling in love with Jesus. All your praying, studying the Bible, and reading books about God will lack intimacy if your heart is not in awe of Him. Even Satan knows the Word of God. As a beloved disciple, you want to foster a deeper relationship with Jesus, not simply more obligations.

> *"Worship should never be pursued as a means to achieving something other than worship. Worship is never a step on our way to another experience. It is not a door through which we pass to get anywhere else. It is the end point, the goal."*
>
> John Piper

He Is Exalted

The word *worship* can mean to "bow down, to reverence, to give honor and adoration." In Revelation 1:17, when John was given a glimpse of the glory of Jesus Christ, he *"fell at His feet as though dead."* Wow...I can only imagine what that will be like someday.

Worship means that you show respect and honor to God. You position yourself to see Him, experience Him, connect with Him, and present your heart to Him. You confess His authority over you. Taking time to worship reminds you of who He is, reassures you that He is in charge, and sets you in your place. You should be amazed by Him – *"Let all the earth fear the Lord; let all the inhabitants of the world stand in awe of Him."*[2]

Worship is humbling. We should *"tremble at His Word"*[3] – He is God. But our society has made God so user-friendly that we have lost a reverential *"fear of the Lord,"* which is *"the beginning of wisdom."*[4] The Lord *"favors those who fear Him."*[5] A. W. Tozer said we need to learn *"astonished reverence, breathless adoration, awesome fascination, lofty admiration of the attributes of God, and something of the breathless silence that we know when God is near."* All these elements make up what the Bible calls the "fear of the Lord."

Created to Worship

You were created to worship. The *"chief end of man is to glorify God and enjoy Him forever."*[6] The question is *what* will you worship? What you're focused on is what you worship. Worship in its simplest essence is attentiveness. What are you "beholding" most of the time?

Worship is your primary responsibility to God. *"You are a chosen people, a royal priesthood, a holy nation, a people belonging to God, **that you may declare the praises of Him** who called you out of darkness into His wonderful light.*[7] You bring Him glory by worshiping Him. You can't add to His glory, but you are commanded to recognize, honor, declare, praise, and reflect His glory:[8]

- *"The people I made will sing songs to praise me."*[9]
- *"All You have made will praise You, O Lord; Your saints will extol You."*[10]

- *"All the nations You have made will come and worship before You, O Lord, they will bring glory to Your name."*[11]
- *"Thou art worthy, O Lord, to receive glory and honor and power: for Thou has created all things, and for Thy pleasure they are and were created."*[12]
- *"You give life to everything, and the multitudes of heaven worship You."*[13]

If praise is the perpetual work of holy angels and the saints of heaven, it should be your primary focus here on earth too.[14] It seems incredible that we can even do anything that brings pleasure to the God of the universe. But it is true, for He has declared that He is well pleased with the praises of His children – *"The Lord is pleased with His worshippers."*[15] And it is the *"praising life"* that honors Him.[16]

Will you *"rob God"*[17] of the *"glory due His Name?"*[18] Refusing to worship Him is prideful rebellion, and it is the same sin that caused Satan's fall. If you don't play your part in praise, *"the stones must cry out."*[19]

When you worship, your goal should be to bring pleasure to God, not yourself. If you leave a church service saying, "I didn't get a lot out of the worship today" you have missed the point. The heart of worship is and always has been blessing Him, coming to intimacy with Him, and giving to Him. HE IS THE CENTER OF WORSHIP. How dare we ever make *us* the center of worship! Worship isn't to please us, it's to please Jesus. Worship is for Jesus, to Jesus, and it's all about Jesus.[20]

> *"The time is coming when the true worshippers will worship the Father in spirit and in truth, and that time is here already. You see, the Father is actively seeking such people to worship Him. God is Spirit and those who worship Him must worship* **in Spirit and truth.***"*[21]

In Spirit and In Truth

In John 4, Jesus was having a conversation with a Samaritan woman at the well. He had already revealed that He knew about her many husbands. This made her uncomfortable, so she attempted to divert His attention to the topic of religion. She questioned Jesus as to the best time, location, and style of worship. Jesus replied that these issues were irrelevant and got right to the heart of the matter. There is no right or wrong place to worship. The most important thing is *who* and *why* you worship and *how much of yourself* you offer to God when you worship. Your greatest desire should simply be to *"worship God in a way that will please Him."*[22]

The Heart of Worship

Worship demands your mind, your body, and your heart...it should encompass your entire being. Mindless worship is meaningless and mechanical. Charles Spurgeon was concerned that *"the very posture of some people indicates that they are going through the hymn, but the hymn is not going through their hearts."* Jesus called this *"vain repetition."*[23] He said, *"These people honor me with their lips, but their hearts are far from me. They worship me in vain."*[24]

In Isaiah 29, God complained about worship that was hypocritical, stale, and insincere. He doesn't want empty rituals recited without meaning or passion. He also doesn't want a showy performance or fake emotions. Your worship should be genuine and heartfelt. It is not just a matter of saying the right thing; you must truly mean what you say. He wants your real, honest expression of love:

- *"Man looks at the outward appearance, but the Lord looks at the **heart.**"*[25]
- *"Sing all you whose **hearts** are right."*[26]
- *"David led them with an innocent **heart.**"*[27]

True worship involves the giving of your heart. You cannot exalt God and your own interests at the same time. David said, *"I will not offer to the Lord my God sacrifices that have cost me nothing."*[28] Authentic worship will cost you time, energy, and attention.

The biggest distraction in worship is yourself – allowing your mind to wander and worrying about what others will think of you. When you start to praise and worship God, choose to lay all other things aside. Deliberately shift the focus off yourself. This requires some preparation. Just as musicians tune their instruments before playing, prepare yourself for worship by "tuning" your heart. Confess your sins. Ask the Holy Spirit to make your soul fit for praising God. Think about specific things you want to worship Him for.

The Presence of the Holy Spirit

God's ultimate goal is to change your heart, to renew it from the inside out. This cannot be done apart from the power of the Holy Spirit. Participating in a great worship service can create a temporary sense of excitement, but it won't alter your life without the

Holy Spirit. Worship in the flesh goes no deeper than superficial emotions. It may look impressive on the surface, but you won't be changed by it. Excited, yes; transformed, no.

When worship is done as God intended, it will bear the distinctive mark of the Holy Spirit. There will be something divine and unexplainable about it. You will know that what has happened can't be duplicated by just bringing the same elements together again (the music, the words, the instruments, etc.). When the Holy Spirit moves during worship, He refines, comforts, and restores. He can penetrate to the depths of your soul. He *"removes your heart of stone"* and *"puts a new spirit within you."*[29] Healing can take place. Minds get renewed. Lives are transformed.

Ceaseless Praise

Worship is a lifestyle, not a Sunday performance. You can worship Him at work, in your kitchen, in your bedroom, or in your car. You can praise Him on Monday, Tuesday, and Wednesday – every day, everywhere. You are encouraged to *"worship continually."*[30] Psalm 113:3 says, *"From the rising of the sun to the place where it sets, the name of the LORD is to be praised."*

If Christians worshipped only when they felt like it, there would be very little worship. Determine to worship no matter what is happening in your life. Praise Him under all circumstances, regardless of your "mood." Worship even when the most difficult thing to do is praise. I understand that choosing to worship requires an incredible step of faith when your world is falling apart. When you praise Him despite your circumstances, your life will overflow with a powerful testimony of the greatness of God. Often when you start to praise God during a hard time, the Holy Spirit will literally come and "lift" your burdens. When you look to Jesus, you feel His promises reawaken your soul.

David was a worshipper. He had worshipped the Lord when he was a young boy, keeping his father's flock. Harp in hand, he had sung to the Lord His Shepherd, whose rod and staff were his comfort. When he was running from Saul, the caves of Engedi resounded with his praise. When he became king of Israel, he daily sang the praises of the God of his salvation. In fact, during his reign over 4000 musicians were assigned to sing and play in the temple both night and day.[31] David also *"danced with all his might"* before the ark of the Lord.[32] Yet in Psalm 71:14, David vowed to praise God *"more and more."*

David resolved to lift his praise higher and higher. I'm sure you already love to worship the Lord – but can you do MORE? Psalms and hymns and praise and worship should abound in your home. Sing as much as you pray – without ceasing!

---◆---

The Powerful Purpose of Worship

Worship can bring transformational power, healing, and restoration to yourself and others. Throughout the Bible, worship served 5 different purposes: celebration, evangelism, spiritual warfare, healing, and seeking God.[33]

1. Celebration and Exaltation

Exaltation means "to increase, to lift up high, to rejoice." It involves raising your heart, voice, and hands to celebrate Him. You want to honor Him with extravagant praise. *"Exalt the Lord our God and worship at His holy mountain."*[34]

Psalm 145 is known as "David's Psalm of Praise." All throughout this Psalm, his desire was for God to be greatly magnified. *"I will exalt You, my God the King; I will praise Your name forever and ever. Every day I will praise You and extol Your Name forever and ever. Great is the LORD and most worthy of praise; His greatness no one can fathom."* (v 1-3). The inspired psalmist wanted to openly declare and joyfully proclaim that the Lord is worthy of praise.

When you worship God, you celebrate all that He has done and will continue to do. You honor Him for who He is. A celebration of worship played a role in every major "movement" in the Bible – the parting of the Red Sea,[35] breaking down the Jericho walls,[36] David returning the ark to Jerusalem,[37] the homecoming of the prodigal son,[38] and Paul and Silas being freed from jail[39] – just to name a few. At the end of this age, *"every creature in heaven and on earth and under the earth and on the sea, and all that is in them, **will be singing:** "To Him who sits on the throne and to the Lamb be praise and honor and glory and power, forever and ever!"*[40]

2. Evangelism

Use your ability to dance, sing, or play an instrument in worship to reflect the love of Christ. If you don't exhibit His love, you are *"just a noisy gong or a clanging cymbal."*[41] But when other people see your authentic worship, they will be attracted to Jesus. They will want salvation too! When Paul and Silas worshipped in jail, the jailer ended up giving his life to Christ.[42]

3. Spiritual Warfare

In 2 Chronicles 20, King Jehoshaphat was about to enter a difficult battle. He appointed men to praise the Lord **ahead of the army** saying, *"Give thanks to the Lord for His love endures forever."* As they began to sing in praise, God defeated their enemy. There is mighty power in the name of Jesus; there is power in praise and worship!

You might be surprised how much is challenged and changed in the spiritual realm through your acts of worship. Psalm 149:5-9 describes your praise as an important means to triumph over the enemy:

> *"Let the saints rejoice and sing for joy on their beds. **May the praise of God be in their mouths and a double-edged sword in their hands,** to inflict vengeance on the nations and punishment on the peoples, to bind their kings with fetters, their nobles with shackles of iron, to carry out the sentence written against them. This is the glory of all His saints. Praise the LORD."*

The work of the devil is to *oppress* – but worship can break oppression through the power of the Holy Spirit. In Acts 16, when Paul and Silas worshipped in jail, the foundation of the prison was suddenly shaken and *"everyone's chains came loose."* You must not overlook the power in worship that can free not only those who are praising, but also those who are listening!

The enemy has no chance in the midst of people who are consumed by the worship of God. A joyful heart is the best weapon against evil. With praise on your lips, you have a harder time complaining and finding fault with others. You cannot fear while you are praising God. Worship displaces darkness.

When the sole motivation is to magnify the Lord, the purity of worship draws the angels of heaven and changes the atmosphere. *"Bless the LORD, O you His angels, you mighty ones who do His word, obeying the voice of His word!"*[43] When you worship, you bring the activity of heaven to earth.

4. Healing

One of the Greek words for worship is *therapeuo,* which means "to cure and to heal." Many times, a worship song can bring comfort and healing. It is not the song itself that ministers, but the anointing on that song that breathes new life into your soul. When anointed with the touch of the Holy Spirit, divine worship can break the bondage of others, bringing healing and restoration. One example of this is found in 1 Samuel 16:23. David would take his harp and play for Saul who was very ill. The scripture says that Saul would feel better, and evil spirits would leave as David played and ministered to him.

I have experienced the healing power of worship myself. After my sister was murdered, I built protective walls around myself (and my emotions) so that nothing could penetrate them. In fact, *nothing made me cry.* For more than 10 years. Then one Sunday our church featured a worship dance. I had never seen anything like it before! I couldn't take my eyes away from it. With tears streaming down my face faster than they could be discreetly wiped away…I was forever changed. I didn't know the dancers and I didn't even know the song, but somehow that worship was able to penetrate my hardened heart and open the floodgates of feeling. I'm now happy to say that *everything* touches me more deeply, and many things can now make me cry – both tears of sadness and tears of joy!

I thank God for anointed worship leaders and song writers. They have gotten me through many a difficult day. Sometimes I will hear a song and it will stop me right in my tracks and bring me down to my knees. There are times I have kept one particular song on repeat for days because it was ministering to my heart. Worship songs are one of the ways that God speaks to me, giving me just the right message that I need for that time or season.

Isaiah 61:3 says that He wants to exchange your *"spirit of heaviness"* for the *"garment of praise."* Open your heart to trust Him with all that concerns you. All the problems in your life will pale in comparison to the promises of God. It is powerful to vocalize those promises and let your spirit rise above it all.

5. Seeking God

Calling His name in worship indicates you are seeking His presence. God *"inhabits the praises of His people."*[44] We are even told that He "enters in" to our worship – He literally sings and dances over us![45] When you bless Him, He draws near. And the reality of His presence is breathtaking.

Never underestimate the power of worship, spending time in the presence of God. Your soul hungers and thirsts for more of Him. Have you ever been away from your church for a long time? Have you ever been unable to sing for an extended period? If so, I am sure you can attest to the insatiable hunger that grows within your soul. There is nothing that compares, as David testified, *"One thing I ask of the Lord, that is what I seek: that I may dwell in the house of the Lord, all the days of my life, to gaze upon the beauty of the Lord and to seek Him in His temple…At His tabernacle will **I come with shouts of joy; I will sing and make music to the Lord.**"*[46] The more you see of Him, the more you want!

The Expression of Worship

"Speak to one another in psalms and hymns and spiritual songs, offering praise with voices [and instruments] and making melody with all your heart to the Lord."[47]

Many forms of worship are mentioned in the Bible, including singing, shouting, kneeling, dancing, making a joyful noise, clapping, leaping, playing instruments, lifting your hands, and even lying prostrate.[48] Psalm 150 says, *"Praise the Lord! Praise Him with trumpet blast; praise Him with harps and lyres. Praise Him with tambourines and dancing; praise Him with stringed instruments and flutes. Praise Him with loud cymbals; praise Him with crashing cymbals. Let everything that has breath praise the Lord."*

Verbalizing our love for Jesus through words and song are the most common forms of worship within a traditional church setting, but we don't want to stop there. We were each created uniquely by God to express our love. Each person has a special way of communicating worship to God – so don't judge. The variety is attractive to Him.

Music

God loves all kinds of music. He invented it all – loud and soft, fast and slow, traditional and contemporary. Unfortunately, I routinely hear complaints in church that the music is too loud, the beat is too fast, someone doesn't like a particular style, or their "favorite" song is not played frequently enough. It is sad to hear that people would leave a church community over something like this – we can get so stuck in our ways! If it grieves my heart, imagine how it grieves the Holy Spirit when we argue about these things.

Christians can passionately defend their preferred style of worship as the most honoring to God. But that's all it is – their own preference, not God's! There is no "best" or most biblical style of music. Worship has nothing to do with style or volume. Whatever is offered to God in spirit and truth is an act of worship and He enjoys it all.

Dance

Scripture gives many references to the use of dance as a form of celebration and of reverent worship.[49] Psalm 149:3 says, *"Let them praise His name in the dance."* Likewise, Psalm 150:4 says, *"Praise Him with the dance."*

However, the body of Christ has been robbed of this gift having its proper place in the church as a powerful tool in worship, warfare, and celebration. Satan has successfully convinced many Christians that dance is carnal in nature and therefore has no place within the church today. This is an understandable point of view because often the only example of dance that many have seen has been that of a worldly nature. We've most often witnessed a distorted, perverted version of what God originally created for a pure and holy purpose. Although the reputation of dance has been severely damaged, its vindication is now taking place in the church. It was created for His pleasure, and it rightfully belongs to the church for its intimate communication of worship.

When dancers dance in worship, they can physically demonstrate a personal relationship with Jesus. They express the emotion and intimacy in a visual way so that everyone can experience it. In our culture, we have lost something by allowing our worship to become a passive thing. We shouldn't just sing the words "we bow down" or "I lift my hands;" we should be doing it! I know the beautiful heart of the worshipping church is bowing down on the inside and understand that not everyone is comfortable expressing their worship in a physical way. But dancers can bring this aspect to corporate worship. It is an offering that pleases the heart of God.

Earlier I mentioned the transformational healing that I experienced while watching a worship dance one Sunday morning at church. Years later I believed He was calling me to dance. Just as it says in Psalm 30:11, He planned to turn my *"mourning into dancing."* I wasn't so convinced. I was 35 years old and had no experience, no training at all. Remember, I grew up in a Mennonite community with a "no dancing" policy. After much procrastination (it took me six more months to even enroll in my first dance class), I decided I would learn to dance – for Him – believing that He would somehow equip those He calls.

I am a very private person and always found it difficult to put myself "out there" on stage when we were invited to minister in dance. But I did it with a prayer that another's heart might be softened through our expression of worship. Hard, protective layers could be stripped away in an instant, as mine had been. And when hearts are open and vulnerable, His Word has a softer place to land – fertile ground in which to take root and grow.

Flags and Banners

The waving of banners and flags has long been a part of worship expression. Psalm 20:5 says, *"May we shout for joy over Your victory and **lift up our banners** in the name of our God."* A banner is typically the standard (or flag) that goes out in front of an army to indicate who it represents. When God defeated the opposition and gave the Promised Land to the Israelites, Moses built an altar and gave it the name *"The Lord is my Banner."*[50]

Song of Solomon 6:10 says, *"...as awesome as an army with banners"* (ESV). Why does it say an army with **banners,** not weapons? Because the banners *are* weapons! We have already addressed how worship can be used for spiritual warfare. Isaiah 59:19 tells us, *"When the enemy comes in like a flood,* ***the Spirit of the Lord will lift up a standard against him"*** (KJV), while Isaiah 31:9 declares, *"Their stronghold will fall because of terror;* ***at the sight of the battle*** *standard their commanders will panic."*

Waving appropriately decorated flags and banners signals which "army" we belong to in the spiritual realm. The many colors of flags each have a specific significance and purpose. You can search the internet for descriptions of the various colors and their Biblical references for associated meaning. Some churches do not allow flags or banners in worship, but where this sort of dynamic expression is offered, there will always be greater liberty in the Spirit for *"Where the Spirit of the Lord is, there is freedom."*[51]

Silence

Some feel they cannot magnify God enough with their worship. Words seem inadequate, no matter how beautiful the song. Sometimes you may simply fall silent in awe of His majesty. Sometimes you just want to lift your hands high. Sometimes you just close your eyes and think about Him. Your silent heart, bowed before God, perhaps more fully expresses your emotion than any song that could ever be sung.

Order in Worship

While there are many means to express worship, there should always be order in worship. First Chronicles 13-15 provides one illustration of the seriousness of God's order. In chapter 13, we see King David wanted to bring the Ark of the Covenant (which contained the original Ten Commandments on stone tablets) back to Israel. God's Word had clearly instructed that only the Levites could transport the Ark, and only by slipping long poles through gold rings attached to the sides. They were to support the poles on their shoulders as they walked. No one was to touch the Ark itself. In fact, anyone who did so would die.

Now David wanted to restore the Ark of God's presence to the people...which was a good thing. However, the people decided to transport the Ark on a newly designed cart. Two men named Uzza and Ahio were driving the cart. King David and all Israel were rejoicing and celebrating with all their might – singing, dancing, and playing all kinds of instruments. It was an exciting day! That is, until they all came to the threshing floor of Chidon. Here, the oxen stumbled, the cart tipped, and Uzza used his hand to steady the ark. *"And the anger of the Lord was kindled against Uzza and He smote him, because he put his hand to the ark; and there he died before God...And David was afraid of God that day."*[52]

This is a frightening story! But what happened in this passage is an important warning for those who have been entrusted as leaders in worship. King David and the Israelites were doing the right thing (restoring the Ark), but they did it in the *wrong way*. The Ark was holy and was not to be touched by human hands. Likewise, worship is holy before God and is not to be touched by "the flesh." Don't presume to know how He wants to be worshipped – always follow His lead and instructions.

When the Ark began to tip, a man with good intentions put out his hand to steady it. Interestingly, the name Uzza means "strength." Do not attempt to uphold the holiness of God in your own strength. Uzza suffered the consequences of acting in his own strength rather than God's direction. Getting overly excited about worship can be dangerous if it causes you to move out in the flesh (e.g., getting attention for yourself, not seeking God's direction, or not allowing the Holy Spirit to flow). God will not allow His holiness to be treated with irreverence – whether intentional or unintentional. Sooner or later the matter will come to the "threshing floor" and be threshed.

Leading Worship

If you have been appointed to lead worship, you should be excited at the absolute honor of bringing people into His presence. You have the unique opportunity to create an atmosphere that prepares the hearts of the congregation to be ready and responsive to the Word as it is preached. It is a privilege and awesome responsibility at the same time.

The minute you are on stage, whenever people can see you – you are leading worship. You are there to lead the congregation into God's presence so that each one of them will be ministered to while spending time with the Father. Parents, struggling teenagers, the elderly, the sick, the discouraged…God wants to touch each of their lives. You are declaring God's promises over broken marriages, broken hearts, and broken dreams. Your purpose is not to show off your skills with your favorite song, but to be a vessel for God as you encourage the people to sing His praise.

Leading worship in ministry is vastly different than performing as a career. In the world, your gift draws attention to you and your ability. In the church, your gift should draw attention to God and His ability. Having your talent recognized is not wrong. What is wrong is when you join the team purely so that your gift will be recognized. If your heart and motives are pure, you exalt God and not yourself.

Remember that Lucifer was the first ever "worship leader." The root of his name, *halel* in Hebrew, literally means "to praise." Scripture tells us that Lucifer was beautiful, anointed, and could sing and play all kinds of instruments.[53] But he became proud in his anointing and wanted to exalt himself above God. God could not tolerate this rebellion and he was cast out of heaven.[54] Worship leaders that are motivated by the desire for recognition and praise from fellow Christians are no different than Lucifer, who wanted the other angels to worship him for his talent and beauty. God will not share His glory; He *"prizes it as His own Name."*[55]

Don't get preoccupied with your own performance. The church is not your personal stage, and the congregation is not your audience. The most beautiful singing in the world is worth nothing if it is intended for an adoring crowd. On "performance" day, make sure you understand the goal of the whole service. Your part may only last a few minutes. You want to contribute to the "whole" in some way. Pray for what you leave behind, *after* you are off stage.

The amount of fruit that you will bear correlates with how apparent it is to others that you are a beloved disciple of Christ. The fruits of the Spirit are love, joy, peace, patience, kindness, goodness, gentleness, and self-control. Are you exhibiting these characteristics *off the stage?* How do you handle problems as they arise? How do you treat other people around you? Do you respect the other members of the team and your pastor?

Leading worship goes far beyond having the ability to sing, dance, or play an instrument. It is a calling that requires you to love God with all your heart, soul, mind, and strength. It also requires sensitivity and submission to the leading of the Spirit. These things come only through a mature relationship with Jesus. You must take time to develop this relationship; otherwise, you will be operating in *"zeal without knowledge."*[56] You will never be perfect; however, there is less room for error when you hop into the spotlight of worship ministry.

Those Who Don't Approve

There is always a chance that someone may not like what you have offered in worship. Someone may think it was not good enough. A cruel comment or criticism may sting. You still need to offer your gift.

King David was full of joy and danced before a great processional as the Ark of the Covenant was finally properly restored to the house of Israel. But Michal, David's wife, looked out the window and saw him leaping and dancing before the Lord; *"and she despised him in her heart."*[57] Notice that it was through a window that she observed David – she had not joined the celebration. When King David returned home, she rebuked him, telling him what a fool he had made of himself. David's response was very clear: *"It was before the Lord, who chose to appoint me ruler over the people of the Lord: therefore, I will play before the Lord. And I will be even more undignified than this!"*[58]

How many of us have put our fear of man before our love for the Lord? There are people who will only hear the message because you are obediently getting into position and proclaiming His Word through your worship. There will be strongholds broken because you are stepping up to the front line of the battle and lifting up the King of Kings with your praise.

For Michal, she paid a high price for her criticism of King David. *"Therefore, Michal had no child until the day of her death."*[59] God didn't want her critical and judgmental nature passed on to future generations. For those who fall into Michal's type of judgmental observation, the price paid is spiritual barrenness.

The Result of Worship

While the primary purpose of worship is to benefit the Lord, it can also edify and strengthen you. The worship songs and hymns you sing have words of life, full of faith and hope. Psalm 135:3 says, *"Sing praises unto His name; **for it is pleasant.**"* Some of the happiest moments in my soul have been during times of intense praise and worship. I have no doubt you can say the same. You were created to worship and, obviously, every creature is happiest doing what it was made for.

When you worship, you are dwelling with Him. And **strength and joy are found in His dwelling place.**[60] If there is anything we need today; it is more strength and joy! Not what the world offers, but the real joy and incredible strength that is found only in God's presence. Exodus 15:2 says, *"The Lord is my strength and my song."* Praising Him gives you the strength to accomplish everything else.

While the joys on earth are many, none compare to drawing near to the One True God. It is a taste of heaven! The atmosphere of heaven is entirely one of praise, gratitude, and adoration. If it is the joyful work of heaven, it should be your continual joy here on earth. Your spirit can anticipate the time when you will enjoy Him forever. I know our church sings loudest when dwelling on the thought of "soon and very soon," "when the trump shall resound," and "the days of Elijah." Sing now as if you are rehearsing to meet the King!

Let the Worshippers Arise

Ultimately, God will allow no detail to escape in your progress of becoming a beloved disciple. Not only should you take care that your relationship with Him is right, but the outward expression of that relationship must also be right. There should be no carelessness in the way you worship God. Oswald Chambers said, *"If you have never had the experience of taking your casual, religious shoes off your casual, religious feet – getting rid of all excessive informality with which you approach God – it is questionable whether you have ever stood in His presence."*

Nothing pleases God more than worship. You must be a participant, not a spectator, in this step toward becoming a beloved disciple. Gaining strength through these last three steps (prayer, thanksgiving, and worship), you will become a mighty instrument of praise in His hand. In the next section, you will move on to bear much fruit.

Prayer

Jesus, I come into Your presence with shouts of praise! I proclaim that you are the King of Kings, Ruler over all the earth! I give You all glory and honor and praise. You are great, You are mighty, You are just, You are Holy. I praise You for Your awesome power. I praise You for Your surpassing greatness. All power belongs to You, Lord. Your kingdom is everlasting. Your glory is everlasting. I celebrate Your faithfulness, for You, O Lord, are greatly to be praised. To You I will lift up my voice. I will bring You the glory due Your Name. I will make a joyful noise and declare all that You have done! You are the One True God. I worship You alone.

I'm waiting here for You with my hands lifted high. Holy Spirit, You are welcome to dwell in this place. Jesus, come and reign in my heart. I invite You to transform my life. Melt my heart of stone. Overwhelm me, flood me with Your spirit and truth. Fill my life with Your holiness. Fill me with Your love. I yield my heart to You. As I come into Your presence, I lay my burdens down. I cast aside my anxious thoughts. I trust myself into Your care. As I set my thoughts on things above, You restore me.

I kneel before Your throne with nothing but an offering of praise to You. I bow down my heart. I ask Your forgiveness for the times I've entered an atmosphere of worship with a casual, irreverent attitude. I repent for every way that I have robbed You of the honor due Your Name. I am sorry for losing a reverential fear of You. At times, I've lost sight of who You are and have become too familiar with You. When I see Your true glory, I fall at Your feet. Gloriously You shine, brighter than the sun. There is nothing to match Your holiness. Jesus, Your beauty is beyond description. The splendor of Your power and majesty is overwhelming. In awe of You I worship. I am amazed at Your great love. Forever faithful, forever true. Face-to-face with the living God, Holy is my only cry.

STUDY

1. What do you learn about the holiness of God in the following verses?

Exodus 3:5-6

Exodus 15:11

Psalm 47:7-9

Psalm 93:4-5

2. Write out the instruction found in Psalm 29:2:

3. What do you think causes the human heart to treat God as less awe-inspiring than He really is?

4. What praise does Daniel ascribe to the Lord in Daniel 2:20-21? How does the sovereignty of the Lord described in these verses impact how you view current world events?

In Spirit and in Truth

5. Charles Spurgeon has been quoted as saying, *"The very posture of some people indicates that they are going through the hymn, but the hymn is not going through their hearts."* What does that mean?

6. How is it possible to worship God *"in vain"* (see Mark 7:6-7)?

7. John 4:23 says that God is seeking *"true worshippers."* What do you think a true worshipper looks like?

8. Does Psalm 63:1 describe your relationship with Jesus today? Read verse 2. What does this suggest about where your intensity for Jesus will come from?

The Expression of Worship

9. In Psalm 141:2, what did David offer God instead of incense for the evening sacrifice?

10. Psalm 63:4 says, *"I will praise you as long as I live, and in your name I will lift up my hands."* Why do we lift up our hands when we praise? Do you feel comfortable doing this?

11. How would you describe your worship recently? What makes your worship feel "authentic"?

12. Which is easier for you – public or private worship? In which do you feel closer to God?

13. Why do you think Christians argue/complain so much about the expression of worship in the church (e.g., style of music, the addition of elements such as dance or flags, etc)?

14. According to 2 Samuel 6:23, what can be the spiritual consequence of rebuking someone else's style of worship? What might you miss?

Let the Worshippers Arise

15. What are some worship songs that have ministered to you?

16. What do you think worship in heaven will be like? How does it affect the way you worship now?

17. Review the Psalms and record your favorite verses of praise/worship.

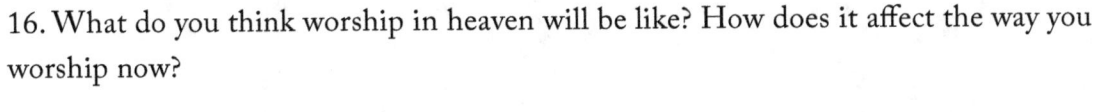

SPIRITUAL MARKER

humility

WORSHIP

Let the Worshippers Arise [Phillips, Craig, and Dean]

Overwhelmed [Darlene Zschech]

I Exalt Thee [Jesus Culture]

A Mighty Fortress [Passion featuring Christy Nockels]

Lamb of God [Tenth Avenue North]

Lead Me to the Cross [Hillsong]

Holy [Jesus Culture]

So Will I [Hillsong United]

Here in the Presence [Elevation]

Defender [Rita Springer]

Raise a Hallelujah [Bethel Music featuring Jonathan & Melissa Hesler]

What a Beautiful Name [Hillsong]

Forever [Kari Jobe]

In Awe of You [Jesus Culture featuring Kim Walker-Smith]

Lord of Lords [Hillsong]

LET EVERYTHING THAT HAS BREATH PRAISE THE LORD

PSALM 150:6

BEAR FRUIT FOR HIM

Bright, colorful, annual flowers are beautiful in the summer. They don't need much time to mature and produce their showy blossoms. But they are here today and gone tomorrow. Strong, fruit-bearing trees require much more time to grow and mature. God is concerned about your maturity. Jesus said, *"This is to My Father's glory, that you **bear much fruit**, showing yourselves to be My disciples."*[1]

In the previous unit, you waited on the Lord. You intertwined yourself with Him while He cultivated, watered, and pruned your life. In your times of prayer and worship, I trust you felt His touch, heard His voice, and soaked in His love. I hope that He is real and personal to you, and you can completely trust Him with your life. Now you will begin to bear fruit. I pray for *"God to fill you with the knowledge of His will through all spiritual wisdom and understanding…that you may live a life worthy of the Lord and may please Him in every way: **bearing fruit in every good work**, growing in the knowledge of God, being strengthened with all power according to His glorious might so that you may have great endurance and patience."*[2]

Spiritual maturity is living out the will of God for your life. He will accomplish incredible things through you. But you will need to make some further changes to bring yourself completely in alignment with His will. Perhaps you have already seen what God wants you to be, but you must still endure the training that will shape you into a vessel to be used by God.

After spending 40 days in the desert (waiting), Jesus came back quoting Isaiah 61: *"The Spirit of the Lord is upon Me, because He has anointed Me to preach good news to the poor. He has sent Me to bind up the brokenhearted, to proclaim freedom for the captives and release the prisoners from darkness, to comfort those who mourn… They will be called oaks of righteousness, a planting of the Lord for the display of His splendor.*[3] In spiritual terms, Jesus was stating His mission to heal, free, deliver, and release people from oppression. This will also become your mission.

Jesus is passionate about freedom. And He needs you healed, whole, well, and strong so that you can free others. Eternal destinies will be impacted by your faithfulness and obedience to His direction. The *"display of His splendor"* will be exhibited in the way that you live. Step by step you proceed in this journey. Step #7 will help open the eyes of the "spiritually blind," while Step #8 will set "captives free." Holy Spirit, walk with us!

PUT YOUR ARMOR ON

In our journey thus far, I have used beautiful imagery to describe your transformation process – a caterpillar turning into a butterfly and a fragile vine intertwining itself with the Lord. But this process would be incomplete without acknowledgement of some other very real imagery in the Bible – terms such as fight, conquer, warfare, struggle, strive, and overcome.

Christians are often described as soldiers fighting an enemy. Paul wrote to Timothy and encouraged him to *"wage the good warfare,"*[1] *"fight the good fight,"*[2] and *"endure like a good soldier."*[3] We aren't fighting a physical enemy; we are constantly engaging in battle in the spiritual realm. And you will be sorely unprepared to bear fruit if you are ignorant of these things. You need to put some armor on!

As you move farther on and higher up, you can expect to encounter increased opposition from the enemy of your soul. Satan hates the true believer – he hates anything the Father loves. His jealousy of God has not subsided in the least. And anything that resembles God fuels his hatred. The Spirit of Christ in you draws his fire. Being a traitor himself, he can't fathom anyone else remaining faithful. Because of your increasing closeness to Jesus, you will be a target for his attacks. He is already rejoicing over anticipated victories. You will have to start claiming yours.

You must understand that this world is a spiritual battleground. God and His forces of righteousness are on one side, while Satan and his forces of hell are on the other. Given that you are participating in this study, you have already chosen sides. Because you have chosen God's side, you can expect great hostility from the enemy. Your adversary is not going to willingly give up without a fight. The fight will be real and last as long as you live on this side of heaven.

"The Spirit-filled life is not, as many suppose, a life of peace and quiet pleasure. It is likely to be quite the opposite. Satan will bitterly oppose the Christian who is pressing on toward a higher life in Christ. Always there is struggle, and sometimes the battle with our own nature is so intense that we become confused, and it seems impossible to tell which impulse is of the Spirit and which of the flesh.

If we want to escape the pressure, all we need to do is pull back and accept a low-key Christian life. That will stunt our growth and render us harmless to the kingdom of darkness. Compromise will take the struggle away. Satan will not bother with a man who has quit fighting. But the cost of quitting is a life of peaceful stagnation. Sons of eternity cannot afford such a thing."

A.W. Tozer

The Battle is Real

Too many Christians do not acknowledge the work of the devil on this earth. From Genesis to Revelation, the Bible contrasts between Christ and the Antichrist, the Spirit of Truth and the father of lies,[4] the sheep and the goats,[5] the wheat and the weeds.[6] As early as Genesis 4:7 you are warned that *"sin is crouching at your door; it desires to have you, but you must master it."* And the New Testament clearly warns believers that *"our struggle is not against flesh and blood, but against the rulers, against the authorities, against the powers of this dark world and against the spiritual forces of evil in the heavenly realms."*[7] Peter told you that the devil *"prowls around like a roaring lion, seeking someone to devour."*[8] You are encouraged to *"put on the full armor of God so that you can take your stand against the devil's schemes."*[9]

How can the devil do so much damage? He is not omnipresent; he cannot be everywhere at once. But he is not operating alone. Most of us are not important enough to be harassed directly by Satan himself – we are not worth his trouble. But he has an entire host of fallen angels under his control that do his dirty work for him. They are called demons, and they are very interested in you.

You can't tell me demons don't exist. After my sister was murdered, our house was full of them. I could "feel" their presence watching me at night. I would get up to turn on a light. It wouldn't turn on. The light simply wouldn't work. I would try a second light. It wouldn't work either. But the next morning all the lights would work again. Other times, I would try to turn on worship music. The player wouldn't work. But 5 minutes later it would come on by itself playing some horrendous music I didn't even recognize.

These kinds of things happened more times than I could count. Clearly, demons were determined to wreak havoc in our home while we were traumatized. And our small Mennonite church had no answers. We were on our own to figure out how to get rid of them. Fortunately, God connected us with another family that seemed to grasp what was going on. We did our best reading books and praying prayers, but we were still pitifully naïve about how to get the house "cleaned out." Beloved disciple, I don't want you to remain *"ignorant of his devices."*[10]

Christians Under Attack

Some don't believe that Christians can be affected by demons. But 1 John 5:19 says that the *"whole world is under the control of the evil one."* If Satan can't touch believers, then why are we instructed to put on our armor to defend ourselves against *"the flaming arrows of the evil one?"*[11] Why would Peter encourage us to be alert, to resist the devil, and to stand firm against his schemes?[12] Why would Paul caution us *"not to give the devil a foothold?"*[13] The Lord's Prayer even urges us to request deliverance from the evil one.[14] All of these warnings are directed to *believers*.

Eve was deceived by Satan.[15] We also know that Satan asked permission to sift Peter like wheat[16] and to devastate Job.[17] He got one disciple to betray Jesus and another to say he did not even know Christ. One day when Jesus was teaching in the synagogue, he encountered a woman who had been sick for eighteen years. The sickness was caused by an evil spirit. She was not an unbeliever; she was a woman of faith. As soon as Jesus released her from her spiritual bondage, the physical problem was cured.[18] All these individuals were walking with God when these events occurred. Those who deny that the church can be influenced by the devil provide no answers for those being attacked within their walls.

As a believer in Christ, Satan can harass you, torment you, and oppress you. As long as you are living on this earth, the possibility of being tempted, deceived, and influenced is continuously present. But the Holy Spirit lives in you and you belong to God. Satan can't possess you. He can't own you; he just hopes to deceive you into yielding control of your life in some way. The father of lies wants nothing more than to limit your effectiveness as a beloved disciple by *"deceiving the very elect."*[19] He will do anything to get you paralyzed with fear. He will do anything to get you painfully discouraged. He will do anything to get you to doubt that your God can take care of you. He will do anything to prevent you from enjoying all that God has planned for you.

Fighting the good fight will take all you've got. But how would you learn to live as an "overcomer" if there was nothing to overcome? God gave the Israelites their Promised Land, but He made them fight for it. In some of those battles, like the one described in Joshua 10, the odds were stacked against them 5:1, they marched all night to get there, they had to fight uphill (literally), and Joshua had to ask for the sun to stand still in order to finish the fight. God clearly didn't hand everything to them on a silver platter. It would be quite simple for God to eradicate every evil obstacle in your path as well, but He's not going to. It is His desire that you achieve victory through a series of battles that will bring you to spiritual maturity. Remember, nothing worth having comes easy!

"Someday the church can relax her guard, call the watchmen down from the wall, and live in safety and peace, but not yet...not yet."

A.W. Tozer

◆

Don't Give the Devil a Foothold

You were created with an insatiable hunger for spiritual things. When you do not turn to Jesus to fill those needs, Satan is ready with a counterfeit solution. First John 2:16 says, *"For all that is in the world, the lust of the flesh and the lust of the eyes and the boastful pride of life is not from the Father but is from the world."* Nothing outside of God's will can satisfy you. It is only those who *"hunger and thirst for righteousness"* that shall be satisfied.[20]

James said, *"We are tempted when we are drawn away and trapped by our own evil desires. Then our evil desires conceive and give birth to sin; and sin, when it is full-grown, gives birth to death. Do not be deceived, my dear friends!"*[21] He also clarified that God is not the one who tempts you. He has nothing to do with evil. In Matthew 4:3, the enemy is called the "tempter." Satan tries to get your cooperation by convincing you to follow your own selfish desires.

With most Christians, the enemy hopes to create confusion on a slippery slope where it's hard to distinguish between healthy and unhealthy levels of something. For example, when does the enjoyment of food become gluttony? When does healthy dieting become an eating disorder? When does appropriate self-care become obsessive striving for perfection? When does love become possessive? When does friendly conversation become gossip? When does rest become laziness? When does showing mercy become enabling bad behavior? When does wise caution become anxious fear?

Satan may also try to cause doubt about whether the tempting thing is really so bad. For example, is there really anything wrong with practicing yoga? Well, yes, actually there is. Every yoga posture was designed to be a position of submissive worship to millions of Hindu gods, including the Shiva god, known as the "Destroyer." Why didn't they share that little detail when you signed up for your first class? So typical of the deceiver. Meanwhile God says, *"My people are destroyed from lack of knowledge."* [22]

Today, many are attempting to meet their spiritual needs with parapsychology, holistic health, Eastern mysticism, and the New Age movement. Consulting with astrologers, palm readers, and psychics has become so acceptable in our culture that they routinely set up their booths at high school prom parties and state fairs. But the Bible warned that *"false prophets will arise, and will show signs and wonders, in order, if possible, to lead the elect astray."* [23] God specifically forbid His people from consulting anyone other than Himself. [24] Leviticus 19:31 says, *"Do not turn to mediums or seek out spiritists, for you will be defiled by them. I am the Lord your God."*

The Bible warns of particularly great deception in the final days before Jesus returns. As that time draws near, more and more voices will contradict the truth of God. Pray for wisdom, discernment, and protection from this deception. Satan isn't going to walk right up to you and say, "Now pay attention, here's a lie for you…" He's going to use the most convincing and persuasive language possible. He will even try to cloak his message in religious language to get you to believe it is some new insight from God. Don't be fooled.

Dealing with Temptation

Demons hope to block your progress in becoming a beloved disciple by turning your attention away from Jesus. Some will tempt you by saying, "I've got something that you really want. It's fun, exciting, and feels good. Come on over and take a look. It's not going to hurt anyone. Don't worry about it." Others will accuse you by saying, "God doesn't really love you. You will never amount to anything. How can you call yourself a Christian when you behave like that?" Some of Satan's other favorite lies include:

- I had to lose my temper. She made me do it. I only hit her a few times. I have to keep her under control.
- It's just harmless flirting at the office. Nothing more. It's not hurting anyone.
- I'm just looking at porn on the computer. I'm not touching anyone, so it doesn't really matter.
- I'll just fudge these numbers a bit. No one will notice. I deserve it. The company owes me anyway.
- It's just a few drinks at night. I've got it all under control. I deserve to relax.
- I deserve to be with this other person. God wants me to be happy, doesn't He?
- I'm never going to change. It's hopeless. I was just made this way.
- I have worn out God's patience and mercy. He cannot forgive what I have done. I deserve to be in this mess. I have no right to ask for His help.

Notice the theme in each of those statements: "**I** deserve, **I** want, **I** think, **I** need…" The devil wants you to believe you need something more than a fully surrendered life with Jesus. Satan's strategies are quite predictable. That's why Paul said, *"We are very familiar with his evil schemes."*[25] He uses the same tactics over and over again. Not very creative! Why do we keep falling for it? We have seen the destruction it causes, why do we keep repeating the same mistakes?

Every temptation presents a choice. You have an opportunity to do the right thing or the wrong thing. You can either act according to your flesh or according to the Spirit.[26] Every time you choose to do the right thing instead of sin, you are growing in the character of Christ. James 1:12 says, *"Blessed is anyone who endures temptation. Such a one has stood the test and will receive the crown of life that the Lord has promised to those who love him."*

Becoming a beloved disciple doesn't guarantee you will live a sinless life.[27] But you no longer *have* to sin – you are not a slave to it.[28] Sin will always be present, available, and appealing, but its power over you is broken. Because of Christ's death on the cross, Satan is a defeated foe. It's now up to you to decide whether you are going to let your body be used as an *"instrument of wickedness"* or for righteousness.[29] It is your responsibility to *"not let sin reign"* in your body.[29]

Resist the Devil

The devil cannot make you do anything you don't want to do. You still have personal control over your own being and the responsibility to make wise choices. Saying "the devil made me do it" is not a valid excuse for bad behavior. You are instructed to *"Resist the devil, and he will flee from you."*[30]

Proverbs 4:26-27 warns, *"Plan carefully what you do…Avoid evil and walk straight ahead. Don't go one step off the right way."* Proverbs 16:17 says to protect yourself by *"watching where you go."* Timothy encourages you to *"flee from youthful passions."*[31] And 1 Peter 5:8 warns you to *"stay alert, be sober, and be vigilant."*

You need to recognize your own weaknesses and patterns of temptation. *When* are you most tempted? *Where* are you most tempted? *What* situations are most likely to cause you to stumble? *Who* is most likely to draw you into temptation? Then don't carelessly and needlessly place yourself in those circumstances. The Bible warns, *"Don't be so naïve and self-confident. You're not exempt. You could fall flat on your face as easily as anyone else."*[32]

You will never be completely free from temptation while on this earth. It is a normal part of living in a fallen world where we are given free will to choose how to behave and what to believe. Don't be surprised or discouraged when you experience temptation. Paul reminds you that *"the temptations that come into your life are no different from what others experience."*[33] It is actually a compliment to be under attack. Satan wouldn't bother tempting you if you weren't a threat. He leaves those alone who are already on the path to destruction – he assumes he has them for eternity. You can't keep Satan from offering you temptations, but you can choose not to be deceived by them or act on them. Temptation only becomes a sin when you give in to it.

The Battle for Your Mind

Temptation always starts in your mind. Satan identifies a desire or need inside of you. He has been watching you since birth to observe your areas of weakness. He notices all the objects of your affection. Like an experienced fisherman, he adapts the bait to your most fragile tendencies. He even knows during which season you will be most likely to bite. When he sees an opportunity, he introduces a thought into your mind to suggest that you give in to the desire. So the battle begins inside you – in your mind. Jesus warned, *"For from within, come evil thoughts, sexual immorality, theft, murder, adultery, greed, wickedness, deceit, lustful pleasure, envy, slander, pride, and foolishness. **All these vile things come from within.**"*[34]

I haven't seen a good explanation for exactly how the devil is able to present thoughts to your mind, but scholars and commentaries agree that is what Scripture clearly teaches. You are warned not to *"follow deceiving spirits and things taught by demons."*[35] You need to distinguish (with your mind) between the Spirit of Truth and the spirit of error.[36] You are instructed to *"guard your hearts and minds in Christ Jesus."*[37] And it is important to filter every thought through Philippians 4:8: *"Whatever is true, whatever is noble, whatever is right, whatever is pure, whatever is lovely, whatever is admirable – if anything is excellent or praiseworthy – **think** about such things."*

The Bible gives several examples of how the devil put thoughts into the minds of people to lead them astray. Satan *"prompted Judas Iscariot, the son of Simon, to betray Jesus."*[38] In the early church, Satan convinced Ananias to lie about a financial gift.[39] And in 1 Chronicles 21, *"Satan incited David to take a census."* What's wrong with taking a census? The strategy here was to get David focused on his worldly resources (number of fighting men) rather than God. Tricky! I'm not sure I would have caught that one either.

How did Satan "incite" David? He didn't speak out loud – that would be too obvious. He put the thought in David's mind. These deceptive thoughts often come in the first person, so you think they are your own thoughts. As you mature and increase your discernment, you will be better able to distinguish between the enemy's thoughts, your own thoughts, and God's voice.

The Path to Self-Destruction

The enemy's purpose is to *"steal and kill and destroy,"*[40] so what he suggests is always negative, disruptive, and destructive. The very first question mark in the Bible came from Satan. In trying to sow seeds of doubt, his words to Eve were *"Did God really say...?"*[41] He usually accompanies his suggestions with a sense of urgency and impulsivity. He wants you to do something wrong *quickly*. Then the outcome produces despair, fear, and hopelessness. Your peace and joy get stolen from you like a thief enters your home to steal treasures.

Anything and everything negative is not from God. All fear and anxiety can be traced back to Satan. While writing this study, I frequently battled thoughts of "Who do you think you are? No one is going to want to hear what you have to say. You are not saying anything new. You are wasting your time. Other people write so much better than you – let them do it."

Likewise, all the anxiety you experience is *internal* – believing the worst, keeping yourself filled with fear and pessimism, or stewing about what might go wrong in the future. It is a sin to allow yourself to get preoccupied with it. You must *fight* fear. Look at fear as something to be attacked and overthrown. Depression is the impression left by fear. Fight that too. Don't entertain it. You waste precious time and energy with destructive thoughts. Your first reaction should be to rebuke them, kick them out, and say "get away from me."

Your negative patterns of thinking have been learned over time. What has been learned can be unlearned. Your mind can be reprogrammed, transformed, and renewed in Christ. This is your inheritance! Renewing your mind will not happen instantly. You may need to slowly replace or overcome negative thought patterns that have been deeply ingrained for years.

Taking Thoughts Captive

Satan knows that if he can influence your thoughts, he can influence your behavior. In 2 Corinthians 10:3-5, Paul explains that to win the war against your flesh, you need to *"destroy speculations and every high thing raised up against the knowledge of God, **taking every thought captive** to the obedience of Christ."* The Bible has long proclaimed what psychologists are just beginning to recognize – you can't change behavior until you change your thoughts. Where you set the focus of your mind determines how you will behave.

The battle for sin is won or lost in your mind. You must be vigilant about what you are focusing on, dwelling on, thinking about, and "entertaining" in your mind. You can't just give your thoughts free rein. Proverbs 4:23 warns, *"Be careful how you think; your life is shaped by your thoughts."* David prayed, *"Keep me from paying attention to what is worthless."*[42]

Have you ever intentionally tried to stop thinking about something? During a lecture on cognitive processes in one of my psychology classes, I ask the students to stop thinking about a Snickers candy bar. I repeat myself a few times and then continue lecturing. At the end of class, I check in to see how often they thought about the candy bar (and how much they want one now!). Psychologists have found the more you try to fight thinking about something, the stronger it seems to get. That's why most diets don't work – you think about eating all the time! By resisting a thought, you actually reinforce and strengthen it.

The same is true for temptation. Remember that a *stronghold* is something that exalts itself in your mind, steals your focus, and causes you to feel overpowered, controlled, or mastered. You can't fight it by just deciding not to think about it anymore. The more you repeat "I must stop doing this," the more obsessed you become with it.

Constantly thinking about what you can't have or shouldn't do sets you up for failure. You must turn your attention to something else: Jesus. That's why the Bible tells you repeatedly to *"fix your thoughts on Jesus,"*[43] and *"always think about Jesus."*[44] Ask Him to help you direct your attention to something else. Using this principle of replacement, you can *"overcome evil with good."*[45] Romans 8:5-6 clarifies, *"Those who live according to the sinful nature have their **minds** set on what that nature desires; but those who live in accordance with the Spirit have their **minds** set on what the Spirit desires. The **mind** of sinful man is death, but the **mind** controlled by the Spirit is life and peace."* The best way to fight the negative is to switch your focus to the positive – and that is Jesus.

"The whole Bible teaches that battles are won before the armies even take the field. The critical moment for any army is not the day it engages the foe in actual combat; it is the day before, the month before, the year before…preparation is vital! The rule is, prepare or fail. We can seek God today to prepare for temptation tomorrow, but if we meet the enemy without first meeting God, the outcome is already decided."

A.W. Tozer

Stay Strong

Ask for divine sensitivity to any thought that breaks your fellowship with Jesus. Nothing else will produce a more immediate change in your life than monitoring your thoughts and taking every one captive that is not obedient to Christ. Victory can become a reality.

You do have control over what you think – not the thoughts that randomly pop into your head from the enemy, but what you *choose to dwell on.*[46] Satan will try to fill your mind with wrong thinking, but you don't have to receive it. If someone gave you a spoonful of poison, you wouldn't choose to swallow it. When a lustful, sinful, destructive thought enters your mind, reject it! Recognize it for what it is. Immediately set your mind on what is pure, honorable, right, lovely, admirable, excellent, and praiseworthy.[47]

Once you get serious about setting your mind on the things of Spirit, you will be shocked at how polluted your mind really is. Take a moment and get a blank sheet of paper. On one half, write down some of Satan's most common lies and deceptions that are impacting your life right now. On the other half, write down God's response – preferably using specific Scriptures that address your current issue. The Word of God is the best weapon for exposing and destroying the lies confronting beloved disciples. Any Bible concordance or online Bible search tool can be helpful to identify relevant verses. If you don't have these available, ask the Holy Spirit what Jesus would think, do, or say in a particular situation. I have found this to be helpful when I am most challenged or harassed by the enemy.

Satan's lies	God's truth
Example: Everyone takes me for granted. I do everything; I give everything. No one takes care of me. They are all selfish. Weapon: *Self-pity*	Love is not self-seeking. Love does not keep score. Love does not keep record of wrongs. Love always looks for the best in others. He will take care of all my needs.
Example: You have no clue what you are doing. You are in way over your head. You are a mess yourself – how are you going to help others? Weapon: *Fear, doubt, discouragement*	He has plans and purposes for my life. I have been set apart for such a time as this. I can bring what no one else can. He equips those He calls. He delights in me.
Example: I don't have money to pay my bills. Where is my next meal going to come from? How am I ever going to get through this? Weapon: *Fear, doubt, discouragement*	His eye is on the sparrow. He will never leave me or forsake me. I will not be anxious about anything. He is my provider. He will make a way when there seems to be no way. I will live for His glory.

With a mustard seed of faith, you can start believing what God says more than what the devil says. You can slowly start making decisions based on the truth. Over time, your mind will be renewed, and you will start behaving in alignment with God's Word.

———————◆———————

Divine Power to Defeat Darkness

You must acknowledge that you have a very real enemy who poses a very real threat, but you must also understand the *infinite strength* available to you through Jesus Christ. Jesus' death and resurrection *"disarmed"* the rulers and authorities of the kingdom of darkness.[48] You don't have to defeat the devil – Jesus already did. You just have to claim your deliverance power! Claiming the truth of Christ's victory and authority is the key to standing firm.[49]

Christ did what He needed to do to set us free, now you assume your responsibility to walk in that freedom. You must make His victory operative in you. No one else can put on the armor of God for you, repent for you, forgive for you, or take every thought captive for you. Freedom is available when you understand your position, identity, and authority in Christ. Second Corinthians 10:3-5 says the weapons you have available to you are *"not the weapons of the world,"* but that they have *"divine power to demolish strongholds."*

You don't have the ability to resist Satan and his demons in your own strength, but *in Christ* you do. Jesus said, *"All authority has been given to Me in heaven and on earth."*[50] And His authority is *"far above all rule and authority and power and dominion, and every name that is named, not only in this age, but also in the one to come."* Then He transferred His authority to His servants to be used in His name[51] – the *"unlimited greatness of His power works with might and strength for us, the believers."*[52] His authority gives you the legal right to rule over the demons.

Defeated believers don't understand this. They envision Satan as equal to God. He is not. He is only a fallen angel, running around on a temporary leash, and will one day be banished for eternity.[53] Satan currently has free reign on this earth, but he is not *your ruler.* You are on his turf, but not under his authority. Unfortunately, that is how many Christians operate in their day-to-day lives. Satan gets his power through deception. As the father of lies, he continues to hold much of the world in bondage.

The Voice of Truth

Walking through this life successfully requires a firm foundation in what Christ has done for you and who you are as His child. If you believe you are a defeated victim, you are going to act like one. If you don't believe you have Christ's authority over demons, you are not likely to exercise it. When you don't understand your identity in Christ, you don't experience the full freedom and fruitfulness that He intends for you.

You need to grasp the dramatic transformation that took place when you accepted Jesus as your Savior. Before you were *"dead in your trespasses and sins,"*[54] but now you are a *"new creation."*[55] Before you were an *"object of wrath,"*[56] but now you have a *"divine nature."*[57] Before you walked in *"darkness,"* but now you are *"light."*[58] You were a sinner, now you are a saint. You are not *being* saved; you *are* saved. Your old self died while your new self, united with Christ, came alive.[59] Yes, the *"the old has gone, the new has come!"*[60]

The following chart establishes further truths about your position in Christ.[61] Read each statement out loud. The spoken word has power!

I belong to Him	I have been set free	I have a future
I am God's child. John 1:12, Romans 8:16	I have been redeemed and forgiven of all my sins. Colossians 1:14	I am assured that all things work together for my good. Romans 8:28
I am Christ's friend. John 15:15	I am complete in Christ. Colossians 2:10	I have been established, anointed, and sealed by God. 2 Corinthians 1:21-22
I am united with the Lord. 1 Corinthians 6:17	I am free from condemnation. Romans 8:1-2, 31-34	I am a citizen of heaven. Philippians 3:20
I have been bought with a price. 1 Corinthians 6:20	I have not been given a spirit of fear but of power, love, and a sound mind. 2 Timothy 1:7	I am confident that the good work that God has begun in me will be perfected. Philippians 1:6
I am a member of Christ's body. 1 Corinthians 12:27	I can find grace and mercy in time of need. Hebrews 4:16	I am the salt and light of the earth. Matthew 5:13
I have been adopted as God's child. Ephesians 1:5	I am born of God and the evil one cannot harm me. 1 John 5:18	I am a branch of the true vine; My Father is the Gardener. John 15:1
I cannot be separated from the love of God. Romans 8:35-39	I am seated with Christ in the heavenly realms. Ephesians 2:6	I have been chosen and appointed to bear fruit. John 15:16
I am hidden with Christ in God. Colossians 3:3	I may approach God with freedom and confidence. Ephesians 3:12	I am God's coworker. 2 Corinthians 6:1

Now the evil one can do nothing about your position in Christ, but he can do a lot to deceive you into believing his lies. Power for the believer comes from hearing the voice of truth. Jesus said:

- *"You will know the **truth**, and the **truth** will make you free."*[62]
- *"I am the way, the **truth**, and the life."*[63]
- *"But when He, the Spirit of **truth**, comes, He will guide you into all **truth**."*[64]
- *"I do not ask Thee to take them out of the world, but to keep them from the evil one... sanctify them in the **truth**."*[65]

The Protective Armor of God

The weapons that God provides His beloved disciples have divine power. And their primary purpose is to reclaim your thoughts and identity in Christ. This armor is spiritual, not physical. Every item provides mental reassurance of His provision and serves as a reminder that God "has you covered." In Ephesians 6:10-18, Paul describes this armor of God:

"Finally, be strong in the Lord and in his mighty power. Put on the full armor of God so that you can take your stand against the devil's schemes. For our struggle is not against flesh and blood, but against the rulers, against the authorities, against the powers of this dark world and against the spiritual forces of evil in the heavenly realms. Therefore, put on the full armor of God, so that when the day of evil comes, you may be able to stand your ground, and after you have done everything, to stand.

Stand firm then, with the belt of truth buckled around your waist, with the breastplate of righteousness in place, and with your feet fitted with the readiness that comes from the gospel of peace. In addition to all this, take up the shield of faith, with which you can extinguish all the flaming arrows of the evil one. Take the helmet of salvation and the sword of the Spirit, which is the word of God. And pray in the Spirit on all occasions with all kinds of prayers and requests. With this in mind, be alert and always keep on praying for all the saints."

Notice that you are instructed to **put on** and **take up** the armor. This requires an active response on your part. To put on your armor, you are essentially taking the truth of Jesus and securing yourself in it:

- **The belt of truth.** Jesus said, *"I am...the Truth"*[63] Because Christ is in you, the truth is in you. The belt of truth is your primary defense against Satan's lies.[4] If a thought comes into your mind that is not in alignment with God's truth, reject it immediately. Don't toy with it, participate in it, or dwell on it. You can only overcome the father of lies with divine truth – not with a physical fight, shouting match, or a debate.

- **The breastplate of righteousness.** When you accepted Christ as your Savior, you were justified before our holy God.[66] You have been given the righteousness of Christ.[67] While your eternal destiny is not at stake when you sin, the extent of your daily victory is. Part of living in agreement with Jesus means you need to daily confess your sins and receive His forgiveness to remain covered in righteousness.[68]

- **The shoes of peace.** Jesus is the Prince of Peace.[69] He brings a peace that *"surpasses all understanding."*[70] The peace of Christ will rule in your heart when you let the Word of Christ dwell in your heart.[71] Your peace is a sign that you are not falling for the devil's lies.

- **The helmet of salvation.** This helmet guarantees your *eternal* victory. It also covers the most important part of your body – your mind, where most spiritual battles are won or lost.

- **The shield of faith.** The more you know and understand about Jesus, the more your faith will grow. The more faith you have, the larger shield you will have to extinguish the *"flaming arrows of the evil one."*[11] These flaming arrows are lies, accusations, and temptations. Whenever he throws one at you, shield yourself with faith in what you know to be true about God and His Word.

- **The sword of the Spirit.** The Word of God is the only offensive weapon listed in Ephesians 6. Paul uses the word *rhema* here to emphasize the spoken word of God. You must proclaim the Word of God out loud when under direct attack by the enemy. While the enemy can introduce thoughts to your mind, he does not know exactly what you are thinking in response. Speaking out loud lets the enemy know you are resisting his schemes. Jesus modeled this behavior when He was tempted in the wilderness. Every time Satan introduced a temptation, Jesus quoted Scripture in response. You must do the same.

The Path to Freedom

We all want immediate deliverance. We want to simply put our armor on and the battle to be over. We want the Lord to strip away every addiction and sinful habit from our lives immediately, even though those addictions and habits may have been entrenched in our lives for decades. The Lord certainly can deliver people instantly. I have known cases where people are never tempted again by the things that held them captive for decades. However, other times the Lord delivers a person slowly over time. Don't get discouraged if your deliverance doesn't happen quickly. Sometimes He will command you to *"Stand firm and you will see the deliverance the Lord will bring you…the Lord will fight for you, you need only be still."*[72] Other times, He wants to see you wield the sword of the Spirit and use your own weapons of warfare in the midst of the battle.

God is committed to getting you the best result in the best timing and in such a way that the stronghold never returns again to your life. The length of the process and the intensity of the struggle are in His hands. It just depends on His objective. Sometimes He may want to reveal His power by instantly demolishing a stronghold. Other times He may be interested in slowly teaching you to cooperate with Him and trust Him as your Deliverer. It can take a long time to reprogram the way you are thinking about something. You may have to walk it out day by day, taking tests that He allows, and learning lessons along the way. But the enemy will be defeated. Count on it!

The path to freedom comes through prayer in Jesus' Name. The steps below are a comprehensive process of submitting to God and resisting the devil (out loud):[30]

1. Acknowledge any sin in your life. Confess your rebellion that resulted in a sinful behavior or habit. Ask Jesus to forgive you for every way that you have tried to control your own life, protect yourself, or rely on your own strength. Ask God to cover your sin with the blood of Jesus. Place the Cross between you and every consequence of your sin. Ask God to redeem everything that has resulted from your sin.

2. Ask God to reveal the true root of the problem. Ask Him to search your heart to reveal hidden things you aren't fully aware of. Acknowledge your inability to deliver yourself. Ask Him to deal with anything that has contributed to your depression, bondage, or oppression. Seek God's help in rejecting and replacing Satan's lies with truth.

3. Forgive others for any way they have hurt you in the past. Unforgiveness is a common way for Satan to gain a legal advantage over you (review the chapter on forgiveness if necessary). Acknowledge that any residual resentment and complaining is considered sin.[73] Ask God to help you release all anger and bitterness from your life. Ask Him to heal any hurtful incident, removing all memory of it.

4. Submit to God – make Him Lord of every day and every situation. Ask Him what you need to do to separate yourself from a person or situation that is unhealthy for you. Ask God to break any unholy soul ties that bind you to them. Ask God to redeem any losses and use the experience for your good.

5. With the authority given you by Jesus Christ, kick out every spirit that is not of God. They must go where Jesus sends them. Declare that you are a child of God. Declare that your house belongs to the Lord. Demons are not welcome there and will not be allowed to stay there. They cannot return or bring anyone else to take their place.

6. Ask the Lord to confuse every scheme of the enemy in your life. Break off every curse, assignment, or attachment that has come to you because of sin. Declare that no weapon formed against you will prosper.

7. Ask the Holy Spirit to fill every void and seal the work that has been accomplished. Ask for protecting angels to surround you and your property – guarding your family, pets, and possessions. Pray that the blood of Jesus would serve as a protective barrier around you so that anything that comes to you must pass through Him first. Revelation 12:11 explains the blood's power against Satan: *"And they overcame him by the blood of the Lamb and by the word of their testimony."*

8. Pray for discernment, knowledge, and faith to understand your position in Christ. Ask for wisdom to distinguish between your own thoughts and those of Satan. Pray that you will not be confused by the enemy. Ask Him to realign every part of you with His truth.

9. Praise Him for His faithfulness. Thank Him that His blood is what makes your salvation and freedom possible. Remember that praise and worship are critical weapons in spiritual warfare.

While this is a comprehensive prayer process against temptation, in the heat of the moment you may only have the time to say the name of Jesus. If you are tempted to engage in a behavior that you are not sure is healthy, the best thing to do is pause and wait. Take a deep spiritual breath. Really, what's the hurry? You want to do the right thing. Jesus will give you the wisdom you need for every situation if you simply stop and ask for it. Repeat His Name several times. Claim His power and authority. Ask for His discernment. If there is evil at work, most likely any frantic sense of urgency will dissipate.

Maintaining Your Freedom

Unfortunately, one victory over the enemy does not mean the battles are over for the rest of your life. The enemy will continue to see where and when he might gain entrance into your life. In Luke 4, we know that Jesus was tempted by the devil in the wilderness. While unsuccessful, the devil went away to wait for a more "opportune time" (verse 13).

Ground that is gained must be maintained. You must continually separate yourself from anything that separates you from Jesus. To protect yourself from further attack, here are some practical steps you can take to maintain your freedom:

- Renounce and seek forgiveness for every association with or activity connected to other religions and the occult. Reject any activity or group that offered guidance through any source other than Jesus Christ. That means horoscopes, crystal balls, hypnosis, Ouija boards, séances, tarot cards, trances, yoga, reiki healing, cults, and other religions. Even if you "innocently" participated in these things as a child, confess and renounce it. Ask the Lord to bring to mind any secret initiations, ceremonies, promises, pacts, or "unholy vows" made in your past – even if you thought it was "just a game" at the time. Break off every curse or demonic attachment that may have come to you as a result of those activities.

- Renounce the sins of your ancestors as well as any curses that may have been placed on your family line. While giving the Ten Commandments, God said He can *"punish the children for the sin of the fathers to the third and fourth generation..."*[74] You may not be guilty of a particular sin, but because of the sin of an ancestor you can still be vulnerable to the enemy's attack in that area. You can be genetically predisposed to struggle with a particular sin. Ask God to reveal anything that is being passed down through your generational line that you need to renounce. Ask God to cancel any demonic rights, curses, or assignments that are being directed toward you. Declare yourself to be fully committed to Jesus and covered by His blood.

- Keep your priorities in alignment with Jesus' plans and purposes for your life. Don't get swayed by idols – anything that consumes your thoughts and devotion other than Jesus. Confess where you have allowed other things or people to become more important than Him. Some possibilities include money, food, possessions, family, children, spouse, friends, pets, work, computers/games, television, physical fitness, personal appearance, knowledge, power, popularity, or hobbies. You cannot expect bondages to be broken unless you are willing to die to yourself and set your life apart in dedication to God and His purposes.

- Keep yourself a pure vessel, to be used as an *"instrument of righteousness."*[29] Avoid gossip, lying, cheating, stealing, quarreling, jealousy, complaining, swearing, laziness, drunkenness, greed, lust, sexual immorality, and anger. Don't drift back into old patterns of behavior.

- Be very selective about what you watch on television. Don't give the devil an opening by watching violent, provocative, or questionable television shows.

The same applies to music – stop listening to any music that gratifies the enemy instead of Jesus. You cannot expose yourself to such content without contaminating yourself.

- Keep worship music playing continuously in your home. All throughout the Bible, there was no successful warfare without worship and prayer. Great victories were always preceded by times of dedication, consecration, and worship (see 2 Chronicles 20).

- Rid your home of all questionable books, movies, and objects. Deuteronomy 7:26 says, *"Do not bring a detestable thing into your house or you, like it, will be set apart for destruction."* Many times, people bring home "cultural artifacts" from travel in foreign countries that honor other gods. Slowly walk through each room in your house and ask God to identify any objects you should remove. When He draws your attention to something, don't argue. Get rid of it. You may be surprised what you have been blind to before you asked for His perspective.

- Watch how you speak – demons can hold against you what has been spoken over your life or the lives of others. James 1:26 says, *"you deceive yourself when you do not bridle your tongue."* If something negative is spoken over your life, break it off and renounce it; declare it not to be true. Speak blessings into your life; what you want or hope to see in the future. Don't make unholy vows using words like "always" or "never." You reap what you sow with your words.

- For daily victory, continue to crucify the flesh, live in faith, walk by the Spirit, and take every thought captive. Don't allow sin to reign. You leave the door open for the enemy by not resisting temptation, accusation, or deception. Never yield ground that you have already won.

If you really want to gain victory over a persistent temptation, you may need the fellowship of other Christians to join you in your struggle. The Bible says, *"You are better off to have a friend than to be all alone…If you fall, your friend can help you up. But if you fall without having a friend nearby, you are really in trouble."*[75] Some patterns are so ingrained that you can't resolve them on your own. Be willing to seek professional help or establish accountability with other believers. James 5:16 says, *"Confess your sins to each other and pray for each other **so that you may be healed.**"* Support groups can encourage, sustain, and love you unconditionally through the recovery process.

Our God is Greater

You must keep one thing in mind: God is greater than any weapon that Satan can fashion against you. God is all powerful, all knowing, and ever present. With His authority, you should be able to defeat the enemy with courage and boldness. God has given you every resource that you need to be successful in the battle.[76] God has promised you victory in the very areas that the enemy hoped for your defeat.[77] The only way that Satan can succeed is if you believe him more than you believe God. Your God is bigger! Stronger! Greater! And He has *"incomparably great power for those who believe."*[51]

Remember that *"the One who is in you is greater than the one who is in the world."*[78] Satan doesn't come close to challenging God in power. You are fighting in the winning army. Satan cannot hinder God's plans and purposes. The battle ultimately belongs to the Lord.[79] You have nothing to fear from the enemy. Jesus, who has all authority, walks beside you – you won't lose your way if you walk with Him. What do small children do when they are frightened? They run and hide with their parents. The devil should drive you straight to Jesus! Can you imagine what it feels like for Him when we put our trusting hand in His? The more you walk in His love, the light of His Word, and the wisdom of the Holy Spirit, the more you will be protected from the schemes of the enemy in this present darkness.[80]

With His authority, you have the legal position to confront and disarm demonic powers that interfere with your life and ministry. This does not mean that you should charge out on your own challenging demons all day long. God does not want warfare to become your focus. The fastest way to lose your balance is to spend more time rebuking the devil than talking to Jesus. Satan derives great satisfaction when he can get you to focus more on him than on God. Your strength will only come through intimacy with Jesus. Keep your eyes fixed on Him. God insists that the most effective strategy in the battle is *prayer* so that you stay constantly connected to Him. And when the battle gets especially difficult (as when the disciples found an evil spirit they could not cast out), Jesus instructs you to *pray and fast* – in other words, double your focus on Him.[81]

> "There are two equal and opposite errors into which our race can fall about the devils. One is to disbelieve their existence. The other is to believe and feel an unhealthy interest in them. They themselves are equally pleased by both errors."
>
> C.S. Lewis

A Way of Escape

You are never out of the hand of God. He acts like a bodyguard to the heirs of His Kingdom. *"The Lord is faithful, He will establish you and guard you from the evil one."*[82] God is always watching over you. He knows exactly how far He will let Satan go. The first time Satan came against Job, God did not permit him to touch Job's flesh.[83] Perhaps that is more than Job could have handled at the time. Where God permits you to endure temptation, He promises to also *"provide a way of escape."*[33]

Job was a better man by the end of the story than he was at the beginning. And his reward was greater too! It's as if God says to Himself, "If Satan does more, I will do more. What he takes away, I will redeem. If he tempts a man to curse, I will so reveal My love for him that he will bless Me. I will help him, I will strengthen him, I will uphold him with My righteous right hand."[84] God helps. God wins. You will see.

You're not thinking of quitting now, are you? God cannot ask the fainthearted to war. He must remove from service those who are only interested in comfort and luxury. A good soldier gives first priority to the armed forces and second place to his own personal security. You are being called to rescue others that have been captured by the enemy, but you are not qualified if you are unequipped to handle the captor yourself. You must have more than resolve – you must have power. You must demonstrate that you can overtake the lion, and then the bear, and then Goliath.[85] And it is when you are called to duty that you will find giants.[86]

Once you understand your position and authority in Christ, you can move on to Step #8, which will fulfill His calling in your life. Jesus' mission was to *"set the captives free."*[87] And He turned His timid group of faithless followers into missionaries, conquerors, and healers. After encountering the risen Christ, Paul's mission became *"to open their eyes, in order to turn them from darkness to light, and from the power of Satan to God."*[88] What will your mission be?

---◆---

Prayer

Jesus, You are my rock, my fortress, my shield, my strong tower, my refuge, my salvation, and my deliverer. I believe You came in the flesh to destroy the works of the devil. I ask You to expose any lies that twist the truth, so that evil has no hiding place in me. I repent for being too busy to pray, too sophisticated to depend on Your Word, too proud to acknowledge my sin, too timid to share the Gospel, and too deceived to discern that the devil is real. I believe that all authority belongs to You Jesus. No power and no enemy can prevail against You. I place myself under the whole armor of God. No weapon formed against me will prosper. No curses spoken against me will be successful. Confusion will completely blind those that dare to tamper with God's purposes for my life.

Open my eyes to any deception, help me to hear You clearly above all other voices. I command all deceiving spirits to be bound, silenced, and stilled. I bind every spirit that is set against my spiritual warfare training. I ask that my eyes and ears be open to all that I need to learn. I want to grow in knowledge and boldness in the army of the Lord. Align my spirit with Your Word and Truth. Lord, only bless and grow what comes from Your hand. Jesus, I give You permission to reprogram any of my thinking that has limited my understanding of You and Your work in my life. All lies and strongholds that have been built in my life are demolished in the name of Jesus.

Thank You for redeeming me, cleansing me, and sanctifying me in Your precious blood. Thank You for providing all that I need. I thank You for guiding my life to this point. I trust You to lead me in ways that bring glory to Your name. Thank You for drawing me deeper and closer to You. I know You are teaching me to trust You completely. I thank You in advance for setting me free from all things and all people that might be considered oppression. Thank You for bringing godly people into my life to support, teach, mentor, and disciple me. Thank You for protecting me when I yoked myself with unrighteous people and for helping me to break any unhealthy relationships in my life.

Lord, this spiritual work is necessary as I strengthen myself in You and begin to bear fruit. I believe that in every area of my life I will be set free. This liberty and knowledge will teach me how to set other captives free as well. Make me a mighty warrior with the sword of Your Spirit. Make me an instrument of Satan's defeat until the day You return to this earth. I trust that every good work You have started in me shall be completed. I ask You to anoint my steps and seek Your favor upon my path. I receive the mind of Christ to guide me. Greater is He that is in me than he that is in the world! I am a conqueror and believe that the best is yet to come!

STUDY

1. Ephesians 6:12 warns believers that *"our struggle is not against flesh and blood, but against* _____

_____

_____*."*

2. How have you been made aware of this "spiritual battle" in your own life?

Don't Give the Devil a Foothold

3. What does James 1:13-15 and Matthew 4:3 tell you about the source of temptation?

4. List several kinds of temptation that you might expect to encounter in this life.

_____   _____

_____   _____

_____   _____

5. *When* do you think you are most vulnerable or susceptible to temptation? *Who* is most likely to cause you to stumble? *Where* are you most tempted? *What* parts of your own nature must you watch carefully?

6. What temptations do you tend to brush off as inconsequential or "harmless"? Even it seems like a small thing, do you get the feeling that you're not supposed to compromise about it? Ask God for discernment as to where it might lead. Could God be insisting on obedience in what seems like a small matter now to prepare you for more difficult tests later?

The Battle for Your Mind

7. Why is the first step of the battle *in your mind?*

8. You may have heard Satan described as the "father of lies." What are some of the lies you must fend off on a fairly regular basis? Provide some examples of God's Truth to fight them.

9. What role has fear played in your life (e.g., fear of the unknown, fear of failure, fear of man, etc)? What compromises have you been tempted to make because of fear?

10. How effective have you found your own willpower to be in defeating temptation or the lies of the enemy? What is more effective?

Winning the War

11. Identify the offensive and defensive "weapons" described in Ephesians 6:13-18.

_____

_____

_____

_____

_____

12. In Matthew 4:1-11, how did Jesus consistently respond to Satan?

13. What are you doing to put on God's armor and protect yourself from the enemy? Describe some of the strategies that David outlined in Psalm 101:1-8.

The Voice of Truth

14. Explain the difference between *absolute* truth and *relative* truth.

15. What are some prevalent false teachings in our culture today? How do you distinguish between absolute and relative truth in these situations?

16. Christians are getting farther removed from the Bible as the source of absolute truth. Instead of relying on Scripture, they turn to worldly ideas, programs, and methods that appear to be the solution to their spiritual problems. What does this mean for our culture? Why is Biblical truth so essential to the Christian life?

17. What are some of your favorite Biblical truths listed in the "Voice of Truth" section of this chapter?

Divine Power to Defeat Darkness

18. For all of Satan's snarl, it takes only one little unnamed angel to seize and bind him for 1000 years (see Revelation 20:1-2). What does that tell you about Satan's power?

19. Read Revelation 20:10 and record what will finally happens to Satan.

SPIRITUAL MARKER

discernment

WORSHIP

Always [Passion featuring Kristian Stanfill]

Voice of Truth [Casting Crowns]

Whom Shall I Fear? (The God of Angel Armies) [Chris Tomlin]

Victor's Crown [Darlene Zschech]

Our God [Chris Tomlin]

In Jesus' Name [Darlene Zschech]

Authority [Elevation]

I Speak Jesus [Here Be Lions and Darlene Zschech]

Who You Say I Am [Hillsong]

See a Victory [Elevation]

You Say [Lauren Daigle]

Tremble [Mosiac MSC]

No Longer Slaves [Bethel Music]

Chain Breaker [Zach Williams]

IF GOD IS FOR US WHO CAN BE AGAINST US

ROMANS 8:31

GO AND MAKE DISCIPLES

Jesus has been drawing you, teaching you, and keeping you for a reason. As a beloved disciple, you do not simply become pious and holy – you become interested in His interests. He brings you into partnership with His plans and purposes. He has called you for a divine assignment, placement, and destiny. Ephesians 2:10 says that you were *"created in Christ Jesus to do good works, which God prepared in advance for you to do."* The Message version of Jeremiah 1:5 says, *"Before I shaped you in the womb, I knew all about you. Before you saw the light of day, I had holy plans for you."*

God has a calling on your life.[1] In Christ, you *"find out who you are and what you are living for."*[2] He didn't call you to have a private Christian "experience." Jesus said, *"I chose you. And I gave you this work: to go and produce fruit, fruit that will last."*[3] The Father is glorified when you *"bear much fruit and so prove to be"* His disciple.[4]

Jesus drew you into His heart to disciple you so that you, in turn, could disciple others. His plan is to first bless you with His fellowship, then for you to bless others. Now that He has captured your heart, you become an *"instrument of righteousness"*[5] and a *"living sacrifice, dedicated to His service and pleasing to Him."*[6] You will *"…shine like stars in the universe as you hold out the word of life."*[7] That is why you are still on this earth.

Your Great Commission

Jesus said to the Father: *"In the same way that You gave me a mission in the world, I give them a mission in the world."*[8] Your Great Commission is to *"go and make disciples of all nations."*[9]

We are each called to testify to God's amazing love and grace. He has *"changed us from enemies into His friends and gave us the task of making others His friends also."*[10] Part of your mission is to attract new believers, while another part will be to support existing believers – growing them into stronger disciples. Some of your work will involve long-term ministry, while other assignments may only be for a short time. Some of your work may be big, while some of it may be small and obscure to others. Some of it pleasant; some of it not.

All your work will have eternal significance. The consequences of your ministry will last forever, making it far more significant than any other job, responsibility, or goal that you might have on earth. Paul said, *"My life is worth nothing unless I use it for doing the work assigned me by the Lord Jesus – the work of telling others the Good News about God's wonderful kindness and love."*[11]

Called to Service

You cannot be in relationship with Jesus and not be on His mission team. Jesus said to His disciples, *"As the Father sent me, I am sending you."*[12] You might think that being "called by God" is reserved for pastors, missionaries, and nuns. But the harvest cannot be brought in by only a handful of preachers. The Bible says that *everyone* is called to service.[13] Now that you belong to Him, you are *"useful in the service of God."*[14]

You represent His hands, His feet, and His heart to the world. Paul says that *"we are workers together with God."*[15] You have a contribution to make. There are people He wants you to meet and lives He wants you to influence. Remind yourself at the beginning of each day that you are God's vessel and let Him order your steps. Interruptions will not be frustrating when they are seen as "divine appointments" that God brings into your life for a purpose. Look for opportunities to minister to those that cross your path every day. The Bible stresses repeatedly:

- *"So then, as we have opportunity, let us **do good** to everyone."*[16]
- *"Use every chance you have for **doing good**."*[17]
- *"Whenever you possibly can, **do good** to those who need it."*[18]

This is not optional; or something to be tacked onto your already busy schedule. It is the core of the life of a beloved disciple. You are meant to live in ministry. You are modeling your Master, who *"did not come to be served, but to serve."*[19]

In the end, you will have to give account for how much time and energy you spent focused on yourself instead of others.[20] All that you have built will be inspected by God. Is He going to find that you watched too much television? Will He see that you spent all your money on yourself? *"Only those who throw away their lives for My sake and for the sake of the Gospel will ever know what it means to truly live.*[21] That doesn't mean you should eliminate all your other tasks and responsibilities, it just means they shouldn't have the highest priority.

God Initiates the Call

God is always at work. When He needs you, He will come and get you for an assignment. Your job is to be prepared to hear Him and immediately obey in faith. When God wanted to rescue the Israelites from Egypt, He went and got Moses.[22] When God was going to flood the earth, He got Noah to build an ark.[23] When God wanted to save Nineveh, He went and got Jonah to preach there.[24] When God wanted to spread the Gospel to the Gentiles, He went and knocked Paul (named Saul at the time) off his horse.[25]

Notice the bigger picture and purpose in each situation. God had a plan and then asked a specific individual to participate in His work. That person didn't come up with the idea. That person didn't create the plan. God did. God didn't come and ask Noah, "So, how would you like to handle this upcoming flood thing?" He didn't ask Moses, "What would you like to do about those Egyptians?" God is not asking you to dream up your own ideas. Wait until He shares His plans and purposes with you. He will tell you what *He* is about to do where you are. That is your invitation to join Him.

To be prepared for Him to use you, you must focus your life on God's purposes instead of your own. Understanding where and how He is moving in the world is more important than telling God how you would like to serve Him. You adjust your life to what He would like to do through you. I know people who say they want to serve God, but don't really want anything to interrupt their comfortable way of living. Give Him the right to help Himself to any part of your life at any time.

The only way you will clearly know He is calling you is through a well-established relationship. You will have to recognize His voice. Whether or not you hear Him correctly depends on the condition of your ears. Every open door is not your call. Every need is not yours to answer. Only what He plans for you will have His blessing.

Pray before you accept a new assignment or make a commitment. Don't *"lean on your own understanding."*[26] Ask for discernment and open eyes to see His activity. Confirm your sense of His direction with the leading of the Holy Spirit and His Word. It's fine to check with other believers (wise counsel) to confirm a call, but make sure you don't replace going to God with going to people. What you should find is that everything starts to line up to bring you a sense of peace in your calling.

This is not the same as moving out on your own and then asking God to stop you or "close the door" if you're wrong. That is just doing as you please and putting all the responsibility on God to intervene if you're going in the wrong direction. He will intervene, if necessary, but it's better to patiently wait and listen for a clear word from God up front. At times He may let you proceed in making a wrong decision. Remember He is interested in developing your character and discernment. Eventually the Holy Spirit will cause you to recognize that you are on the wrong path. He will then clarify what He wants. He can even take your disobedience and turn it around for good as He gives you another chance.[27]

God doesn't usually give you just one assignment and leave you there. He is far too creative for that! Don't lock yourself into one line of work by saying, "God called me to be a _____, so this other assignment couldn't possibly be from Him." God wants you to bear all kinds of fruit – not just one variety. You must be open to His call changing *daily*. He is calling you into a relationship where He is Lord of your life, and He has access to use you whenever He chooses. If you are willing to obey, you are in for the ride of your life!

◆

Obeying the Call

Jesus made it clear that obedience to His call is a condition for every beloved disciple. He said, *"You are my friends if you do what I command."*[28] You obey Him out of love and gratitude for all He has done for you. He is your Shepherd, and you trust that He knows what is best for you. The more you obey and trust Him, the deeper your relationship becomes. Jesus said, *"When you obey Me, you remain in My love."*[29]

What He asks of you will require faith. When God calls you for an assignment, it will be something bigger than you can do alone. You will not be able to complete the assignment in your own strength, wisdom, and power. But with God, *"all things are possible."*[30] In faith, you can proceed confidently knowing that He will bring to pass whatever He has planned. He told Isaiah, *"I've said it, and I'll most certainly do it. I've planned it, so it's as good as done."*[31]

One Step at a Time

When He says *"Go,"* most of us want a precise roadmap to follow. We want to know where we are going, how long it will take to get there, which route we are going to take, and what we are going to do along the way. That's definitely how I prefer to operate, but He has never let me get away with it for long! He won't let you operate that way either. He said, *"I am the way."*[32] He wants you to follow *Him,* not a plan. That means one step at a time.

Look at the call to Abraham. God said, *"Leave your country, your people, and your father's household and go to the land I will show you."*[33] Hebrews 11:8 says, *"He went out, not knowing where he was going."* Abraham didn't get a Google map, he didn't get a spreadsheet of instructions, he wasn't shown a picture of the house he would be living in, he wasn't assured of the job he would have when he got there, he didn't know what the weather would be like, and he wasn't told where the nearest grocery store would be to buy food. Just "go." Abraham went and was abundantly blessed for his faithfulness.

I can't think of any example in the Bible where a beloved disciple knew the end from the beginning. Daniel certainly didn't know how captivity, interpreting dreams, and a lion's den would all fit together. Joseph didn't see how slavery and imprisonment would one day fulfill God's purposes in Egypt. Noah didn't know how the ark would turn out. Even Mary couldn't comprehend how her Savior's birth would one day end in death.

God gives you guidance on a "need to know" basis. He doesn't owe you an explanation for everything He asks you to do. You won't know the how, when, or where of His will until He tells you. But the Bible says He will *"order your steps."*[34] He eventually gave Noah very specific details about the size of the ark, the type of materials to use, and how to put it together. He didn't say, *"Build any boat you want to."* The Bible tells us that Noah *"did everything exactly as God had commanded him."*[35] And God eventually gave Abraham more details about the son to be born to him, the number of his descendants, and the territory they would inhabit.

He wants you to follow by faith, not by sight. You are more likely to depend solely on Him when you don't know all the details in advance. When He seems to be withholding instructions, it may be that He wants you to seek Him more intently. Pray and wait. Stay patient. Only go where He wants you to go and say what He wants you to say. Psalm 85:13 says, *"He will make His footsteps our pathway."* Stay in step with Him, and you'll be right in the center of His will.

Make the Necessary Adjustments

When God gives you an assignment, your life may need to change. You demonstrate your faith by making the necessary adjustments to cooperate with God. Some of these adjustments may be significant:

- Abraham left his homeland.[36]
- David left his sheep.[37]
- Amos left his farm.[38]
- Jonah left his home (and his prejudices) behind.[39]
- Peter, Andrew, James, and John left their fishing business.[40]
- Matthew left his tax collecting business.[41]
- Paul left his status as a prominent Jewish leader.[42]

These are enormous changes! All these people had to leave behind the lives they comfortably knew to venture into the great unknown. Their very existence had to be yielded to God.

Sometimes you may be tempted to give partial obedience – picking and choosing which commands seem best to you while ignoring the ones that seem too difficult, unreasonable, or costly. Let's take a closer look at the call of Moses. When you think of Moses, you tend to think of the burning bush, the Egyptian plagues, the Red Sea, and the Ten Commandments. But you may have skipped right over three short verses: Exodus 4:24-26. Moses had just been called by God and had packed up everything to go to Egypt. It looks like he was being obedient. But now God was mad enough to kill him. What happened?

Apparently, Moses had neglected to circumcise his youngest son. Commentaries suggest that this is perhaps due to his Midianite wife, Zipporah, who was too indulgent of the child, while Moses was too indulgent of her.[43] This was a sin of omission, as Moses knew that circumcision was a requirement of the covenant with Abraham.[44] God now reminds Moses that without circumcision any Israelite would be cut off from that covenant. Zipporah immediately performs the circumcision, though angrily, telling Moses he is a "bloody husband." This incident serves as a warning that commissioned servants must obey God *completely*. Out of deference to his wife's wishes, Moses almost forfeited his opportunity to serve God and wasted eighty years of preparation![45]

If you want to become a beloved disciple, you will have to make some adjustments in your life to obey God. Your adjustments may involve your circumstances, beliefs, commitments, priorities, and actions. He may ask you to adjust where you live, your relationships, or how you handle your finances. When He sees something amiss in your life, He will let you know. Don't let *anything* hinder your love for God or take you away from His call. Until you can faithfully demonstrate your commitment to make any adjustment He asks, you will be of little use to God.

Overcoming Obstacles

When you finally begin to step into your calling, you can expect to face obstacles and opposition. Before you even get started, the enemy is planning your defeat. He will attempt to convince you there is no point in trying to continue. But God loves to see any progress, any cooperation – even a mustard seed of faith.

Whether it is criticism from others, your old ways of thinking, or the devil himself... you will need the strength of the Lord to sustain you through these eight common obstacles:[46]

1. Unworthiness – Many believers have found this to be the first obstacle they had to overcome. God is used to hearing these objections! But you are essentially doubting God's ability to accomplish something through you.

- When called by God to free the Israelites from slavery in Egypt, Moses offered numerous objections. *"They won't listen to me! They won't believe me! They won't understand me! I don't speak well!"* He even said, *"Please send someone else!"*[47]

- When Samuel told a young Saul that he would one day be king of Israel, Saul replied, *"But am I not a Benjamite, from the smallest tribe of Israel, and is not my clan the least of all the clans of the tribe of Benjamin? Why do you say such a thing to me?"*[48]

- When God appointed Jeremiah to be a prophet to the nations he said, *"Ah, Sovereign LORD, I do not know how to speak; I am only a child!"* God rejected his excuse saying, *"You must go to everyone I send you to and say whatever I command you. Do not be afraid of them, for I am with you."*[49]

2. Distractions – Many people never accomplish their mission because they get side-tracked with worldly pursuits and other obligations.

- King Solomon loved many women – Moabite, Ammonite, Edomite, Sidonian, and Hittite women. These were foreign nations that the Lord had told the Israelites, *"You must not intermarry with them, because they will surely turn your hearts after their gods."* Nevertheless, Solomon had seven hundred wives and three hundred concubines from these nations. And as Solomon grew old, these women turned his heart toward other gods.[50]

- While Nehemiah was rebuilding the walls around Jerusalem, he was incessantly harassed by his enemies. The surrounding village leaders sent repeated invitations to meet with him. But Nehemiah realized this was a trap – they were plotting to kill him. If he had taken the bait, he would not have finished his mission.[51]

- As Jesus was walking along a road, He asked a man to follow Him. But the man replied, *"Lord, first let me go and bury my father."*[52] Sometimes even noble obligations get in the way of following Jesus.

3. Fear – You may never fully step into your calling if you are too afraid. You demonstrate courage when you follow despite your fear.

- Ahab told Jezebel everything Elijah had done and how he had killed all the false prophets. Jezebel sent a message to Elijah to say, *"May the gods deal with me, be it ever so severely, if by this time tomorrow I do not make your life like that of one of them."* Elijah was afraid and ran for his life. After a day's journey into the desert, he prayed that he might die. *"I have had enough, Lord, take my life."*[53]

- The Israelites were hiding in mountain caves from the Midianites when an angel appeared to Gideon saying, *"Mighty warrior, the Lord is with you!"* He was commissioned to raise up an army to fight the Midianites. But Gideon asked, *"How can I save Israel? My clan is the weakest in Manasseh, and I am the least in my family."* He was convinced of his calling only after he received three miraculous signs from heaven.[54]

4. Impatience – Sometimes you are tempted to hurry things along and don't have the patience to fulfill your calling. God never calls you to act impulsively or in reckless haste. Often one of the most difficult things you will have to do is *wait*. And God is good at stretching your faith to the eleventh hour!

- Moses killed an Egyptian in a fit of anger over how the Israelites were being treated.[55] But the timing (and method) was not right for him to rescue the Jewish people. Moses ended up herding sheep for the next forty years.

- Samuel had told Saul to wait seven days for his arrival to make an offering to the Lord. When he didn't come, Saul decided to sacrifice a burnt offering himself. Just as he was finishing, Samuel arrived. *"You acted foolishly,"* Samuel said. *"You have not kept the command the LORD your God gave you; if you had, He would have established your kingdom over Israel for all time. But now your kingdom will not endure."*[56]

- Jesus explained to His disciples that He must go to Jerusalem and be killed. Peter began to rebuke Him. *"Never, Lord!"* he said. *"This shall never happen to You!"* Peter had better plans for this new leader he was following. Jesus turned and said to Peter, *"Get behind me, Satan! You are a stumbling block to me; you do not have in mind the things of God, but the things of men."*[57]

5. Prejudice – Sometimes God will call you to minister to people that you dislike. He will confront your attitude that certain people "don't deserve" God's grace.

- When God asked Jonah to preach to Nineveh, he initially refused and tried to hide. His objection was that he didn't want to preach to his *"pagan enemies."* He wanted God to destroy them instead. God was angry with his disobedience and had him swallowed by a whale. When God gave Jonah a second chance, he reluctantly obeyed. Because of Jonah's faithfulness, God saved 120,000 people through the one-sentence sermon.[39]

- John did not like the Samaritans. In fact, he and James once asked Jesus if they could call down *"fire from heaven to burn them up"* because the Samaritans had refused to let them lodge there on the way to Jerusalem.[58] Later, John was sent to witness and minister there.[59]

6. Rejection from others – Sometimes those closest to you can be the most critical of your calling. Often it is your own family that rejects your attempt to move forward in it. Remember, God ultimately determines your success.

- When David set out to bring his brothers some lunch, he discovered all the Israelites trembling at the threat of the Philistine giant Goliath. When David suggested that he might take on the battle, his oldest brother burned with anger and he asked, *"Why have you come down here? And with whom did you leave those few sheep in the desert? I know how conceited you are and how wicked your heart is."*[60]

- When Joseph shared his dream of future power with his brothers, they mocked him and threw him in a pit. They sold him into slavery, where he was then thrown in prison, falsely accused by his master's wife. But this was all part of God's plan to position Joseph for the promise he received in that very first dream. He ended up saving his family, and an entire nation, from starvation.[61]

7. Complaints from others – It can be hard to fulfill your calling when everyone around you is complaining, criticizing, and whining.

- After Moses led the Israelites out of Egyptian slavery, they quickly became discontent in the wilderness. They cried out, *"If only we had meat to eat! We remember the fish we ate in Egypt at no cost – and the cucumbers, melons, leeks, onions, and garlic. But now we have lost our appetite; we never see anything but this manna!"*[62]

- When the Israelites finally arrived at the Promised Land and were called to take possession of it, ten spies came back with a bad report. The Israelites then grumbled in their tents and said, *"The LORD hates us; so He brought us out of Egypt to destroy us. Where can we go? Our brothers have made us lose heart. The people are stronger and taller than we are; the cities are large, with walls up to the sky."* They complained against Moses and Aaron, *"If only we had died in Egypt! Why is the LORD bringing us to this land only to let us fall by the sword? Our wives and children will be taken as plunder. Wouldn't it be better for us to go back to Egypt?"*[63]

8. Apathy from others – Sometimes you will not get the help you need for your mission because others are lazy or unprepared.

- Deborah had summoned the military leader, Barak, to mobilize for battle. First, he was too afraid to go without her. Then, four of the tribes of Israel wouldn't go either. The Reubenites *"stayed among the campfires."* The Danites *"lingered by their ships."* Asher *"remained on the coast"* and Gilead *"stayed beyond the Jordan."*[64] These apathetic tribes were listed by name in the Bible as unwilling to assist in the plans of the Lord.

- Jesus told a parable of ten virgins who took their lamps and went out to wait for the bridegroom. Five were foolish and five were wise. The foolish ones didn't take any extra oil with them. The bridegroom was a long time in coming and they all fell asleep. At midnight the cry rang out: *"Here's the bridegroom! Come out to meet him!"* All the virgins woke up to light their lamps. But the foolish ones didn't have enough oil. They said to the wise, *"Give us some of your oil; our lamps are going out."* They replied, *"No, there may not be enough for both of us. Instead, go to those who sell oil and buy some for yourselves."* But while they were on their way to buy the oil, the bridegroom arrived. The virgins who were prepared went in with him to enjoy the wedding banquet. The door was shut. Later the others also came saying, *"Sir! Sir! Open the door for us!"* But it was too late.[65]

It will take a lot of prayer, hard work, and determination to overcome these kinds of obstacles. Your calling may require long hours, frustration, and times of testing. It may be scary and uncomfortable. It is here that many give up and turn back. Don't lose heart! God will work everything together to ensure His plans unfold.

When you get discouraged, refresh yourself in worship. Refuel yourself with His Word. Get reenergized with His presence. He can supernaturally bring His wisdom and favor to your situation. Sense His reassurance that everything is going to be ok. *"If you fully obey the Lord your God and carefully follow all His commands, the Lord your God will set you high above all the nations on earth…The Lord will send a blessing on everything you put your hand to."*[66]

"I hope you have not missed something good from God's hand because you felt you did not measure up to Gideon or Isaiah. In this, your generation, give God all your attention! Give Him all your devotion and faithful service! You do not know what holy happy secret God may want to whisper to your responsive heart."

A.W. Tozer

Gifted for Service

God will give you a supernatural empowering to accomplish whatever He has asked you to do. In your own flesh, you will never feel prepared enough. Never strong enough. Never smart enough. If you feel up to the task on your own, I wonder if the call is even from God?

Jesus promised His disciples *"power from on high"* before they were sent out to disciple others.[68] A definition of the word *power* means "the ability to act or produce a result." You will be given a dynamic, powerful ability to do what you have been called to do. You will receive it. It will *"come upon you."*[67]

Use Every Gift You've Been Given

God has established a unique role for you to play in ministry. And He will "gift" you specifically for that assignment: *"A spiritual gift is given to each of us as a means of helping the entire church."*[68] Spiritual gifts are special abilities that God provides believers to enable them to serve Him effectively. You don't choose your own gifts. Paul said, *"It is the Holy Spirit who distributes these gifts. He alone decides which gift each person should have."*[69]

He expects you to use all that you've been given. Everything that has happened in your life is related to how He has shaped you for ministry. Nothing is wasted. No one has the exact same set of skills and experiences to make the contribution that He intends for you to make. *"There are different kinds of spiritual gifts...different ways of serving...and different abilities to perform service."*[70] No one else can play the role that God has planned for you. Your interests, abilities, talents, and life experiences are all intended for His glory. There is no other story exactly like yours, so only you can share it.

Even your most painful experiences in life can be used by God for ministry. I'll repeat myself here: nothing is wasted. God has allowed every circumstance for the purpose of molding and shaping you. The experiences you have resented and regretted in life are the very ones that God wants to use to help others! But you must be willing to share them. Stop hiding your faults, fears, and failures. Paul frequently talked about his weaknesses and that is what made him an effective minister.

Serving Others

The primary purpose of your spiritual gifts is for building up *others*. If you decide that to be holy you must always be alone with God, then you are of no use to Him. You are just putting yourself on a pedestal. His plan is to meet the needs of His people *through* His people. *"As each one has received a special gift, employ it in **serving one another**, as good stewards of the grace of God."*[71] None of us *"live to ourselves alone."*[72] When you use one of your gifts to help another believer, you are serving as the hands and feet of Christ. When you exercise your gifts, the grace of God flows through you.

The Christian life is more than just commitment to Jesus; it involves a commitment to other believers as well. No matter how far you advance in your personal holiness, you will always need other believers. Not because God isn't enough for you, but because He planned it that way. It is by His design. Unlike other religions in which individuals seek a solitary, Zen-like state to discover truth, Christianity calls us to follow God in loving community. Jesus modeled this behavior as He invested in His disciples. They didn't sit around on pillows silently meditating. They hiked all over Israel. They got their hands dirty together. They walked, talked, and worked together. Mark 3:14 says that Jesus appointed the twelve *"so that they would be **with Him**."* He wanted their fellowship!

Our Western individualism and independence (along with modern technology) has allowed us to minimize our contact with others – to our own detriment. God never intended for you to live separately from others. It is much easier to be holy when no one else is around to frustrate you, but a "lone ranger" receives no godly counsel and sets himself up for deception. An isolated person seeks only his own desires; he *"rages against all wise judgment."*[73] Alone, it is difficult to see areas of your life that may need to change.

Since He created us to function together as parts of one body, you cannot live a healthy life separated from other believers. Various Bible translations say that we are *"put together,"* *"joined together,"* *"built together,"* *"members together,"* *"fitted together,"* and *"held together."*[74] Spirit-filled Christians actively pursue relationships with other believers. They look for ways to be involved in their local church and parachurch ministries.

In the Body of Christ

The church is the body of Christ.[75] Jesus is the Head of the church, and every member is placed in the body as God sees fit.[76] The whole body is fashioned together by the Father. We are each equipped by the Holy Spirit to perform certain functions within the body. The body works together until *every* member comes to the fullness of Christ.[77]

In the church body, you are connected to other believers. A single body part cannot function on its own. You can't survive on your own either. The Message version of Romans 12:4-5 says, *"Each part gets its meaning from the body as a whole, not the other way around. The body we're talking about is Christ's body of chosen people. Each of us finds meaning and function as a part of His body."* God made us interdependent. We need each other. What one lacks, someone else in the body can supply. In Paul's illustration he said, *"The eye cannot say to the hand, 'I have no need of you;' or again the head to the feet, 'I have no need of you.'"*[78] This is true for the body of Christ as well.

To become a beloved disciple, you need to be firmly rooted and planted in His body – the church. The discipling process takes place within the body. We help each other walk out obedience to His commands. We hold each other accountable. We challenge each other. We correct each other. We share insights with each other. We encourage each other. We bear each other's burdens. We pray for each other. We love one another. We are devoted to each other. We are a family in Christ. When we become Christians, we are among brothers and sisters in faith. No Christan is an only child.

Ask God to carefully choose a church for you. Then stay there until He clearly tells you to go somewhere else. The Bible doesn't say, "God has set the members, each one of them, in the body just as *they* please." It says, *"God has set the members, each one of them, in the body just as **He** pleased."*[79] He will place you within a very specific community of people where He wants you to give and receive love. The enemy will try to get you offended so you leave the body God has chosen for you. Don't let him win! Psalm 92:13 says, *"Those who are planted in the house of the LORD shall flourish."* You're never going to flourish if you keep transplanting yourself every few years. You need a strong root system to withstand the storms of life. And Christians who hop around, constantly changing churches, cut off their own ability to produce lasting fruit.

In Love

The Bible tells us that the church could stay together in *"perfect harmony"* if we all walked in love.[80] God is love and the most important thing He wants you to learn on earth is to love. Jesus said, *"The whole Law can be summed up in this one command: 'Love others as you love yourself.*"[81] Ephesians 5:1-2 suggests that love is best expressed through your lifestyle: *"Be imitators of God, therefore, as dearly loved children and **live a life of love**…"* You are called to literally live love.

If you are in love with Jesus, your love for others will show. *"By this all men will know that you are my disciples, if you love one another."*[82] Any service will be futile and exhausting unless it springs from a heart overflowing with love. The book of 1 John repeatedly says that your relationships with Christian brothers and sisters reflect your relationship with God:

- *"Anyone who claims to be in the light but hates his brother is still in darkness. Whoever **loves** his brother lives in the light."*[83]
- *"This is how we know who the children of God are and who the children of the devil are: Anyone who does not do what is right is not a child of God; nor is anyone who does not **love** his brother."*[84]
- *"We know that we have passed from death to life because we **love** our brothers. Anyone who does not **love** remains in death."*[85]
- *"This is how we know what **love** is: Jesus Christ laid down His life for us. And we ought to lay down our lives for our brothers."*[86]
- *"Dear friends, let us **love** one another, for **love** comes from God. Everyone who **loves** has been born of God and knows God. Whoever does not **love** does not know God, because God is **love**."*[87]
- *"Dear friends, since God so **loved** us, we also ought to **love** one another. No one has ever seen God; but if we **love** one another, God lives in us, and His **love** is made complete in us."*[88]
- *"If anyone says, "I **love** God," yet hates his brother, he is a liar. For anyone who does not **love** his brother, whom he has seen, cannot **love** God, whom he has not seen. And He has given us this command: Whoever **loves** God must also **love** his brother."*[89]
- *"This is how we know that we **love** the children of God: by **loving** God and carrying out His commands."*[90]

Learning to love unselfishly is not an easy task. You must be in regular and close contact with other believers to practice love. Maintaining strong relationships with others should be a priority in your life. It is the only way to leave a legacy and impact others. The Bible tells us that faith, hope, and love are eternal, but *"the greatest of these is love."*[91] Galatians 5:6 says, *"The only thing that counts is faith expressing itself through love."*

It's not enough just to say that relationships are important, you actually have to devote time, energy, and attention to them. Jesus said, *"My children, our love should not be just words and talk; it must be true love, which shows itself in action.*[92] One of the enemy's favorite strategies is to keep you so overwhelmed with activity that you don't have time to invest in relationships. When God brings people to you that need His touch, the tendency is to give them a quick word of Scripture or leave them with a hurried word of counsel before rushing on your way. Nothing can substitute for your focused attention. This means that you will often have to give up your preferences, comforts, and time for the benefit of someone else.

Do You See Your Calling?

You are being called to represent Jesus to the world and He is love. Service is simply the overflow of a life filled with love and devotion. When you are moving in divine relationship with Him, service should be a natural part of your life. John 7:38 says that when you believe in Him, *"streams of living water"* will flow out from you. That living water is meant to touch the world.

You will bring the Kingdom into places where it has never been before. The weak need His strength. The strong need His comfort. The tempted need His grace. The lonely need His companionship. Give all your best to all who need it.

"Many are called, but few are chosen."[93] The chosen ones have emptied themselves of themselves and say, *"Here am I, send me!"*[94] Anytime. Anywhere. He can accomplish great things through a believing, yielded vessel. Remember, you are *"not your own."*[95] To someday hear *"Well done, good and faithful servant,"*[96] you must fulfill His calling in your life.

As you move forward, remember that God is far more interested in you having a relationship with Him than He is in getting a task accomplished. You can't make more disciples if you are not a disciple yourself. Never neglect seeking Jesus, even at the cost of laying your ministry aside. In Luke 10:38, Martha's walk looked like work while Mary's walk looked like devotion. So, in the final unit, we are going to learn to *abide* with Jesus like Mary did. Steps #9 and #10 will remind you of your humble position and refresh you in His quiet rest.

---◆---

Prayer

Jesus, teach me to be a vessel that draws others to You. I repent of closing my eyes and ears to the needs of others because I want more for myself. I repent of any priorities, actions, or decisions that demonstrate that I exalt myself, my friends, my family, my career, or my finances above You. I am honored to be Your hands and feet for those that need to feel Your presence. Help me demonstrate Your love in all I say and do.

Prepare my heart in prayer so that I can clearly discern Your plans and purposes for me. I don't want to miss any opportunities You have for me. Entrust me with tasks that fulfill Your eternal Kingdom purposes. Help me to respond joyfully in whatever way you choose to use me. Keep me from striving to do things in my own strength, my own way, or my own time. Keep me in step with You. Increase my discernment for anything done outside Your calling; realizing it is a waste of my time and strength. Lord, I don't want to go anywhere that Your presence is not with me. Walking in step with You, I won't grow weary. Give me perseverance. Help me to remain faithful.

There is still much to be done here! Lord, give me opportunities to witness and the courage to speak up. Help me lay aside all fear and apprehension to boldly proclaim Your glory and grace. I repent of caring more about my own reputation than Yours. I am sorry for any way that I have compromised my witness of You because I want to seem inclusive and tolerant of everyone. Lord, You did not worry about opposition. Don't let me live in fear either. Help me let go of my own comforts to step out in faith to wherever and whatever You call me to. Help me to live completely "sold out" for You, no matter how radical it appears. When You say "Go," I'll go. Don't let me count the cost. Let me forfeit everything for whatever Your Kingdom requires.

Help me to make a difference in this world. Fill me with compassion and give me a heart for the harvest. Open doors for Your Gospel to go forth to the nations. Prepare receptive hearts for Your truth. Give me Your eyes so I can see. Give me Your ears so I can hear. Help me to see my whole life as a mission. I am sorry for giving You my leftover money and my leftover time implying that You are second-best in my life. Show me how to best support Your work physically, spiritually, emotionally, and financially. I want to play a role in fulfilling Your words that the Gospel must be preached to all nations before the end of time.

STUDY

1. According to John 15:8, how will you demonstrate that you are Jesus' disciple?

2. Are you bearing fruit? Where would you place yourself on this scale?

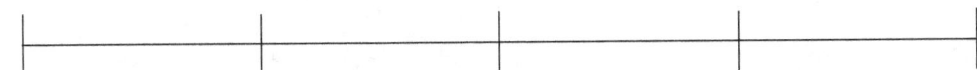

No fruit   Some fruit   Much fruit

3. What does 1 Corinthians 3:6-10 say about how your fruit will grow?

Your Great Commission

4. How consistent are you in declaring what you have *"seen and heard"* concerning Christ (see 1 John 1:3)? What has been your most recent "testimony" about Jesus?

5. What are some typical fears and stereotypes that people have when they hear the word "evangelism?" What keeps *you* from sharing the Gospel with others?

6. Identify one way that you've noticed our culture becoming less tolerant of Christians. How does this personally impact your willingness to share your testimony with others? What risk is Jesus asking you to take to share the Gospel with others?

7. Do you believe that each day is an opportunity to be on "mission" with Jesus? How does that impact your day?

Questions that can spark a spiritual conversation:	1. What does your culture say about Jesus? 2. Do you consider yourself spiritual? 3. I just learned something in the Bible that's really helping me deal with _____. May I share it with you? 4. I'm in a season of prayer. Do you have any prayer requests?

Obeying the Call

8. How would you describe your current mission in life? Do you feel you are in the right place in relation to God's present will for your life or are you currently doing one thing but feeling called to do another? What work is still undone in your life?

9. Do you need to see the whole picture before moving forward? How do you walk *"by faith and not by sight?"* Identify several examples of others (from the Bible or personal experience) who took a step without knowing where they were going.

10. Have any of these obstacles ever taken the wind out of your sails and left you discouraged in your pursuit of God's calling on your life?

☐ unworthiness　　　　　☐ distractions

☐ fear　　　　　　　　　☐ impatience

☐ prejudice　　　　　　　☐ rejection from others

☐ complaints from others　☐ apathy from others

How can you respond in a way that is pleasing to God?

Gifted for Service

11. Review the parable of the Talents (see Matthew 25:14-30). List some of the talents you have personally been given. Which gifts have you chosen to use (multiplied)? Which have you chosen not to use (buried)?

12. How have you seen God combine your upbringing, experiences, and passion to accomplish something? How have difficulties in your life prepared you to serve God better?

Serving in the Body of Christ

13. In Galatians 6:10, whom does Paul suggest we should help as often as we can? Why?

> *"Therefore, as we have opportunity, let us do good to all people, especially to those who belong to the family of believers."*
>
> Galatians 6:10

14. Do you tend to be a spiritual "lone ranger?" Why is it important to fellowship with others who share your beliefs?

15. What are the most common excuses people give for not joining a church, and how would you answer them?

16. First Corinthians 12:7-31 describes the church as the body of Christ. Verse 25 says there should be no division in the body. Is this true of your church? What can you do to protect and promote the unity of your church?

Serving in Love

17. We might say we're being called to "love difficult people" when in reality we are being challenged to love "people we find difficult." What's the difference?

18. Review 1 Corinthians 13. List the phrases that describe what Christian love is and is not:

Love is...   **Love is not...**

_____   _____

_____   _____

_____   _____

_____   _____

_____   _____

SPIRITUAL MARKER

love

WORSHIP

If We Are the Body [Casting Crowns]

Give Me Your Eyes [Brandon Heath]

My Own Little World [Matthew West]

Only You Can Save [Chris Sligh]

I Refuse [Josh Wilson]

For the One [Brian and Jenn Johnson]

By Our Love [Christy Nockels]

Available [Elevation]

The Blessing [Elevation, Kari Jobe, & Cody Carnes]

Revival's in the Air [Bethel Music featuring Melissa Hesler]

This is a Move [Brandon Lake]

Reckless Love [Bethel Music featuring Cory Asbury]

All the Way My Savior Leads Me [Chris Tomlin]

Stay and Wait [Hillsong United]

YOU ARE THE LIGHT OF THE WORLD

MATTHEW 5:14

UNIT 4

ABIDE IN HIM

"Abide in Me, and I in you. As the branch cannot bear fruit by itself, unless it abides in the vine, neither can you, unless you abide in Me."[1]

In the previous steps, you learned to win battles against the enemy and serve other disciples. But "works" can easily shift your focus away from God. Jesus doesn't call us to work – He calls us to Himself. The remainder of this book is a reminder that apart from Him, *"you can do **nothing.**"[2]* The only requirement for a fruit-bearing life is that you abide in Jesus the same way a branch remains securely attached to the vine. You must remain completely dependent on Him to accomplish all He wants to do through you and in you.

You have come a long way, but don't think for a moment that you need His support any less! You need Him, no matter how mature you have become. Don't stop now in contentment with the progress you have already made. Like the Israelites, it is possible to be dramatically delivered from slavery and leave your "Egypt" behind but wander through the wilderness and never make it to your Promised Land of peace and rest.

Hold His hand even more firmly as you journey on. *"Remain in His love."[3]* Dwell in it, linger in it, soak in it. With Jesus at the center, every aspect of your life will bear fruit for Him. But don't rejoice that God has used you, rejoice that your name is written in heaven.[4] In Step #9, let Him do His finishing work to make you patient and humble. In Step #10, you will find the calm, peaceful assurance that He is directing every detail of your life. Therein lies the secret of sustaining comfort for the beloved disciple of Christ.

HUMBLE YOURSELF IN THE SIGHT OF THE LORD

Beloved disciple, you have come too far to lose your way now. Sadly, many do. Just as ministries start to rise, the minister falls. What came before that fall? *Pride.*[1]

This is the time to stay strong. Keep your eyes fixed ahead. There's further to go; there's more to be done. You are nearing the finish line, but to climb the next hurdle you must bring yourself lower.

> *"We have only to become acquainted with the big names of our time to discover how wretchedly inferior most of them are. We turn away from them sick to our stomach and wonder for a discouraged moment if this is the best the human race can produce. But then we gain our perspective again as we think upon some of the plain folk we know, who live unheralded and unsung lives, but are made of stuff infinitely finer than the braggarts who occupy the highest places in the land. The Church also suffers from this evil. We have learned to equate popularity with excellence and in open defiance of the Sermon on the Mount, give our approval to the assertive, not the meek."*
>
> A.W. Tozer

The Way Up is Down

Jesus repeatedly taught His disciples to be humble. Instead, they argued multiple times over who was the greatest.[2] James and John asked Jesus if they could be seated on His right and left in heaven, the highest places in the Kingdom.[3] How slow they were to learn! These disciples loved Jesus and had forsaken *all* for Him. But deep down was this dark, deceptive need for their own power and glory.

The disciples had come so far in their training while humility was still so terribly lacking. As it is today. We find ministers, missionaries, public servants, teachers, and evangelists who sincerely love the Lord but eventually fall prey to personal pride. Beloved disciple, you are not yet humble. I am not yet humble. That is why we are so strongly encouraged to pursue it.

In the Old Testament:

- *"This is the one I esteem: he who is humble and contrite in spirit, and trembles at My word."*[4]
- *"When pride comes, then comes disgrace, but with humility comes wisdom."*[5]
- *"Humility and the fear of the LORD bring wealth and honor and life."*[6]

In the Gospels of Matthew, Mark, Luke, and John:

- *"Whoever wants to become great among you must be your servant, and whoever wants to be first must be your slave."*[7]
- *"Whoever exalts himself will be humbled, and whoever humbles himself will be exalted."*[8]
- *"Therefore, whoever humbles himself like a child is the greatest in the kingdom of heaven."*[9]
- *"Take My yoke upon you and learn from Me, for I am gentle and humble in heart, and you will find rest for your souls."*[10]
- *"Blessed are the poor in spirit; for theirs is the kingdom of heaven. Blessed are the meek; for they shall inherit the earth."*[11]

In the writings of other disciples:

- *"Humble yourselves in the sight of the Lord, and He shall lift you up."*[12]
- *"All of you, clothe yourselves with humility toward one another, because 'God opposes the proud but gives grace to the humble.' Humble yourselves, therefore, under God's mighty hand, that He may lift you up in due time."*[13]

From the letters of Paul:

- *"Do not be proud but be willing to associate with people of low position. Do not be conceited."*[14]
- *"Love does not parade itself, is not puffed up; does not behave rudely, does not seek its own."*[15]

- *"Let nothing be done through selfish ambition or conceit, but in lowliness of mind let each esteem others better than himself."*[16]
- *"Therefore, as God's chosen people, holy and dearly loved, clothe yourselves with compassion, kindness, humility, gentleness and patience."*[17]

The way to a higher life is lower down! Let your only purpose and prayer be to serve. No place should be too low, no task too menial, and no service beneath you.

"Your attitude should be the same as that of Christ Jesus: Who, being in very nature God, did not consider equality with God something to be grasped, but made Himself nothing…He humbled Himself and became obedient to death—even death on a cross!"[18]

He Humbled Himself

Jesus is your example. He left the light of heaven to be born in a filthy stable. The One who hung the stars now had to have His diaper changed. He had to learn to walk and talk. He experienced what it was like to grow tired and hungry. As His ministry began, He walked hundreds of miles on dusty roads with crowds pulling at Him from all directions. Days, months, and years…walking, talking, and serving.

His whole life was yielded to God. He never failed to obey the will of the Father. His beloved disciple, John, was taking good notes. He quoted Jesus saying:

- *"For I have come down from heaven not to do My will but to do the will of Him who sent Me."*[19]
- *"I do nothing on My own but speak just what the Father has taught Me."*[20]
- *"I tell you the truth, the Son can do nothing by Himself; He can do only what He sees His Father doing, because whatever the Father does the Son also does."*[21]
- *"The words I say to you are not just My own. Rather, it is the Father, living in Me, who is doing His work."*[22]
- *"By Myself I can do nothing; for I seek not to please myself but Him who sent Me."*[23]
- *"I am not seeking glory for Myself."*[24]

- *"I do not accept praise from men."*[25]

Jesus never asserted His own power or sought His own glory while on this earth. He even shared the spotlight with His disciples saying, *"I have given them the glory that you gave Me."*[26] Can you think of anyone else that has ever lived like this?

Give Him All the Glory

You may be an incredible teacher. You may have a gift for preaching. You might have a fabulous testimony to share. You may be a talented writer or great singer. You might be a charismatic leader. But you are trying to become a beloved disciple, not a crowd pleaser. Don't get preoccupied with what a wonderful thing He is going to make out of you. Success is not your goal; a relationship with Jesus is the goal. You were created to glorify Him. True humility is bowing at His feet in recognition that everything good has come from His hand. John 3:27 says, *"A man can receive only what is given him from heaven."*

Some believers are unable to handle the wealth, position, blessings, gifts, or talents that God gives them. Without realizing it, they slowly drift into self-worship. They feel they are "God's gift to the world" or have "arrived." Their ego starts to believe that *they* have done the sowing, growing, watering, and harvesting. God can't bless that kind of prideful work. First Corinthians 3:6-10 explains that while you may plant and water the seeds, only God can make them grow. *"We are simply God's servants...Each one of us does the work which the Lord gave him to do."*

God wants you to bear much fruit. He wants to grace you with incomparably great power. He wants to accomplish mighty things through you. But when He starts showing you off, don't get proud in your anointing! It's not that God wants you to feel your efforts are pitiful or meaningless. You will do amazing things, but only *through* Christ.[27] God wants to be sure you understand that He is the One behind your victories. He cannot tolerate any attempt to share His glory. You are responsible to do your part, but God always gets the credit. As it is written: *"Let him who boasts boast in the Lord."*[28]

You can either choose to humble yourself[29] or He will have to do it for you.[30] Every time you start to think highly of yourself, fall to your knees! Doing this voluntarily is much better than the alternative, trust me. Allow any weaknesses and "thorns in the flesh" to do their work to cultivate humility. Paul admitted, *"I have received wonderful revelations from God. But to keep me from getting puffed up, I was given a thorn in my flesh to keep me from getting proud."*[31]

Pride Before the Fall

Pride – the opposite of humility – is always destructive. Wars among nations, bitter and broken relationships, and the daily striving with ambitions and jealousies can all be traced back to the curse of pride. Indifference to the needs of others, harsh and hasty judgments, temper, and touchiness have their root in nothing but pride.

Pride is what got Satan cast out of heaven. And really, *what was he thinking?* He had a good thing going on up there! He was beautiful, anointed, and already held a very high position. But he started to believe he could be better than God. Then he successfully deceived the hearts of the first people on earth, Adam and Eve, with the very same evil desire. As a result, they had to be cast out of the Garden of Eden. Many have forfeited great things because they wanted more…and more…and more.

It is clear that self-exaltation is Satan's preferred means of destruction. When he wanted to tempt Jesus, he took him to the pinnacle of the temple to promise him power. He hasn't changed his approach since then. He still wants to destroy the lives of God's children. And his primary strategy to keep you from being full of the Spirit is to get you full of yourself – full of self-righteousness, self-pity, self-confidence, self-sufficiency, self-admiration, and self-love. When you are increasing, God is not.

Pride can be a subtle trap. You may find yourself walking with God one minute and falling right into the enemy's snare the next. Moses had spent many years in faithful and humble obedience before he stole God's glory by striking the rock and declaring, *"Listen, you rebels, must we bring you water out of this rock?"*[32] Notice the word "we." Ooops. God was the only One who would bring water out of the rock. This one slip-up cost Moses dearly. He was never allowed to enter the Promised Land with the rest of the Israelites because of that mistake.

Uzziah is another example.[33] He became King of Judah when he was only sixteen years old. He *"did right in the sight of the Lord"* and reigned for 52 years. As long as he sought the Lord, God prospered him. Unfortunately, as he gained wealth and military strength, he started to believe he no longer needed God. One day, he entered the temple of the Lord to burn his own incense. This was against the law as only the appointed priests were supposed to enter the sanctuary to offer sacrifices. Blinded by his pride, he assumed the law didn't apply to him. When the priests reprimanded him, he became defiant. *"While he was raging at the priests before the incense altar in the LORD's temple, leprosy broke out on his forehead."* He spent the rest of his life cut off from God's goodness.

These accounts should be strong warnings to you – prideful disobedience can be very costly. These are sad outcomes for men who showed such promise. The consequences sound harsh, but *"from the one trusted with much, much more will be expected."*[34] If you are not vigilant, the same attitude that destroyed their lives can corrupt yours too. Just because you respond properly one time does not guarantee you will the next time. Instead of praying and asking for discernment, you may move forward believing you know what is best. You might rush into doing things that are not yours to do. Beloved disciple, His commands are in place to ensure you live the best life possible – with humility.

The Poison of Pride

Those pursuing the heights of holiness are most in danger of falling prey to the depths of pride. Remember the Pharisee who entered the temple and prayed, *"I thank you, God, that I am not a sinner like everyone else, especially like that tax collector over there!"*[35] While the saint is thanking God, he is really congratulating himself.

You may never have the nerve to say, *"Stand back...for I am holier than thou,"*[36] but you might act like it. Just listen to the way a Christian couple speaks to each other in the church parking lot, observe the Elders arguing over how to disperse the funds, see a worshipper attracting attention to herself, watch the Pastor dismissing much of the church work as "beneath" him, and hear the congregation criticizing the Pastor. Here, holiness loses its humility.

Pride exalts self rather than Christ. It is your defense against anyone or anything trying to subtract from your worth. And this excessive self-focus leads to comparison, competition, jealousy, defensiveness, perfectionism, and entitlement. Poison fruits from the root of pride.

Comparison and Competition

"How do you expect to get anywhere with God when you spend all your time jockeying for position with each other, ranking your rivals, and ignoring God?"[37]

These days, many of us wonder with every status update, picture, tweet, and blog whether we're liked or popular enough. We fantasize about going viral on the latest social platform. Then, we'll finally belong. We clamor for fame, success, and recognition. We want the "good life", and we want to make sure everyone else knows we have it. Comparison is what makes you proud: the pleasure you find in being above the rest. This struggle for belonging and importance represents all the ways you still want the throne, rather than a simple seat at a round table alongside everyone else.

One of your greatest challenges will be watching others operating effectively in their gifts while your own ministry seems to struggle. Comparison says, "Why them and not me?" Competition says, "Am I better than her?" You never (or rarely) say these things out loud, but the thoughts are still destructive. Paul said, *"We will not compare ourselves with each other as if one of us were better and another worse. Each of us is an original,"*[38] and *"Do your own work well, and then you will have something to be proud of. But don't compare yourself with others."*[39]

What happens when your ministry role is taken away by a younger person? What happens when the other girl gets the dream date or dream job or acceptance to your dream school? What happens when you experience failure or rejection at work? If you truly trust God with your future, you should not be threatened by blessings given to another person. Everything isn't a marker to make you feel ahead or behind. Just because someone else is enjoying favor doesn't mean that God will withhold His goodness from you. You are not insignificant. He will not leave you empty-handed. He has a variety of gifts planned for you. You just need to be patient and wait for the right time. He knows what it will take to prepare you for the blessings He has in store. Ask Him to help you see your life from His perspective.

There are times He may allow you to face situations in which you have to battle feelings of competition and comparison. Take a step back. *"Drop the vicious habit of depersonalizing everyone into a rival."*[40] You will always find someone better than you. Stop worrying about getting taking advantage of – He will provide all you need. And remember, you are not responsible for the outcomes. It's His work.

True humility comes when you are content to see yourself as nothing and no longer compare yourself to others. You can handle others getting praised and not being noticed yourself. You can give credit where credit is due without feeling forgotten. Jesus has taken the place of self.

Jealousy

You are tempted to become jealous when you are afraid someone else will take your position; when you see someone getting something you think you should have. Even

Peter had to be reminded, *"What's it to you? Follow Me!"* when he got jealous over the fate of the disciple Jesus loved.[41]

Jealousy usually starts by devoting time and energy to some idol, and then deciding you are not getting as much of that thing as you should be. Your life starts to feel empty, incomplete, and unsatisfying. All the while, you overlook God's goodness and sovereignty. Jealousy prevents you from fully enjoying the gifts that God placed in you. You get so caught up in what others are gaining that you lose sight of what you already have.

James 3:16 says that *"where you have envy and selfish ambition, there you find disorder."* Because you are operating outside of God's will in jealousy, you won't be able to hear Him clearly. You can't focus and make proper decisions when you are obsessed with who has more than you. You may get distracted and lose sleep. You may try to manipulate your circumstances to come out ahead. You might distance yourself from others, becoming critical and resentful. And others will steer clear of you. Insecurity, tension, and bitterness will be written all over your face.[42]

It is not Christ's nature to be jealous, and you want to become more like Christ. It is never His plan that you become envious of what others have or do. He wants you to live in harmony with others. It's no accident that several of the Ten Commandments involve jealousy. And 1 Corinthians 3:33 says, *"For since there is jealousy and quarreling among you, are you not worldly?"* Getting gripped by jealousy means you are out of step with His plan for your own life. Jealousy is listed as sin that is carnal, fleshly, and demonic.[43] Consider the source! It is always Satan's goal to shift your focus off God and onto yourself.

Jealousy begins with a single thought. You can choose to entertain it or let it pass through your mind. It is a matter of choice; you must choose not to be envious. It is a normal temptation, but you must turn away from it. If you leave it unaddressed, it will eventually take a toll on you physically and emotionally. You will wind up working long and hard to reach goals that were never meant for you to chase.

To win this battle, you must believe that He loves you and has not forgotten you. Why would you want anything more than He is giving you right now? Set your heart solely on pleasing Him. Only consider His purpose for your own life. He intends to use everyone mightily. He has work set apart for you that no one else can do. Quit keeping score. When your eyes are focused on Jesus, you are not concerned about who is getting ahead.

Be willing to confess your feelings of jealousy to God. Acknowledge that it places you in conflict with Him. Open your heart to receive His instruction. Find ways to encourage and compliment the other person. They are not the enemy! They are just being who God created them to be and living out His plan for their life. Thank Him for what He has done in your own life. Ask Him to help you rest in His presence. The feelings of jealousy will eventually fade with the help of the Holy Spirit.

Self-protection

Almost all the anxiety, worry, and stress in your life can be traced back to self-protection. Perfectionism is self-protection. Independence is self-protection. Defensiveness is self-protection. You are trying to protect your status, your image, your rights, and your "territory." You must protect yourself against every slight, challenge every word spoken against you, and shield your touchy honor from the bad opinion of friend or foe. How then can you hope to have any inward peace? This leads to hyper-vigilance; strategizing how you can best control the circumstances in your favor.

Protecting yourself means you are not trusting God to protect you. Jesus calls us to rest, and meekness is His method. Trust Him with your reputation. Trust Him with your relationships. Trust Him with your possessions. If there is something He wants you to have, you will have it. And there will come a time when God asks you to lay down the right to be recognized, defend yourself, or isolate yourself from someone that deserves your distance.

You can tell how much self-protection is operating in you by your reaction to criticism. I remember having a *miserable* week a few years ago. First, a junior colleague gave me a less-than-perfect evaluation of my classroom teaching. She pointed out that I wasn't using as much "modern technology" as she was. Later that week, I gave a leadership workshop where the feedback was not as stellar as I thought it would be. That same week, I got "demoted" in a church ministry that mattered a great deal to me. The last straw was a house appraiser that evaluated our home well below market value and criticized our "out of date" interior. I felt defeated and deflated everywhere. But why did it matter so much to me? By dumping it all in the same week, God was definitely making a point! The fact that all these things pierced me like a knife demonstrated that I was clearly not free from my self-protection tendencies. I wanted so badly to defend myself in each situation. I desperately needed to re-fill my heart and mind with His truth.

Jesus never defended Himself. *"He was oppressed and afflicted, yet he did not open His mouth."*[44] He made Himself of *"no reputation"* so He didn't have to worry about keeping it.[45] We must stop defending ourselves against any perceived gain or loss of our worth. Romans 8:33 says that *"God justifies us; we don't have to justify ourselves."* Yes, beloved disciples experience hurt and disappointment just like everybody else. They feel frustration when they are treated unfairly. But what makes them different is their response. They refocus their attention on the big picture and God's purpose in the situation. They remind themselves that *"all things work together for good."*[46] They don't *"repay evil for evil."*[47] They allow God to work it out in His way and in His timing. They rest their minds on things above.

Selfishness

Pride keeps you from caring about others. Instead of thinking about how you can help or serve others, you only think about your own needs and wants. You strive to be the center of attention. You surround yourself with people who stroke your ego. And when your ego inflates, you start to believe you are better than everyone else. You lose touch with those less fortunate. When Nebuchadnezzar gained power and prosperity, he announced, *"I am, and there is none beside me."* God was displeased with this arrogance and gave him a year to change his attitude, renounce his sins, and *"minister to the poor."*[48]

Isaiah 58:10-11 suggests that we are *"healed"* when we help the poor. I believe that one of the things we are healed from is our own pride. True humility means focusing on others more than yourself. Paul preached, *"Forget yourself long enough to lend a helping hand."*[49] The Message version of Philippians 2:1 says, *"If you've gotten anything at all out of following Christ, if His love has made any difference in your life…don't push your way to the front; don't sweet talk your way to the top. Put yourself aside, and help others get ahead. Don't be obsessed with getting the advantage."* When you stop thinking about your own needs, you become more aware of the needs around you. You invest in God's work, God's way.

The Grip of this World

To eliminate pride from your life, Jesus must eliminate the grip of this world in you. The world says, "Seek status!" The Bible says, *"Seek first His kingdom and His righteousness."*[50] Paul reminded the Ephesians, *"You were taught to change the way you were living. The person you used to be will ruin you through desires that deceive you."*[51] As a beloved disciple, you exchange the call of the world for the call of God because *"What good is it for a man to gain the whole world but lose his own soul?"*[52] The Message Bible says, *"Don't love the world's ways. Don't love the world's goods. Love of the world squeezes out love for the Father."*[53]

"It will require a determined heart and courage to wrench yourself loose from the grip of this world and return to Biblical ways. But it can be done."

A.W. Tozer

I need to hear this message myself, again and again. I am wired by nature to love the same toys that the world loves. I want to fit in. I start to love what the world loves. I begin to think of this earth as my "home." Before I even realize it, I am calling luxuries "needs" and spending my money the same way unbelievers do. I don't think much about people perishing. Mission work drops out of my mind. I thank God for His constant, gentle reminders that building a life around appearance, affluence, and achievement is no life at all.

Do you want satisfaction from Him plus satisfaction from the world too? If so, you are trying to serve two masters. You are trying to claim the wages of both God and the world. If you are working for God, you will have your reward in due time. Don't then turn to human beings and expect rewards there too. Paul proclaimed, *"We were not looking for praise from men, not from you or anyone else."*[54]

The desire to impress, gain momentary attention, or appear better in comparison to others is the opposite of what Jesus taught His disciples. But those disciples argued about who was the greatest 2,000 years ago and Christians still find themselves jockeying for position today. "How big? How many?" are the questions frequently asked. Don't be led astray by worldly numbers. God ignores all this status-seeking and looks only at your character. And it's never about quantity; it's all about quality.

The World's Measuring Stick

We tend to see as the world sees; to judge as the world judges. We are impressed by power, charmed by charisma, fascinated by glamour, and hypnotized by wealth. This is out of touch with the Spirit of God. *"What is highly esteemed among men is an abomination in the sight of God."*[55] What the Bible clearly describes as sin – taking matters into your own hands, being your own god, grabbing all you can while you can get it – is now considered "common sense:" improving yourself by whatever means necessary, getting ahead regardless of the price, taking care of yourself first.

The "servant" message is not a popular one. Our culture is obsessed with best of the best lists: the most beautiful person list, the most influential person list, the richest person in the world list. Do you find yourself striving to make it on "the list" where you work? Once you're on the list, you feel pressure to move up higher on the list! The goal is recognition, recognition, recognition. You want to be the most gifted. You want to be the first choice. You want to be the top priority. You want to be the best. You want to be noticed. You want to win. *Anything less hurts your pride.* Our world supports, encourages, and promotes a sense of pride.

You can't measure your success by the world's standards. According to these standards, Jesus died an apparent failure; rejected and forsaken. The world did not want a meek and modest leader. They questioned the authority of a King born in a stable. And the public ministry of the strangely dressed, locust-eating John the Baptist lasted only about six months. He didn't perform a single miracle.[56] Hardly fit to make the cover of TIME magazine as one of the world's most influential people. But Jesus said, *"There is no one greater than John."*[57]

God's standards are different. Leadership and greatness in the Kingdom are not based on appearance, power, influence, or reputation. When you feel weak and ordinary is when God can best use you! Paul said God intentionally seeks out the *"despised"* because He can achieve the greatest glory through them.[58] Dwight L. Moody was a poorly educated shoe salesman who became one of the greatest evangelists of modern times. Peter and John were uneducated, ordinary fishermen. The Bible says, *"God chose the foolish things of the world to shame the wise; God chose the weak things of the world to shame the strong."*[59]

One day you will be judged, not by fame, fortune, or achievements, but by how much of the character of Jesus is found in you. Beloved disciples must treat this life as a temporary assignment and await their promised reward in heaven. John 12:25 teaches, *"The man who loves his life will lose it, while the man who hates his life in this world will keep it for eternity."* The Message version of 2 Corinthians 4:18 says, *"The things we see now are here today, gone tomorrow. But the things we can't see now will last forever."*

"The moment we make up our minds that we are going on with this determination to exalt God over all else, we step out of the world's parade."

A.W. Tozer

The Riches of This World

You were created for eternity. Wealth is temporary. And God had more to say about the pursuit of riches than most anything else in the Bible. Proverbs 23:4-5 says, *"Do not weary yourself to gain wealth. Cease from your consideration of it. When you set your eyes upon it, it is gone."*

Money has the potential to displace Jesus in your life. The *"cares of this world"* and the *"deceitfulness of riches"* will choke the life of God in you.[60] You must consider everything *"a loss compared to the surpassing greatness of knowing Jesus."*[61] No one can serve two masters. *"Either he will hate the one and love the other, or he will be devoted to the one and despise the other. You cannot serve both God and Money."*[62] Notice that He didn't say "you should not" serve two masters; He said you "cannot." It is impossible to have a strong relationship with both.

As a beloved disciple, you must orient your life to the purposes of God, not your own. Make sure you are investing in things that will not pass away. *"Do not store up for yourselves treasures on earth, where moth and rust destroy, and where thieves break in and steal. But store up for yourselves treasures in heaven…for where your treasure is, there your heart will be also."*[63] God will use money to test your faithfulness as a beloved disciple. He said, *"If you have not been trustworthy in handling worldly wealth, who will trust you with true riches?"*[64] Think of yourself as His servant; managing His estate. Only seek financial gain when that gain will gain more for the Kingdom.

The Approval of Man

Another powerful "grip of this world" demands that you please people to gain their approval. You try to conduct yourself in ways that bring attention and admiration. You strive to protect your reputation at all costs. You collect possessions to further your status in the eyes of your neighbors. Your longing to be loved and admired runs deep. I know this all too well.

The need for approval makes you do all kinds of things to "fit in." You play the part that's needed in any given situation. Soon you resemble a chameleon. John 7:18 says, *"He who speaks on his own does so to gain honor for himself, but he who works for the honor of the One who sent him is a man of truth; there is nothing false about him."* Can you say there is nothing false about you? That you have never acted fake or inauthentic to protect your reputation?

The force behind what makes you "false" is the fear of man. You want praise and admiration so much you will do *anything* to avoid criticism. You don't want to disappoint anyone, so you say "yes" to things you don't want to do out of guilt, pressure, and obligation. Sometimes you may even compromise your faith…

Part of the reason I kept my personal and professional lives separate in the past was that I didn't want to ruffle any feathers. I didn't want to come across as too "Christian."

I wanted to blend in with the very liberal institution where I currently work. After all, a practicing Wiccan has her office just down the hall from mine. I realize that by publishing this book, I am taking a risk that others may not approve. I am not the first to consider job security over faith. Why did Nicodemus visit Jesus at *night?* John tells us that *"many among the leaders believed in Him. But because of the Pharisees they would not confess their faith for fear they would be put out of the synagogue."*[65] They denied Jesus because they didn't want to lose their seat in church!

What will others think? How will they react? Peer pressure made Peter deny Jesus three times. Concern about the consequences made the parents of a blind son say they had "no idea" how he got healed.[66] Fear of repercussions made Elijah run and hide in a cave.[67] Self-protection made Abraham lie and pretend that Sarah was his sister.[68] Fear is a powerful force.

We have seen examples of the consequences of standing firm in the faith. Shadrach, Meshach, and Abednego refused to bow down and got put in a fiery furnace. Daniel refused to stop praying and he got put in the lion's den. The disciples refused to stop preaching and most of them were martyred. The list of beatings that Paul endured sounds like more than one person could bear. Today, employees lose their jobs for views that don't align with our current culture. Freedom of speech is enjoyed only by those who speak what others want to hear. The pressure is strong to keep your mouth shut and "fly below the radar."

The heart of the world is breaking under this load of fear, pride, and pretense. Beloved disciple, you are either for Him or against Him. First Corinthians 10:21 warns, *"You cannot drink the cup of the Lord and the cup of demons too; you cannot have a part in both the Lord's table and the table of demons."* God says He will eventually spit the "lukewarm" out of His mouth.[69] And Jesus warned, *"Whoever denies me before men, I also will deny before my Father who is in heaven."*[70] It would be nice if you could please everyone here on earth, but the One you are most trying to please is Jesus. A day is coming when you will be placed in the position where you must choose. It will take courage and strength not to be double-minded.

"When we are baptized in the criticism of man, it inoculates us from the praise of man, so that we die to the control of man."

Francis Frangipane

Of No Reputation

Neither success nor fame had any hold on Jesus. He lived free of the fear of man. He experienced the praise of the crowds one day and the contempt of the Pharisees the next – without altering who He was.

You have been sent to bless the world, not compromise with it. And to be branded as belonging to Him will bring a certain amount of criticism from the world. That just doesn't sound appealing to most of us. Jesus pointed out that few would find His way acceptable. The only thing that will free you from the desire to receive the glory of men is to give yourself entirely to the glory of God. Accept anything and everything that humbles you before Him. Death to self is the only cure for the shackles of pride.

Expect to be outnumbered. Noah's culture was completely depraved, and yet he remained faithful and righteous.[71] He was the *only one* in his entire generation that walked with God. Elijah was outnumbered 850 to 1 when he engaged in the fire-starting competition on Mount Carmel.[72] When it comes to true religion, the crowds are always wrong. Accept the fact that you will have a different perspective than most of those around you.

Expect to be ridiculed. Your motives may be misinterpreted. You may be wronged. You may be provoked. You may even be persecuted. All the prophets and disciples before you were mistreated. And 2 Peter 3:3 warns us that the scoffers will get more vocal as the end of time nears. Will your faith waver?

"The humble man is not afflicted with a sense of his own inferiority. Rather he simply knows that the world will never see him as God sees him and he has stopped caring. He will be happy to let God defend him. He rests perfectly content to allow God to establish His own value. He will be patient to wait for the day when everything will get its own price tag and real worth will come into its own. Then the righteous shall shine forth in the Kingdom of their Father. He is willing to wait for that day."

A.W. Tozer

God's Work, God's Way

Imagine being unknown, ordinary, embracing your irrelevance and unimportance. Does this thought scare you? It used to terrify me. Achievement – and being recognized for it – used to be a stronghold in my life. I believed I was only worthy when I was accomplishing something. Perhaps, like me, you equate your value with your level of success. What you'll come to learn is that your heart doesn't really want *importance,* it actually craves *unconditional acceptance,* found only through Jesus.

To become a beloved disciple, you must value the unconditional acceptance of Jesus more than the conditional approval of man. You cannot be truly humble until you have a deep understanding of how much you are loved. Paul said, *"The love of Christ compels us…"*[73] He acted as he did because he was gripped by the love of God. People thought he was crazy – he did not care. You won't be able to take a firm stand for Jesus until you are totally grounded by His love.

The key to continually saying "yes" to God is a matter of trusting Him in all things. Every time you think you have surrendered all, you will find yourself at another crossroads where He asks for an even deeper commitment to Him. All your desires to be noticed, to be somebody, or to do something great have to be given up to the Lord. Your dreams now have to be His dreams, the ones *He* places on your heart. To become a beloved disciple, all excess baggage will have to be eliminated, and most of that will include your*self*.

You must find your security in Christ alone. Only insecure people worry about how they appear to others. When you base your worth on your relationship with Christ, you are free from the evaluations of others. Isaiah 33:6 reminds you that He is your stability, security, and firm foundation. He is the only thing you live for. Whether you accomplish anything great or not, you are valuable to Him. That should bring great comfort.

Jesus at the Center

Pride brings striving – always trying to prove something, having to be someone you're not. Humility brings peace. Simplicity brings rest.

Pride will no longer drive you when you keep Jesus at the center of your life. Beloved disciples don't seek the approval or applause of others. They live for an audience of One. In 2 Corinthians 10:18, Paul reminds you that the only approval that counts is the Lord's approval. He said, *"We make it our goal to please Him."*[74]

God has assigned you a sphere of influence. Your goal is *"to stay within the sphere"* that He has set for you.[75] Sometimes God will test your faithfulness in small ministries before giving you bigger ones. Can He trust you with power and influence as He did Daniel? Or do you grab the spotlight and put yourself "front and center?" When you compare, compete, and overextend your reach, you will experience stress. Satan will try to tempt you to compromise your ministry to gain the approval of others. These are deadly traps.

Jesus' parable of the talents demonstrates that those who are faithful stewards of what the Master gives them will be given more.[76] If you are not faithful with what God entrusts to your care, no doubt He will postpone giving you more opportunities. A.W. Tozer said, *"If you are too big for a little place, you are too little for a big place."* Depth of character must come before height, breadth, or length of service.

Clothe Yourself with Humility

You can live your life with humility, but it won't happen by accident. Humility is something you must choose to put on and wear, the same way you put on clothes each day. First Peter 5:5 says, *"Clothe yourself with humility."* It is a state of mind that impacts your behavior.

I still find myself struggling with pride, despite my life experience and relationship with Jesus. It is far easier for me to write this chapter on humility than it is for me to practice it! And simply reading this chapter is not going to forever liberate you from pride either. I don't believe that any of us will gain complete freedom from this tendency on this side of heaven. The devil is always at work and pride is his favorite weapon. That's why humility is a constant struggle; a lesson you will have to relearn over and over.

Walking in humility requires *daily* submission to God and death to self, which is never any fun. There is nothing pleasant about it. To tear away the dear and tender stuff that life is made of is deeply painful. But the more you pamper your flesh the more it will demand of you. To begin to deal with pride, take the following steps:

- Confess the presence of pride in your life. Ask for His forgiveness for your vanity, compromise, and insincerity in the past. Ask the Holy Spirit to help you turn from pride.
- Remember God's faithfulness and how He has sustained you in the past. Your life belongs to Him now. Trust Him with it. Seek Him first above all else.
- Stop comparing yourself to others. Refuse to compete. Be vulnerable and honest about your weaknesses. Stop pretending you have it all together.
- Be willing to endure adversity that may serve to humble you. Accept that He may

not remove a "thorn in the flesh" to prevent further pride. God often attaches a major weakness to a major strength to keep your ego in check.

- Practice humility in simple ways – pick up the trash, acknowledge the cleaning and serving staff, be patient with weakness in others, compliment others. Don't think of any work as beneath you. To be utterly unnoticeable yourself makes you absolutely His.

Deliverance can only be found through the blood of Jesus. The Bible says, *"As the Spirit of the Lord works within us, we become more and more like Him and reflect His glory even more."*[77] It is the Holy Spirit's job to produce Christ's character in you. It would be a hopeless task if you had to save yourself from pride! Your part is to yield and trust. Only the indwelling of the humble Christ can make you humble. Ask that He accomplish that work in you.

Leave the Right Legacy

Our lives here on earth have been described as a vapor in the wind, a blink of an eye, a blade of grass, and as transient as a shadow. David pleaded, *"Lord, remind me how brief my time on earth will be. Remind me that my days are numbered, and that my life is fleeing away."*[78] Living for an earthly legacy is short-sighted. If you read enough history, you will find that the Christians who did the most for this present world were those who thought most of the next.

Applause dies, awards are forgotten, records are broken, and fame only lasts 15 minutes. Leaders, speakers, and writers come and go. Only He remains. Paul indicated his change in priorities when he said, *"I once thought all these things were so very important, but now I consider them worthless because of what Christ has done."*[79]

He is the reason we are here. You are not here for your own personal success. *"A pretentious, showy life is an empty life; a plain and simple life is a full life."*[80] He provides an infinitely higher and fulfilling purpose. When you live in light of eternity, your values are different. *"The world is fading away, along with everything it craves. But if you do the will of God, you will live forever."*[81] You find your life when you lose it for Him.

The devil promises you can have it all now...if you just compromise a bit. But you have a promised future with the King of Kings. You will eventually reign with Him in glory. Once you grasp that your true home is heaven, you stop trying to "have it all" here on earth. *"Friends, this world is not your home, so don't make yourselves cozy in it. Don't indulge your ego at the expense of your soul."*[82]

Godliness with Contentment

"Godliness with contentment is great gain."[83] This great gain is resting peacefully in His provision, whether that is much or little on this earth. Jesus found His perfect peace through absolute surrender to the Father's will. God honored His trust and obedience and has now exalted Him to the highest place of honor.

This is the same self-denial to which He calls you – to be an empty vessel that He can use however and whenever He wishes. Humility is not just a prayer posture; it is the core of your spiritual life. For a beloved disciple, *"He becomes greater; I become less."*[84] This level of humility is rarely taught or sought. Yes, beloved disciples are rare and unique… and counted as precious in His sight.

"Take a good look at my servant. I'm backing him completely. He's the one I chose, and I couldn't be more pleased with him. I've bathed him with My Spirit, My life. He'll set everything right. He won't call attention to what he does with loud speeches or gaudy parades. He won't brush aside the bruised and the hurt. He won't disregard the small and insignificant. But he'll steadily and firmly set things right. He won't tire out and quit. He won't be stopped until he's finished his work. To set things right on earth. Far-flung ocean islands wait expectantly for his teaching."[85]

◆

Prayer

Jesus, where would I be without You? Reveal to me the degree of pride in my life. Awaken in me the deepest depth of humility. Transform my greed into simplicity, my frustration into contentment, my envy to joy, and my worldly comforts to Your peace. Be exalted over my possessions. Be exalted over my relationships. Be exalted over my reputation. Be exalted over my comfort. I am determined that You are exalted above all. Forgive me for forfeiting my peace to pursue the riches of this world. Make my only desire to please You, even if it means I live in obscurity and my name is forgotten. Rise above my ambitions, my preferences, even my life itself.

Lord, forgive me for remaining focused on my own status, worth, and being "the best." I am sorry for being concerned about my own reputation and accomplishments. I have not been focused on Your glory. I will resist the devil and his schemes to steal, kill, and destroy through pride. I renounce the sin of jealousy and all that it entails – fear, control, selfishness, and restlessness. I repent of being offended and resentful when someone else receives more attention or seems more fruitful than I am. Help me submit to any bruising that is necessary to keep me humble. Let the hurting make me sweeter, deeper, and richer. Let me choose to be weak, to be nothing, to be low. Then the power of Christ can rest upon me.

Lord, forgive me for seeking the approval of others. I repent for being so intimidated by the opinions of others that I have remained silent and not boldly proclaimed who You are. Forgive me for pursuing popularity and perfection here on this earth to elevate my own status and self-worth. Forgive me for getting my security from the gifts You have given me rather than You. Lord, give me a passion for the truth that is stronger than my need to be praised. Help me lose the fear of losing out on something in this world. Help me loosen my grip on things that I want but don't really need. Help me to hold fast to Your path and Your ways.

Jesus, give me the ability to enjoy the gifts you have given me without striving for more. Keep me from working myself to death for man's approval or grasping for gain beyond what you intend for me. I want to find my identity in You alone, Jesus. Help me to understand my worth through Your eyes and by Your standards. Help me to recognize the unique qualities You have placed in me and appreciate them, without getting prideful in them. Give me the peace and security of knowing that I am fully loved and accepted by You. Free me from a self-focus and self-consciousness that will imprison my soul. Quiet the enemy's voice telling me lies; give me ears to hear Your voice telling me that it will not be my own perfection that gets me through this life, but Yours. Help me to see who You really are so that I can know who I really am.

Lord, do not enlarge my territory if You know I'm not going to be faithful in it. Don't give me a bigger ministry if I will lose You in the process. Don't answer my prayers to become strong if I will cease to rely on You for strength. Give me wisdom and grace in responding to those who scoff and ridicule Your work. Don't let me be easily provoked. Forgive me for all the ways I have defended myself and acted as my own protector to "right the wrongs" done to me. I step back and hand the outcome over to Your sovereign control. I trust that You will someday exalt me; I don't need to exalt myself! Give me peace in the night; a calm assurance that You are always defending me. No matter what happens in this life, Jesus, I am Your beloved.

STUDY

1. Read John 12:23-25 below. What does it mean to you?

> Jesus replied, "I tell you the truth, unless a kernel of wheat falls to the
> ground and dies, it remains only a single seed. But if it dies, it produces
> many seeds. The man who loves his life will lose it, while the man
> who hates his life in this world will keep it for eternal life."
>
> John 12:23-25

2. Matthew 23:12 says, *"For whoever exalts himself will be humbled, and whoever humbles himself will be exalted."* Proverbs 22:4 suggests, *"Humility and the fear of the LORD bring wealth and honor and life."* Why does the Bible contain so many paradoxes – being poor to become rich, giving to receive, dying to live, etc?

3. Read Mark 10:42-45 and Luke 9:24-25. How does this contradict the norms of our current culture?

4. What does it mean to *"clothe yourself"* with humility (see Colossians 3:12)?

Give Him All the Glory

5. When you wake up in the morning, where do your first thoughts go?

    a. The cares of this world – your agenda, work, schedule

    b. How well you are doing spiritually

    c. God's glory

6. How well are you living out 1 Corinthians 10:31?

So whether you eat or drink or whatever you do, do it all for the glory of God.

1 Corinthians 10:31

---

7. How would your life look different if your *only* desire was to glorify God? What keeps God's glory from being your only ambition?

Pride Comes Before a Fall

8. In which of the following ways has pride impacted your life?

☐ thinking of myself more highly than I should

☐ considering myself better than others because of my abilities or accomplishments

☐ feeling my needs are more important than someone else's needs

☐ being driven to attain recognition through titles or positions

☐ thinking I am more humble, spiritual, or devoted than others

☐ being concerned about getting the credit I deserve

☐ being more concerned about pleasing people (or not offending them) than pleasing God

☐ finding it hard to admit when I am wrong

☐ being too busy doing "important" things to take time to do little things for others

☐ trying to control or change others instead of changing myself

☐ trying to do things in my own strength rather than relying on the power of the Holy Spirit

☐ leaning too much on my own understanding rather than seeking God's guidance on a matter

☐ having a stronger desire to do my own will rather than God's

Confess each one now and choose to humble yourself before Him.

Thank Him for forgiving you.

Choose to place all your confidence in Him and not in your own flesh.

9. Proverbs 8:13 says, *"I hate pride and arrogance, evil behavior and perverse speech."* Why does God hate pride so much?

10. What warning do these verses have in common: Isaiah 63:10 and 1 Peter 5:5?

Comparison, Competition, and Jealousy

11. In John 21:21-22, what emotion do you think Peter was experiencing? Was it jealousy? Have you ever felt like asking a similar question – *"why them"* or *"what about me?"*

12. Do you feel jealous of anyone else's success? Who represents "competition" to you? If one of your current struggles involves comparison, competition, or jealousy, what will lead to freedom?

13. What does 1 Peter 5:6 say is the answer to our quest for significance?

> *Humble yourselves, therefore, under God's mighty hand,*
> *that He may lift you up in due time.*
>
> 1 Peter 5:6

14. Where does your self-worth come from? Is it difficult to describe your value in terms other than your performance or others' opinions of you?

15. What is the difference between low self-esteem and humility? (Hint: low self-esteem is still preoccupation with self).

The Approval of Man

16. Whose approval matters most to you right now? Whose opinion do you value most? If you look to others for approval, who is really in control of your life?

17. Describe a time when "fear of man" controlled your actions or behavior. Where, or in what ways, are you currently feeling this pressure now?

18. Jesus didn't seem at all concerned about His reputation or the perception of others. The firm stand of Jesus made certain groups and individuals want to crucify Him. What beliefs might make you unpopular today?

19. How do you think Jesus' insistence on the Truth impacted His disciple's strength or resolve? What did they learn from seeing Him walk with freedom and confidence in His own identity?

20. Second Peter 3:3-13 warns us that many scoffers will rise up vocally in the last days – similar to those who doubted the destruction of the flood in Noah's day. How might this affect you? Are you willing to look foolish to others? In the midst of feeling outnumbered, do you think you will ever question whether your minority position is wrong?

Leave the Right Legacy

21. How do you spend most of your time? Your money? Examine your checkbook and calendar if necessary. What are some of the reasons you do these things (e.g., to gain the approval of others, to be a success, to honor Christ, to fulfill someone else's expectation, to help people)? How many of your activities are designed to help you "get ahead" in this world?

22. How should a believer in Christ define success? What do you most desire to be "rich" in?

23. If everyone understood that life on this earth is really *preparation for eternity*, how would we act differently?

24. Matthew 6:19-21 addresses the futility in storing up earthly treasures.

Identify some examples of things that will pass away:

Identify some examples of things that have eternal value:

25. Revelation 4:10 says all the elders *lay their crowns before the throne.* How can we keep our "crowns" (achievements, gifts, responsibilities, unique identities) cast before the throne while still here on earth?

> # SPIRITUAL MARKER
>
> ## wisdom

WORSHIP

Jesus at the Center [Darlene Zschech]

Lord, You're Beautiful [Jesus Culture]

Legacy [Nichole Nordeman]

Be Thou My Vision [Various Artists]

Christ the Rock [Kim Walker-Smith and Skyler Smith]

Steal My Show [tobyMac]

He Knows My Name [Francesca Battistelli]

The Cause of Christ [Kari Jobe]

O Praise the Name [Hillsong]

Holy One [Rush of Fools]

More Like Jesus [Passion featuring Kristian Stanfill]

Only Jesus [Casting Crowns]

None but Jesus [Darlene Zschech]

I Will Look Up [Elevation]

When It's All Been Said and Done [Robin Mark]

HUMBLE YOURSELVES IN THE SIGHT OF THE LORD AND HE WILL LIFT YOU UP

JAMES 4:10

REST BESIDE STILL WATERS

Beloved disciple, you have traveled long and far. We are nearing the end of our journey together. Now it is important to remember to rest. *"In returning and rest you shall be saved; in quietness and confidence shall be your strength."*[1] While the world sees strength in action; God says your strength will come from quietness and rest.

"You are my hiding place."[2]

You will not be able to fulfill your earthly destiny if you don't take care of your physical and mental health with periods of rest. God took a rest after creating the world.[3] Jesus needed periods of quiet communion with the Father, away from the noise, crowds, and activity.[4] Surely you need time alone with Him too. You need to regularly take a "Selah," a mental pause that allows you to separate yourself from the ordinary.

There's no denying that life in this world is stressful! Most of us are overwhelmed by our own calendar and phone. We believe we are not productive unless we are multitasking and juggling several commitments at the same time. In fact, we often hear, *"Don't just sit there. Do something!"* But God would say, *"Don't just do something. Sit here awhile and rest with Me!"*

Your relationship with Jesus must come before anything else. Don't miss His precious presence by frantically trying to please Him through your work. In her desire to minister to Jesus, Martha missed out on His friendship. Many Christians still worship work today. He will use you, yes, but not destroy you in the process. You may destroy yourself if you lack discernment or fail to listen to His guidance about which assignments you are to take. You will soon get burned out and defeated if He isn't your source of strength and stability.

Set your heart at rest and sit at His feet. Carve out areas of your life where you are not striving – open spaces where your soul is available for any sweet thing He wishes to share. Allow intervals in which you do nothing, think nothing, and plan nothing. Your mind will be refreshed and renewed in the absence of strain. Only He can replenish what the world takes from you. You will need these times of intimate rest as He has deeper lessons to teach you. It is not a place of stagnation, but a place of glorious unfolding. You emerge stronger, braver, and more loving than you were before.

Returning to Rest

Jesus said to His disciples, *"Come with me by yourselves to a quiet place and get some rest."*[5] *"Learn from Me, for I am gentle and lowly of heart, and you will find rest for your souls."*[6]

The physical and psychological benefits of rest should not be underestimated. Rest impacts your well-being, productivity, and ability to think. There is a reason that surgeons, pilots, and truck drivers have mandated periods of rest – lives are at stake. A landmark study by Dr. Ericsson demonstrated that elite performers – including musicians, athletes, actors, and competitive chess players – maximized their achievements through predictable patterns of rest. They practiced their craft in focused sessions no longer than 90 minutes. Then they would take a break to ensure complete recovery. They also got more than 8 hours of sleep each night.[7]

The average American gets only 6-7 hours of sleep each night. With all the things you need to accomplish in a day, sacrificing sleep may seem like a good way to find some extra time. But rest is not a luxury; it is a necessity. Sleep deprivation raises blood pressure, increases inflammation, increases your risk for heart disease and stroke, and raises the likelihood of catching a cold or the flu.[8]

Your physical, mental, and spiritual health are all closely intertwined. When your body is completely exhausted, your attitude is affected. Physical weariness can turn into depression, despair, and feelings of hopelessness. Your physical and mental state can then affect your diet. Lack of sleep not only increases hunger, but causes you to crave foods high in calories, sugar, and carbohydrates. This kind of diet can then contribute to anxiety and fear. And that mental stress has been linked to heart disease, high blood pressure, digestive problems, cancer, and other degenerative diseases.

John wrote, *"Dear friend, I pray that you may enjoy good health and that all may go well with you, even as your soul is getting along well."*[9] As long as your spirit resides in a physical body, it will be impacted by its condition. Where there is disease in your heart and soul, there will be disease in your body. There was no sickness in Jesus. Consider how amazingly worry-free His life was! He never got caught up in the frenzy of activity that we so often see today.

Rest for Your Soul

True rest for your soul is not found in books, not gained through human effort, and not provided by New Age gurus. Rest comes from an **absence of inner conflict** – a lack of panic and confusion; a refusal to be anxious and afraid. *"For anxiety produces tension, and tension erodes joy; and when joy is gone, victory is lost, faith is weakened, and spontaneity is destroyed. The spirit falls ill."*[10]

Only when your mind is free from anxiety can your body be at rest. Worry, fear, bitterness, and anger are poison to the soul. Psalm 37:8 says, *"Do not fret – it only causes harm."* Your physical health is a gift from God, entrusted to you to be used for His purposes and for His glory. It grieves Him when you waste your health on toxic emotions. He commanded us not to worry.[11] Not about clothes, not about food, not about friends, not about money, not about the weather, and not about the future. But you may be thinking, "I have to worry about this stuff. You don't understand what I'm going through..." Jesus knows your circumstances better than you do and He says *not* to worry to the point where they become your primary focus.

"Worry is believing God won't get it right. Bitterness is believing God got it wrong."

Timothy Kellor

Anxiety and worry are the early warning signs that God has been pushed to the side in your life. Much of what disturbs your rest is actually sin, even though you don't recognize it as such. Fretting comes from a determination to get your own way. Worry means that you don't trust that God is taking care of the details of your life. Every time you lose ground with God it is because you have allowed the *"cares of this world"* to take His place.[12]

Jesus said, *"Come to Me, all you who are weary and burdened, and I will give you rest."*[13] When you cease all your striving and give your life entirely to Him, *then* you will know freedom and release. You don't need to go through life confused and tired. There is one place you can go for direction and rest. The moment your calm is broken, run immediately to Jesus. Be on guard against any unrest in your mind; any disturbance in your soul. Those are the times when the enemy can gain a foothold. No matter who or what upsets you, stop everything until complete calm is restored through Him. This might mean clearing your calendar to read His Word. It might mean asking others to join you in prayer. It might mean sitting quietly until you can surrender, forgive, pray, or worship.

He desires to take the tensions of life away from you. Where there is confusion and chaos, He will reorder and reorganize. There is no point in worrying about what lies ahead and whether you will have the strength to endure it. He will provide the strength when you need it. Jesus said, *"Therefore do not worry about tomorrow, for tomorrow will worry about its own things. Sufficient for the day is its own trouble."*[14] You can bear the weight of 24 hours, nothing more. Adding the weight of years past and fear of the days ahead will cause you to stumble. No one has ever effectively worried themselves out of any crisis. Surrender your worries so that He can work them out on your behalf. Hand them over – again and again and again. Ask for quick conviction when you take them up again. The more time He has them in His hands, the better off you will be.

The moment you put Jesus back in the center of your life, you will experience peace. You can see things from His point of view, interpret circumstances as He does, and respond as He would. The Bible says, *"It's wonderful what happens when Christ displaces worry at the center of your life."*[15]

"Let the peace of God rule in your hearts."[16]

Peace Like A River

God wants to provide consistent, ongoing peace in your life. The only way to get His peace is through constant connection with Him. Isaiah 26:3 says that those whose minds are steadfast and trusting will be *"kept in perfect **peace**."* Isaiah 32:17 says the *"fruit of righteousness will be **peace**; the effect of righteousness will be quietness and confidence forever."* And Isaiah 48:18 says, *"If only you had paid attention to My commands, your **peace** would have been like a river, your righteousness like the waves of the sea."* In other words, peace comes *after* things like surrender, trust, righteousness, and obedience.

His peace is provided to *"guard your heart and mind."*[17] When you get off track, you lose your sense of peace. You can't always put your finger on exactly why, but you know something is not right. This is called a "check in your spirit." In times of uncertainty, do not go against this feeling of restraint. When you lose your peace about something, it is the Holy Spirit's way of guarding you against error or deception. When you begin to tune in to the presence or absence of His peace, you will be amazed at the consistency with which He is guiding you.

The things that are most likely to threaten your peace are busyness, bitterness, idols, jealousy, fear, rebellion, and pride. You have been instructed to *"lay aside every weight"* and the sin that so easily entangles you.[18] How? Surrender brings peace (Step 1). Laying down your Isaac brings peace (Step 2). Forgiveness brings peace (Step 3). Prayer brings peace (Step 4). Gratitude brings peace (Step 5). Worship brings peace (Step 6). Your protective armor brings peace (Step 7). In other words, becoming a beloved disciple should bring more peace! When you come to Jesus, His peace should flow through you like a river – carrying away bitterness, pain, and pride. Let Him bring you to rest beside the still waters.

Psalm 23

The still waters described in Psalm 23 have brought peace to many beloved disciples through the centuries. David was a young shepherd, so he used imagery of God as a shepherd to express His loving care in writing this passage. Jesus referred to Himself as the *"Good Shepherd."*[19] A good shepherd knows each sheep by name as each one must be personally led to green pastures and still waters. To know that Jesus is deeply concerned about you, as an individual, should bring great comfort and peace.

For a short period of time, we raised sheep on our farm as I was growing up. The baby lambs were just precious. Bottle feeding some of them was the highlight of my day. But sheep are a lot of work. They need endless attention. They are easily agitated. The slightest disturbance frightens them to the point of stampeding right out of their pens. They are stubborn and impulsive. They are prone to disease and injury. They must be moved to new grazing grounds frequently. Their wool coats need to be tended regularly. On top of all the other animals and crops we maintained, we soon tired of the commitment the sheep required. Thank goodness Jesus never tires of us. He is always working on our behalf to ensure we benefit under His care.[20]

I Shall Not Want; He Makes Me Lie Down in Green Pastures

It is the responsibility of the shepherd to ensure that his flock is free from want or need so that they can lie down and rest peacefully. It is his duty to ensure that the sheep are well fed and safe from predators. He is the one who makes it possible for them to rest, relax, and be content. The same is true for you. You can rest in the assurance that your Shepherd is watching over all your affairs. It is only His presence that can dispel panic and fear. He makes all the difference.

"For God has not given us the spirit of fear; but of power, and of love, and of a sound mind."[21] A sound mind is at peace – it is not consumed with anxiety and fear of the unknown. It is the Holy Spirit that brings serenity and strength in the midst of frustrating and frightening circumstances. When you permit Him to take over in the situation, He soothes frazzled nerves and restores wasted energy. Because you sense His activity on your behalf, you can settle into a place of peaceful contentment. You can lie down and rest.

David was not referring to material wealth when he made the statement, *"I shall not want."* He was simply suggesting that he would never lack the care of His Shepherd. Many of God's cherished sheep are asked to endure hardship, disaster, or the struggle to stay afloat financially. But it is possible to maintain a calm assurance in Jesus despite a difficult situation. Paul said, *"I have learned to be content whatever the circumstances. I know what it is to be in need, and I know what it is to have plenty. I have learned the secret of being content in any and every situation, whether well fed or hungry, whether living in plenty or in want. I can do everything through Him who gives me strength."*[22]

One of the distinguishing marks of a beloved disciple should be a peaceful, quiet contentment. You have ceased any striving, competing, and quarreling to get ahead of others. You have forgiven others and no longer feel a need to defend your own rights. You have laid your idols down that consume needless energy and attention. Your eyes are fixed on the glory of the Lord rather than your own. You recognize that whoever is last now will be first later. A humble heart walking closely with Jesus can relax and be content to let the rest of the world go by.

He Leads Me Beside Still Waters; He Restores My Soul

There is something about sitting by a babbling brook, a still lake, or the gentle waves of the ocean that brings peace and comfort. *"Deep calls to deep"* and quiets our soul.[23]

Water is the source of life. For sheep, water determines their health, strength, and vitality. If they are not led to fresh clean water, they become desperate enough to drink from polluted water holes that contain parasites and disease. The shepherd knows where the best drinking places are. In fact, he is often the one who has prepared them.

Jesus declared, *"If anyone is thirsty, let him come to Me and drink."*[24] And He told the woman at the well, *"Everyone who drinks this water will be thirsty again, but whoever drinks the water I give them will never thirst. Indeed, the water I give them will become in them a spring of water welling up to eternal life."*[25]

To drink means to "take in or accept." To drink of Jesus means to assimilate Him into your life. The problem is that so many who are thirsty drink from polluted watering holes instead. They try to find fulfillment in careers, achievements, adventures, social activities, unhealthy relationships, and lusts of the flesh. God said to Jeremiah, *"My people have forsaken Me, the spring of living water, and have dug their own cisterns, broken cisterns that cannot hold water."*[26] Jesus purposely created you with a need that only He can meet. Satan will continually cast idols before you – don't settle for anything less than Jesus!

Isaiah declared that God's intention for believers is that our souls be well-watered:

- *"Waters shall burst forth in the wilderness, and streams in the desert. The parched ground shall become a pool, and the thirsty land springs of water."*[27]
- *"I will open rivers in desolate heights, and fountains in the midst of the valleys; I will make the wilderness a pool of water, and the dry land springs of water."*[28]
- *"The Lord will satisfy your soul in drought and strengthen your bones; you shall be like a watered garden, and like a spring of water, whose waters do not fail."*[29]

A beloved disciple who takes the time to soak in the refreshing waters of Jesus comes away calm, composed, and able to cope with life's complexities. Hope is restored and life finds new beginning. In fact, the word *restore* means "1. To bring back into existence or use. 2. To bring back to its original state. 3. To make restitution, to give back, to return." When God *"restores your soul,"* it means that He can return you to the state or condition you were in before you strayed from His perfect path for you. He has the power to restore whatever has been lost, whether that loss was your own fault or the fault of enemy. How awesome is that!

He Guides Me in Paths of Righteousness for His Name's Sake

Sheep are notorious for getting lost. They are easily led astray by the slightest distraction. We all, *"like sheep, have gone astray, each of us has turned to his own way."*[30] Our "own way" means doing whatever we want. Most of us can be as stubborn as sheep. Carrying out our own plans and ideas is the opposite of a surrendered life under the control of the Shepherd. We continue this self-destructive behavior even though it is clearly to our own detriment. Proverbs 14:12 reminds us, *"There is a way that seems right to man, but in the end, it leads to death."*

Jesus knew we would need a lot of guidance and He clearly outlined the cost of being led by Him. Self-interest cannot exist in the life of a beloved disciple. This makes the cost prohibitive for most people. Independence and pride are difficult obstacles to overcome. We don't want to deny ourselves, take up our cross, or lay our Isaacs down. We don't want to be told what to do. Of course, most would passionately deny this. We insist we are "following the Lord." But as far as truly living it out, there are few that forsake all to be led in *"paths of righteousness."*

Becoming a beloved disciple entails a whole new set of attitudes – it is not the natural, normal way a person would typically live. Taking the back seat, laying down your rights, enduring criticism, and renouncing self-importance are all forward movements onto higher ground with God. Most of what constitutes becoming a beloved disciple lies in the surrender of your will. Surrender is obedience. You do what He asks you to do. You go where He invites you to go. You say what He wants you to say. You react to every situation in a way that maintains His reputation. All this is for *"His Name's sake."*

This way of living may seem impossibly difficult. And it would be if you had to depend on your own strength. But He works in you *"to will and to do His good pleasure."*[31] He makes it possible for those who are willing to be willing. He is the one who breaks up the hard ground of your heart. He clears out the thorns of unbelief. He tears out the roots of bitterness and pride. Then He sows seeds from His precious Word. And He waters them with the Holy Spirit to bring forth fruits of love, joy, peace, patience, kindness, goodness, faithfulness, gentleness, and self-control. He is the one who prunes and cultivates your life, making it rich and productive.

The Holy Spirit is constantly at work to change you into the image of Jesus. *"For all of us are being transformed into the same image from one degree of glory to another…this comes from the Lord who is the Spirit."*[32] This process of changing you to be more like Jesus is called sanctification. It is the pursuit of holiness and God's will for every believer. *"God wants you to live a pure life."*[33] Not to become a perfect specimen of holiness to be put on display for others to admire, but to become one with Jesus – keeping your body, soul, and spirit for His purposes alone. For this to become a reality requires the work of God in your life. Paul prayed, *"May God Himself, the God of peace, sanctify you through and through."*[34]

Even Though I Walk Through the Valley; Your Rod and Staff Comfort Me

As sheep make the long trek from one grazing ground to another (often with a change of season), they stay in constant contact with the shepherd. He must protect each one from the dangers of harsh weather, poisonous plants, and predators. His "rod" is a weapon of power, authority, and defense. It is not used to beat the sheep, but rather placed alongside the animal with gentle pressure to guide it through a dangerous or difficult route.

The rod and staff can symbolize the guiding authority of the Holy Spirit in your life. While it can be a sweet comfort for your protection, it can also be used for gentle correction. It can separate truth from error amid confusing chaos. It can convict your conscience when you are going astray. It can also be used to pull you close for intimate examination. In this way, you are kept under the control and authority of the Shepherd who guides you in paths of righteousness. It is He that quietly, lovingly, and tirelessly says, *"This is the way – walk in it."*[35]

Over your life, you will be carefully led through some dark and treacherous valleys. Notice that in this Psalm, David didn't say "I die in the valley" or "I remain in the valley." He said, *"I **walk through** the valley."* The Shepherd's rod and staff will comfort you along the way. Jesus reminds you, *"Surely I am with you always."*[36] With this assurance, your soul can remain at rest.

Most of us do not want valleys in our lives; instead, we yearn for "mountaintop" experiences. We long to live in intense intimacy with Jesus, above the daily striving of life. But we have no idea how to get there. We don't simply get "airlifted" to this higher ground. Nor is it a straight shot to the top. When herding sheep, you get to higher ground by slowly winding (in a circular fashion) through the valleys in a gradual climb. Every mountain has valleys, ravines, and gulches. It is through these that you make your way higher.

The question is not how many valleys there will be in your life, nor how deep they are, but how you react to them. Your disappointments do not need to bring death and destruction. Each trial can be a trail that leads to higher ground with God. Thank Him for the difficult days, knowing that He is there with you and gently leading you upward. Even in the darkest valley, you will sense His guiding presence and comfort. You can remain calm and confident that all things are under His control.

It is only the beloved disciple who comprehends this that can encourage the weaker ones around him. Just as water flows through the deepest ravines, the life of God will flow through the valleys that have been carved out in your life. It is through these channels that you can minister to others. The deeper your valleys, the more blessings they can hold.

In the end, you will look back over your life and see how He has guided and sustained you in every crisis. You will notice how your faith grew in the darkest hours. Over and over, He will have proved His care and compassion. And because He has led you through before, you trust that He will do it again, and again, and again. Your confidence in Him is multiplied. You comprehend His deep concern for your welfare. You are His.

You Prepare a Table Before Me; You Anoint My Head with Oil

The high plateaus of sheep ranges around the world are often referred to as "mesas" – also a word for "tables." David was likely referring to the broad grasslands typically used for summer sheep grazing when he said, *"You prepare a table before me."* The shepherd takes great care to prepare these tablelands by making several advance expeditions before the sheep arrive. He will find the best bedding grounds, prepare fresh watering holes, remove any poisonous weeds, hunt down predators, and supply salt and minerals in areas where the grass and vegetation look weak.

Despite a shepherd's best efforts to prepare a place of safety on the mountaintop plains, predators can still attack, weeds can still grow, and fierce storms can still arise without warning. And so it is with you. Your attentive Shepherd goes before you in every situation, anticipating what dangers you might encounter, and praying that your faith will not fail despite your circumstances. He makes every possible provision to provide a "way of escape" when you must cope with temptation and sin.[37] It is His advance preparation and watchful eye that prevent you from falling prey to the enemy or getting consumed with panic and fear. The Shepherd is your one sure place of safety. Walk close to Him so He can protect you. He applies the "oil" of His Spirit to your mind and makes the rough places smooth. Read His Word. Pray and worship. Spend time sitting with Him. Listen to what He says.

Jesus told us that He came to bring us life – abundant life.[38] Nothing pleases Him more than to see you enjoying the tablelands He has prepared for you. His heart is to see you living on a higher plane. He delights in watching you walk in holiness, peaceful serenity, and contentment in His care. To enjoy this tableland is to experience the Savior's love for you.

You should appreciate the advance preparation required to arrange such a table for you. When you come to the "Lord's table" to partake of communion, consider the great personal sacrifice required for Him to prepare this place of freedom for you. He traded incredible splendor for ridicule, mocking, shame, and malicious charges that lead to His own slaughter. This divine level of self-sacrifice is staggering. He literally *"laid down His life"* for His sheep.[19]

Surely Goodness and Mercy Will Follow Me

In Psalm 23, David proudly exclaims that his life is securely in the Shepherd's capable hands. Can you say the same? Even in difficult times, you should be able to rest assured that His goodness and mercy follow you. You will not always understand what He is doing. Your natural inclination might be to worry or ask "why." But if you follow Him long enough, you will eventually see that His tenderness, mercy, kindness, and goodness have never left you. You trust that no difficulty or disaster will arise without some eventual good coming out of the chaos. This is a firm foundation of faith.

All this care, concern, watchfulness, protection, and sacrifice are the result of His love. He loves His sheep. He loves His work. He loves His role as Your Shepherd. Hopefully, you have become convinced of this love by now. You love Him because He first loved you.

He had a purpose in mind when He called you and set you apart in His special flock. He wants you to pass along this goodness and mercy to others. The overflow of loving kindness should not stagnate in your own life. It can benefit others. Bring peace wherever you go. Practice forgiveness and mercy. Share your wisdom and discernment. Demonstrate gratitude and joy. Plant seeds of prayer and worship at every opportunity. Spread hope.

I Will Dwell in the House of the Lord Forever

A sheep who is completely satisfied with its owner has no desire to leave. It knows it will flourish under infinite care and protection. And you can boast about how good Your Shepherd is! You should be eager to express your confidence in Christ. You can look back over your life at the remarkable ways He has provided for your welfare. You can share your testimony of how He has brought you safely through every trial and temptation. You should freely and boldly state that you belong to Him. By your contentment, you should demonstrate what a distinct advantage it is to belong to His flock.

David wanted nothing more than to remain in the presence of God. The Amplified version of the last verse in Psalm 23 says, *"I will dwell in the presence of the Lord forever."* It is the presence of the Shepherd that ensures abundant life, green pastures, still waters, and plentiful tablelands. There will be freedom from fear, protection from enemies, and places of restful quiet when you belong to Him. And this will continue for eternity!

There are incredible things in store for His flock of beloved sheep. The Bible says,

"God has reserved a priceless inheritance for His children. It is kept in heaven for you, pure and undefiled, beyond the reach of change and decay."[39] And Paul said, *"I want you to realize what a rich and glorious inheritance He has given to His people:"*[40]

- You will dwell with Him forever.[41]
- You will be transformed into His likeness.[42]
- You will be freed from sin, pain, and suffering.[43]
- You will share in God's glory.[44]
- You will be rewarded and assigned positions of authority and service.[45]
- You will wear the crown of life.[46]

Let your heart be encouraged. Jesus told John, *"I am the Alpha and the Omega, the Beginning and the End…who is and who was and who is to come, the Almighty."*[47] You stand on the threshold of a new heaven and a new earth.[48] It has never been more important that you recognize and hear His voice. You need direction like never before. Truly you are in the world, but not of this world. He has fit you for the path of holiness. He is doing a work of righteousness for the coming days. He has begun a good work in you and promises to complete it. You shall come forth as gold, having been tried by fire. You will flourish and be made fruitful.

This is a time of great outpouring of the Spirit.[49] This is the day of preparation for the coming of the Lord. None of your training has been in vain. We will soon be gathered together with Him. Scoffers and doubters will be swept away. Much of the world remains lukewarm. Half-heartedness will not do for you at this point. Stand firm. Never waver. Hebrews 10:35 says, *"Do not throw away your confidence; it will be richly rewarded. You need to persevere so that when you have done the will of God, you will receive what He has promised."* His Word shall be fulfilled. Keep your eye on the prize. Let your stability be apparent to all.

"I have fought the good fight, I have finished the race, I have kept the faith."[50]

◆

Finishing the Race

Something made you choose this study and persevere in the journey thus far. Jesus is drawing you closer to Himself. He wants your life, character, and personality to be as beautiful as He envisioned you when He created you – before this world tainted you. Let Him remake and remold what has not developed properly. *"He will see to it that everything is finished correctly."*[51] Steadily, and without conscious effort, you will be transformed.

You may be saying, "Hurry up and make me mature." But remember this is a process. Becoming a beloved disciple takes days, months, and years of an unwavering desire to conquer self. Don't get discouraged if things don't change overnight. God said, *"These things I plan won't happen right away. Slowly, steadily, surely, the time approaches when the vision will be fulfilled. If it seems slow, do not despair, for these things will surely come to pass. Just be patient! They will not be overdue a single day."*[52] Given that He has eternity in mind, He is not in a hurry. Be patient. Endure to the end.

Like the sun coming up in the morning, little by little light overtakes the darkness. If you sit and watch it, it seems to take forever, and you barely see any progress. In the same way, spiritual growth is often imperceptible. Don't think it is taking too long or that it's too late. Don't take matters into your own hands. The Bible says, *"Our lives gradually become brighter and more beautiful as God enters our lives and we become like Him."*[53] God only allowed the Israelites to take over their Promised Land *"little by little"* so they wouldn't be overwhelmed.[54] In the same way, He will work in incremental and orderly steps in your own life. You don't need to look too far ahead. One step at a time. Months from now you'll look back and perceive all the ways God has been transforming you, all because you are cooperating with the Spirit's work in your life.

God is more interested in your strength and stability than in how fast you are growing. When you are ready for the next step, He will bring new truth into your life. Even after the disciples had walked closely with their Rabbi for three years, they still had much to learn – more than they could *"now bear."*[55] Jesus had more to teach them, but they were not ready to receive it. Jesus knew that the Holy Spirit would have to continue to gradually guide the disciples in all they needed to know.

It's also important to understand that we cannot change ourselves by ourselves. We trust God to do the work in us that needs to be done. There are many fears, strongholds, and worries that used to paralyze me that no longer do. But I didn't renew my own mind. He did it. I just told Him when I was ready and willing for Him to work on each area. I can't pinpoint exactly when things changed, I just know that I feel and respond differently than I did in the past. And He is not finished with me yet. I am still somewhere along this journey with you. There is more work to be done!

You are still a work in progress and your spiritual transformation will take the rest of your life. *"I am sure that God who began the good work within you will keep right on helping you grow in His grace until His task within you is finally finished on that day when Jesus Christ returns.*"[56] He will strengthen you until you are able to carry heavier loads and withstand more intense pressures. He will continually say, "Come up even higher." Through a multitude of tests and refining fire, you will develop the characteristics of Christ (our spiritual markers throughout this study):

1. FAITH	**6. HUMILITY**
2. HOPE	**7. DISCERNMENT**
3. MERCY	**8. LOVE**
4. PATIENCE	**9. WISDOM**
5. JOY	**10. PEACE**

With these spiritual markers evident in your life, He can assign you critical missions, confident that you are equipped to fulfill them. You will be unashamed to testify about Him, for you will know the words you speak are not your own.[57] You will be able to distinguish between truth and error. You will speak the truth in love. You will rebuke the enemy in Jesus' Name. You will bring healing to others. With God in your midst, *"you shall not be moved."*[58] You are building an unshakeable faith!

"You have been faithful with a few things; I will put you in charge
of many things. Come and share your master's happiness!"[59]

Well Done, Good and Faithful Servant

The ten steps outlined in this study represent a series of progressive forward movements that continually shift the focus off yourself and onto Jesus. Any area not fully surrendered will be the place He goes to work. To summarize our journey, here are ten transformations found in the life of a beloved disciple:

1. Your Life is Not Your Own	give up control over every detail of your life
2. Lay Your Isaac Down	surrender every idol (keep Him first), accept every circumstance as ordained by God
3. Forgive 70 x 7	show others the same mercy you have been shown
4. Pray Without Ceasing	walk in constant contact with your Savior
5. Count Your Blessings	cultivate an attitude of gratitude
6. Worship in Spirit and Truth	give Him all the glory
7. Put Your Armor On	depend on Him for Truth, your identity, and protection from evil
8. Go and Make Disciple	keep your focus on God's activity around you
9. Humble Yourself in the Sight of the Lord	seek first His Kingdom and His righteousness
10. Rest Beside Still Waters	dwell in the presence of the Lord forever, knowing you are His beloved

Beloved disciples exist all over this earth. Every now and then you will recognize one. Their very voices and faces are different: stronger, quieter, happier, peaceful, and more radiant. They do not look like the "religious people" you find in ceremonial services. There is a real giving up of self. They hold nothing tightly. They love others more but need them less. They usually seem to have a lot of time; you wonder where it comes from. They do not draw attention to themselves. They begin where many leave off in their pursuit of Jesus.

He wants to be Lord of your life. Because He loves you, His will is always best for you. Any adjustment He asks you to make will be for your good in the end. Allow Him to interrupt your life anytime He wants. Your steps should be *"ordered by the Lord."*[60] He is inviting you to join Him for eternal purposes. You are no longer working for God according to *your* abilities, *your* interests, *your* goals, or *your* preferences. Your ways will not bear lasting fruit. Apart from Him, you can do nothing. But *everything* is possible with God.[61]

Jesus has challenged you to pray so that you learn to lean on Him. He has encouraged you to rejoice at all times so that you do not get swallowed up in anxiety and fear. He has asked you to forgive so that your heart is free to receive His forgiveness. He has instructed you to remain humble to keep you from the pride which precedes a fall. He has circumcised your heart so that you are free from worldly entanglements which hinder your love for Him. He has taught you how to use spiritual armor in defense against your enemy. He has given you eyes to see and ears to hear His call to serve those around you. Put all of these into practice. Paul said, *"Practice these things. Devote your life to them so that everyone can see your progress."*[62]

This study has merely been a tool to guide you into deeper intimacy with Jesus. But classes, study guides, and prepared programs cannot take the place of a relationship with Him. It is extremely important to understand that your relationship with Jesus overrides everything else. It is not work for the Lord, suffering in the name of the Lord, witnessing for the Lord, teaching Sunday School for the Lord, or praying three hours a day to the Lord. A list of rules cannot change a human heart; only a radical relationship with Jesus can transform your life. Your connection to Jesus must become real to you. He can become just as personal and dear to you as He was to John, the beloved disciple.

The Holy Spirit does the work as you surrender more and more to Him. This study is not doing the work. I am not doing the work. I can only pray that you pursue Jesus passionately. I pray you find your satisfaction in Him alone. I pray you surrender all to Him. I pray you grow in the knowledge of His deep love for you. I pray you crucify the flesh and let the Spirit thrive. I pray you put the devil on alert. I pray you trust the Lord more every day. I pray that you learn to relax and rest in His power and faithfulness. I pray you find new ways to love God and new opportunities to love others. I pray you glorify Him by all you do and say. I pray that you worship Him with all your heart, soul, mind, and strength. I pray you experience His peace. I pray you enjoy the crowning gift of His presence forever. And having been in His presence, you are forever changed…

"May the God of peace equip you with everything good for doing
His will, and may He work in us what is pleasing to Him, through
Jesus Christ, to whom be glory for ever and ever. Amen."[63]

◆

Prayer

Jesus, You have captured my heart. You have called me friend and taken me into Your flock of precious sheep. You rescued me because You delighted in me. You have chosen me. I choose You. Now I rest in You. I am safe with You. Though mountains may shake all around me, Your love can never be moved. Help me to comprehend the breadth and width and height and depth of it. I pray that I will be firmly rooted and established in that love.

You are the God of heaven and earth. There is none beside You. I rest in the knowledge of Your powerful reality. I will testify to what I have seen and heard in these days since You have drawn me closer to You. Show me more! Never stop teaching me more of who You are. I want to be filled with the fullness of You. I want to declare Your power, Your goodness, Your mercy, and Your love to others. I want to scatter everywhere the fragrance of You.

I am not yet fully mature, but I want to make every effort to take hold of the life You have given me. I want to be an instrument in Your hand, set apart for such a time as this. Do not abandon the work You have started in me. I want to honor You with every part of my life. I turn from evil and choose to pursue righteousness, love, and peace. I choose to remain grounded in faith, not moving one inch from the truth and hope of the Gospel. I forget what is behind and look forward to all You have planned for me. I pursue the prize promised by Your heavenly calling. Your grace abounds in me so that I have everything I need to accomplish every good work You have prepared for me. I stand secure in knowing that You equip those You call.

I will run this race with endurance. I will keep my eyes on You, the author and finisher of my faith. I will soar with wings like eagles. I will run and not grow weary. I will walk and not faint. I won't lose heart. This world will soon pass away, but You will remain forever. Soon the day will come when You Yourself will descend from heaven with a shout, with the voice of the archangel, and the trumpet of God. I look forward to the day I will meet You face to face. Then I will always be with You. I will worship in Your very presence. No more sorrow, no more tears. I press on knowing that what lies ahead will be worth it all. How awesome it is that no eye has seen, and no ear has heard what You have prepared for those who love You. Come quickly, Lord Jesus, come quickly!

STUDY

1. How do you replenish your energy? How often?

2. Can you become overly concerned about your physical health? What's the balance here?

3. What percent of your day is spent truly at rest (in perfect peace)? What would the ideal look like? What is one small step you could take to get you closer to that ideal?

He Leads Me Beside Still Waters

4. What kinds of benefits do you find after spending time with Jesus? How do your attitudes or perceptions change?

5. Describe what a lack of contentment or peace looks like. What symptoms would you look for?

6. What threatens your sense of peace?

7. What are we told to do instead of worrying about tomorrow (see Matthew 6:33-34)?

"But seek first his kingdom and his righteousness, and all these things will be given to you as well. Therefore, do not worry about tomorrow, for tomorrow will worry about itself. Each day has enough trouble of its own."

Matthew 6:33-34

---

8. Isaiah 26:3 says, *"You will keep in perfect peace him whose mind is steadfast, because he **trusts** in you."* Is there an area in your life where you could trust God more?

Even Though I Walk Through the Valley...

9. Consider some of the defining moments in your relationship with Jesus. Have any of them involved suffering? How did God use the pain or trouble to help you grow? Did you feel His peace that surpasses understanding?

I Will Dwell in the House of the Lord Forever

10. Read 2 Corinthians 4:16-18 below. How do you distinguish between what is *seen* and what is *unseen?*

> *"Therefore, we do not lose heart. Though outwardly we are wasting away, yet inwardly we are being renewed day by day. For our light and momentary troubles are achieving for us an eternal glory that far outweighs them all. So, we fix our eyes not on what is seen, but on what is unseen. For what is seen is temporary, but what is unseen is eternal."*
>
> 2 Corinthians 4:16-18

11. What does it mean for Christians to live with the end in mind? What are you most looking forward to with Jesus?

12. Which of these promises from God's Word are most precious to you?

☐ *Jesus will never leave me.* Matthew 28:20, Hebrews 13:5

☐ *He will abundantly provide for my needs.* Philippians 4:19

☐ *I will be in heaven with Him.* John 14:1-3

☐ *I will reign with Him.* 2 Timothy 2:12

☐ *He will strengthen me.* Isaiah 40:29

☐ *He will give me His peace.* John 14:27

☐ *He will accomplish His purposes in my life.* 1 Thessalonians 5:24

13. What important points about God are being made in Revelation 1:8, 21:6, and 22:13?

Finishing the Race - Well Done, Good and Faithful Servant

14. Losing heart and giving up is not an option for a believer in Christ. Read the following verses and record what you learn about how to finish the race:

Luke 18:1

2 Corinthians 4:1

Galatians 6:9

Ephesians 6:10

15. This study involved some spiritual training. What does 1 Timothy 4:7-8 have to say about the necessity and value of spiritual training?

16. How has this study drawn you closer to Jesus? In what ways would you say your personal faith has grown? What are some spiritual insights that you will never forget from this study?

17. Who does God bring to mind that you could share the life-changing message of this study with? Would you be willing to disciple and grow other believers in a study like this?

18. What are the rewards for those who remain faithful until the end?

1 Corinthians 9:25

2 Timothy 4:8

1 Peter 5:4

Revelation 2:17

SPIRITUAL MARKER

peace

WORSHIP

The Glorious Unfolding [Steven Curtis Chapman]

Psalm 23 [Jason Upton]

Still [Hillsong]

Be Still and Know [Steven Curtis Chapman]

Resting [Rita Springer]

All My Days [Rita Springer]

I Will Rise [Chris Tomlin]

I Can Only Imagine [Mercy Me]

Soon [Hillsong United]

Heaven's Song [Phil Wickham]

Resurrecting [Elevation]

Abide [Worship Initiative featuring Aaron Williams]

One Day (When We All Get to Heaven) [Matt Redman]

Til I See You [Hillsong United]

All That is to Come [Christy Nockels]

I Am Your Beloved [Bethel Music, Jonathan David & Melissa Hesler]

BE STILL AND KNOW
THAT I AM GOD

PSALM 46:10

REFERENCES

*NIV unless otherwise noted

PREFACE
1. John 3:16
2. John 15:16
3. John 15:5
4. Isaiah 55:11
5. Colossians 3:16
6. Adapted from Bebo Norman,
   The Only Hope
7. 1 Corinthians 2:9

INTRODUCTION
1. Written by Zach Neese. Gateway Create
   Publishing/Integrity's Praise Music.
   CCLI #1596342
2. 1 John 1:3-4, John 15:9-11
3. Psalm 16:11
4. John 10:10, Romans 8:11
5. Ephesians 5:18
6. 2 Chronicles 16:9
7. Hosea 6:6
8. 1 Chronicles 28:9, Matthew 7:8
9. Hebrews 11:6 KJV
10. Proverbs 8:17 ESV
11. Matthew 7:13-14
12. Proverbs 3:32 KJV
13. Matthew 13:11-12
14. Exodus 33:11
15. Isaiah 41:8, 2 Chronicles 20:7
16. Genesis 5:24
17. Daniel 9:23
18. Luke 1:28
19. Job 1:8
20. Acts 13:22
21. John 20:25
22. John 17:20-23
23. 2 Corinthians 6:17
24. Matthew 11:28
25. Exodus 33:11
26. Exodus 33:10-11
27. Numbers 13
28. Exodus 25:8
29. Exodus 25:9
30. Matthew 27:51
31. Luke 10:1
32. 1 Corinthians15:5-7
33. John 13:23 KJV, MSG
34. Spangler, A. & Tverberg, L. (2009).
    Sitting at the Feet of Rabbi Jesus.
    Zondervan.
35. Luke 9:62
36. Luke 14:26
37. Joshua 24:15
38. John 13:23, John 21:7
39. Mark 1:17-20
40. Matthew 4:18-22
41. Mark 9:2-10
42. Mark 5:35-43
43. Luke 22:8
44. Matthew 26:37
45. John 19:26-27

46. Mark 9:32-34, Luke 22:24, Mark 10:35-41
47. Mark 3:14-17
48. Luke 9:49
49. Luke 9:51-56
50. Matthew 26:36-40
51. 1 John 1:3 MSG
52. 2 Peter 1:5
53. Philippians 3:12
54. Revelation 1:17
55. Luke 14:33
56. Matthew 4:19
57. Luke 11:9–13

UNIT 1: SURRENDER
1. Romans 6:13
2. Luke 9:23
3. Colossians 3:3
4. Ephesians 1:3
5. Philippians 4:19
6. Psalm 81:10

STEP 1 - YOUR LIFE IS NOT YOUR OWN
1. Proverbs 16:4 NLT
2. 1 Corinthians 6:19
3. 1 Corinthians 6:20
4. Romans 12:1
5. Job 1:21
6. Harvey, B. (1998). *George Mueller: Man of Faith*. Barbour Publishing.
7. Mark 8:34-38
8. Galatians 2:20
9. Chambers, Oswald (1992). *My Utmost for His Highest: Updated Edition in Today's Language*. Discovery House.
10. Philippians 1:21 NCV
11. John 13:37
12. 2 Corinthians 5:15
13. Luke 9:61
14. James 4:7
15. Genesis 3:5
16. Philippians 3:8
17. John 12:25 MSG
18. Galatians 5:24
19. John 16:12-15
20. Romans 8:14
21. Acts 20:22
22. Acts 20:23
23. John 16:8-11
24. Romans 8:26
25. Galatians 5:18
26. 1 Corinthians 2:11
27. John 16:13
28. 1 Corinthians 3:16
29. Proverbs 3:6 KJV
30. Galatians 5:16 ESV
31. John 15:5
32. John 13:13
33. Luke 9:23
34. Mark 10:21
35. 1 John 4:18
36. 1 John 4:9-10
37. Romans 9:33
38. Jeremiah 45:5 NKJV
39. Jeremiah 29:11
40. Colossians 2:6-7
41. Hebrews 11:39
42. 2 Corinthians 5:7
43. Hebrews 11:6
44. Romans 4:3
45. 2 Corinthians 13:5
46. John 20:29
47. Romans 4:20 ESV
48. 1 Corinthians 15:31
49. Luke 9:23 NCV
50. Henry Varley to D. L. Moody, 1867

STEP 2 - LAY YOUR ISAAC DOWN
1. Mark 12:30
2. Luke 14:28
3. Genesis 22:1-17
4. Romans 4:18
5. Judges 6:2, 1 Samuel 23:14
6. Joel 3:16
7. Psalm 27:1
8. Isaiah 44:20
9. Deuteronomy 4:35
10. Ecclesiastes 1:14
11. Psalm 63:3

12. Matthew 7:11
13. Luke 14:34
14. Psalm 81:9, Leviticus 26
15. 1 John 5:21 AMP
16. Colossians 2:10 KJV
17. Psalm 42:1-2
18. John 4:10,14
19. Romans 12:2
20. 2 Corinthians 10:5
21. 2 Chronicles 20:15
22. Philippians 4:13
23. Matthew 5:30
24. Genesis 22:3
25. 1 Samuel 3:18 NLT
26. Matthew 6:34, John 16:33
27. 1 Peter 4:12
28. Hebrews 5:8-9, Hebrews 2:10
29. Romans 8:17 MSG
30. Psalm 30:6
31. 2 Corinthians 4:17
32. 1 Kings 12:24
33. Genesis 50:20
34. Acts 12:1-3
35. Matthew 11:11
36. Daniel 3:16-18
37. Job 13:15
38. 2 Corinthians 12:10
39. 2 Corinthians 1:9 NLT
40. 2 Timothy 4:17
41. Isaiah 61:3
42. Job 1:6-22
43. Job 12:9
44. 1 Corinthians 10:13 GNT
45. James 1:12
46. Romans 5:3-4
47. Hebrews 12:29
48. 1 Peter 1:6-7 ESV
49. Hebrews 3:13
50. Isaiah 48:10
51. Malachi 3:3
52. James 1:3 MSG
53. James 1:4 MSG
54. Job 23:10

55. Ecclesiastes 7:3, 1 Peter 5:10,
    Hebrews 12:11
56. John 12:24 MSG
57. Psalm 126:5-6 AMP
58. Genesis 41:52
59. Hebrews 12:10 MSG
60. Jeremiah 29:11.
61. 1 Thessalonians 1:6-7, Romans 12:15,
    Galatians 6:2, 2 Corinthians 1:3-5
62. Romans 5:3, James 1:3-4, Hebrews 10:36
63. Psalm 27:13-14 NAS
64. Psalm 46:1
65. 2 Corinthians 4:16-18
66. 2 Corinthians 4:8-9
67. Psalm 62:5-7 NLT
68. Isaiah 40:31
69. Romans 15:4
70. Psalm 146:5
71. Hebrews 12:1-19 (selected verses) MSG
72. Hebrews 11:26
73. John 6:66-69
74. John 18:11 GNT

STEP 3 - FORGIVE 70 x 7
1. Genesis 45
2. Genesis 33
3. Exodus 16-17, 32
4. 1 Samuel 24-26, 2 Samuel 1, 2 Samuel 9
5. Matthew 6:12
6. Mark 11:25
7. John 20:22-23
8. Luke 23:34
9. Luke 17:1 KJV
10. Matthew 24:10 KJV
11. Isaiah 53:5
12. 2 Corinthians 5:21
13. Hebrews 10:22-23 ESV
14. 1 John 1:7
15. Jeremiah 31:34
16. Psalm 103:12
17. Romans 8:1
18. 2 Corinthians 5:17
19. Luke 23:34
20. Matthew 18:21

21. Matthew 18:23-35
22. Colossians 2:13-14
23. Matthew 5:7
24. Mark 11:26, Matthew 6:14-15, Luke 6:37
25. Hebrews 12:15 KJV
26. Matthew 7:19-20
27. Proverbs 4:23
28. Luke 6:45
29. Matthew 7:1-2
30. James 4:12, 5:9
31. Matthew 7:3, Luke 6:42
32. 1 Peter 3:4 KJV
33. Reed, G. L. (2007). Is It Time for Forgiveness? A Living Narrative of Transformation. http://www.leaderu.com/common/journeyofforgiveness.html
34. 1 Corinthians 11:30-31
35. Luke 6:37-38
36. Hosea 4:6
37. Isaiah 61:1
38. Romans 12:19 ESV
39. 1 Samuel 26:9-11 ESV
40. Matthew 5:38-42
41. Matthew 5:44, Luke 6:28, Romans 12:14
42. James 4:1-2
43. Matthew 10:30
44. Psalm 121:8, Psalm 139:1-6
45. John 14:3
46. Job 42:8-12
47. Acts 24:16 KJV
48. Ephesians 4:30-32 KJV

UNIT 2: WAIT

1. Isaiah 30:18
2. Isaiah 64:4
3. Psalm 27:14
4. Isaiah 40:31
5. Ephesians 4:13

STEP 4 - PRAY WITHOUT CEASING

1. Isaiah 56:7, Matthew 21:13
2. John 14:23, 1 Corinthians 6:19
3. Psalm 50:15
4. Job 22:27-28
5. Joel 2:32 Acts 2:21

6. Psalm 115:5-6
7. Genesis 17:1-2
8. Genesis 22:14
9. Exodus 15:22-26
10. Jeremiah 33:16
11. Exodus 17:15
12. Judges 6:24
13. Ezekiel 48:35
14. Romans 9:29
15. Psalm 23
16. John 15:16, 16:23
17. Hebrews 6:19-20, 10:12
18. Exodus 32:12, Numbers 14:13-16, Joshua 7:9
19. Numbers 23:19
20. John 15:15
21. Revelation 5:8, 8:3
22. 1 Samuel 1:15
23. Acts 13:22
24. Psalm 119:97, Psalms 143:5, Psalms 63:6
25. Psalms 104:34, Psalms 19:14
26. Joshua 1:8
27. Philippians 4:8
28. Psalm 36:9
29. 1 John 4:1-3
30. Matthew 6:8
31. Psalm 142:1-2
32. Matthew 21:22
33. Psalm 70:5
34. John 16:24
35. John 11:41-42
36. Matthew 26:39
37. Philippians 4:6
38. Isaiah 41:21
39. 1 Corinthians 3:21, 23
40. Galatians 6:2
41. Genesis 18:16-33
42. Matthew 5:44, Jeremiah 29:7
43. Philippians 2:5
44. 1 Samuel 12:23
45. Psalm 51:4
46. Matthew 6:6 NKJV
47. Isaiah 30:15

48. Psalm 119:164
49. Daniel 6:10
50. Colossians 4:2
51. 1 Thessalonians 5:17
52. Luke 18:1
53. Lawrence, Brother (1982). *The Practice of the Presence of God.* Whitaker House.
54. Luke 11:1
55. 2 Timothy 3:16
56. Psalm 119:105
57. 2 Samuel 7:28
58. Romans 4:21
59. John 8:31 ESV
60. Matthew 4:4 NLT
61. 1 Peter 2:2, Matthew 4:4, 1 Corinthians 3:2, Psalm 119:103
62. Psalm 27:4
63. Romans 8:26
64. 1 Corinthians 14:2 GNT
65. Matthew 17:21 KJV
66. Matthew 6:16-18
67. John 8:47
68. John 10:2-4, 14
69. Isaiah 58:11, Proverbs 3:5-6
70. James 4:7, Luke 10:19
71. Luke 8:18
72. Amos 8:11-12
73. John 11:6
74. Daniel 10:12-13
75. Exodus 24:16
76. Psalm 69:13, Micah 7:7
77. 1 John 5:14
78. Psalm 10:1
79. Isaiah 8:17 GNT
80. St. John of the Cross, Henri Nouwen, A.W. Tozer
81. Deuteronomy 31:8, Psalm 37:28, John 14:16-18, Hebrews 13:5
82. Isaiah 45:15
83. Job 23:8-10

STEP 5 - COUNT YOUR BLESSINGS

1. Hebrews 13:15 KJV
2. Psalm 116:17 KJV
3. Luke 17:11-19
4. 1 Timothy 6:17 GNT
5. Ephesians 1:3
6. James 1:17
7. Psalm 126:3
8. 1 Chronicles 16:7-36 AMP (selected verses)
9. Psalm 103:1 ESV
10. Spangler, A. & Tverberg, L. (2009). *Sitting at the Feet of Rabbi Jesus.* Zondervan.
11. Psalm 89:15-16
12. Ephesians 5:20
13. Colossians 3:17
14. Philippians 4:4
15. 1 Thessalonians 5:18
16. Psalm 9:10
17. Psalm 42:3
18. Psalm 88:18 AMP
19. Cohen, S. (2007). Psychological Stress and Disease. *JAMA 14,* page 1685.
20. James 3:4
21. James 3:6
22. Proverbs 18:21
23. James 3:8
24. 2 Corinthians 4:13
25. Numbers 13, 14:1-4
26. Psalm 50:14 NAS
27. James 3:9-10
28. 2 Corinthians 5:17
29. John 15:16
30. Isaiah 49:16
31. Isaiah 45:2, 4
32. 2 Corinthians 1:21-22
33. Philippians 1:6
34. 2 Timothy 1:7 KJV
35. 1 Corinthians 2:16
36. Ephesians 2:10
37. Romans 8:35
38. Psalm 106:7
39. Psalm 106:12-13
40. 2 Peter 3:1 KJV

41. Emmons, R. A., & Kneezel, T. T. (2005). Giving gratitude: Spiritual and religious correlates of gratitude. *Journal of Psychology and Christianity,* 24.2, 140-48.

42. Cameron, K. S., Dutton, J. E., & Quinn, R. E. (2003). *Positive Organizational Scholarship.* San Francisco: Berrett-Koehler Publishers.

43. McCullough, M. E., Emmons, R. A., & Tsang, J. (2002). The grateful disposition: A conceptual and empirical topography. *Journal of Personality and Social Psychology,* 82, 112-127.

44. Wood, A. M., Joseph, S. & Maltby, N. (2009). Gratitude predicts psychological well-being above the Big Five facets. *Personality and Individual Differences,* 45, 655-660.

45. Wood, A. M., Joseph, S., & Linley, P. A. (2007). Coping style as a psychological resource of grateful people. *Journal of Social and Clinical Psychology,* 26, 1108–1125.

46. Wood, A. M., Joseph, S., Lloyd, J., & Atkins, S. (2009). Gratitude influences sleep through the mechanism of pre-sleep cognitions. *Journal of Psychosomatic Research,* 66, 43-48.

47. Seligman, M. E. P., Steen, T. A., Park, N.,& Peterson, C. (2005). Positive psychology progress: Empirical validation of interventions. *American Psychologist,* 60, 410-421.

48. Oatman Jr., J. (1897). In *Songs for Young People* by Edwin Excell. Chicago, Illinois.

49. Galatians 5:22

50. Psalm 16:11 ESV

51. Psalm 45:7

52. Isaiah 35:10

53. 1 Chronicles 16:25

STEP 6 - WORSHIP IN SPIRIT AND TRUTH

1. Spurgeon, C. (1998). *Prayer and Spiritual Warfare.* New Kensington, PA: Whitaker House.

2. Psalm 33:8

3. Isaiah 66:5

4. Leviticus 25:17, Deuteronomy 10:12, 2 Chronicles 19:7, Job 28:28, Psalm 19:9, Psalm 111:10, Proverbs 1:7

5. Psalm 147:11, Psalm 33:18, Psalm 34:7, Psalm 128:1

6. Ecclesiastes 12:13AMP and Westminster catechism, 1647

7. 1 Peter 2:9

8. 1 Chronicles 16:24, Psalm 29:1, Psalm 66:2, Psalm 96:7, 2 Corinthians 3:18

9. Isaiah 43:21 NCV

10. Psalm 145:10

11. Psalm 86:9

12. Revelation 4:11

13. Nehemiah 9:6

14. Revelation 4:8

15. Psalm 147:11

16. Psalm 50:23 MSG

17. Malachi 3:8

18. Psalm 29:2

19. Luke 19:40

20. From the Vineyard UK "I Love Your Presence"

21. John 4:23-24

22. Hebrews 12:28 NCV

23. Matthew 6:7 KJV

24. Mark 7:6-7

25. 1 Samuel 16:7

26. Psalm 32:11 NCV

27. Psalm 78:72 NCV

28. 2 Samuel 24:24

29. Ezekiel 36:26

30. Psalm 105:4 GNT

31. 1 Chronicles 9:33, 23:5

32. 2 Samuel 6:14

33. Zschech, Darlene (1996). *Worship.* Hillsong Music Australia.

34. Psalm 99:9

35. Exodus 15
36. Joshua 6
37. 2 Samuel 6
38. Luke 15:24-25
39. Acts 16:25-26
40. Revelation 5:13
41. 1 Corinthians 13:1
42. Acts 16:25-34
43. Psalm 103:20 ESV
44. Psalm 22:3 KJV
45. Zephaniah 3:17 GNT
46. Psalm 27: 4
47. Ephesians 5:19
48. Hebrews 13:15, Psalm 7:17, Ezra
    3:11 Psalm 149:3, Psalm 150:3-4,
    Nehemiah 8:6
49. 1 Samuel 18:6-7, Psalm 30:11, Jeremiah
    31:13, Luke 15:25
50. Exodus 17:15
51. 2 Corinthians 3:17
52. 1 Chronicles 13:10-13
53. Ezekiel 28:13-17 KJV
54. Isaiah 14:11-14
55. Isaiah 42:8
56. Romans 10:2
57. 2 Samuel 6:16
58. 2 Samuel 6:21-22
59. 2 Samuel 6:23
60. 1 Chronicles 16:27

UNIT 3: BEAR FRUIT
1. John 15:8
2. Colossians 1:9-13
3. Luke 4:17-19

STEP 7 - PUT YOUR ARMOR ON
1. 1 Timothy 1:18 ESV
2. 1 Timothy 6:12
3. 2 Timothy 2:3
4. John 8:44
5. Matthew 25:31-46
6. Matthew 13:24-30
7. Ephesians 6:12
8. 1 Peter 5:8
9. Ephesians 6:11
10. 2 Corinthians 2:11
11. Ephesians 6:16
12. 1 Peter 5:8-9
13. Ephesians 4:27
14. Matthew 6:13
15. Genesis 3
16. Luke 22:31
17. Job 1
18. Luke 13:10-17
19. Matthew 24:24
20. Matthew 5:6
21. James 1:14-16
22. Hosea 4:6
23. Mark 13:22 ESV
24. Leviticus 20:6, 27
25. 2 Corinthians 2:11 NLT
26. Romans 8:12-13
27. 1 John 1:8
28. 1 John 2:1, Romans 6:1-11
29. Romans 6:12-13
30. James 4:7
31. 2 Timothy 2:22 ESV
32. 1 Corinthians 10:12 MSG
33. 1 Corinthians 10:13 NLT
34. Mark 7:21-23 NLT
35. 1 Timothy 4:1
36. 1 John 4:6
37. Philippians 4:7
38. John 13:2
39. Acts 5:3
40. John 10:10
41. Genesis 3:1
42. Psalm 119:37 GNT
43. Hebrews 3:1
44. 2 Timothy 2:8
45. Romans 12:21
46. Matthew 5:28
47. Philippians 4:8
48. Colossians 2:15
49. Matthew 28:18
50. Matthew 28:18, Ephesians 1:20-21,
    Colossians 2:10
51. Luke 10:17-19

52. Ephesians 1:19
53. Ezekiel 28:13-17, Isaiah 14:11-14,
    Revelation 19-20
54. Ephesians 2:1
55. 2 Corinthians 5:17
56. Ephesians 2:3
57. 2 Peter 1:4
58. Ephesians 5:8
59. Romans 6:6, Galatians 2:20
60. 2 Corinthians 5:17
61. Adapted from *The Bondage Breaker* by
    Neil Anderson
62. John 8:32
63. John 14:6
64. John 16:13
65. John 17:15, 17
66. Romans 5:1
67. 1 Corinthians 1:30, Philippians 3:8-9
68. 1 John 1:9
69. Isaiah 9:6
70. Philippians 4:7 ESV
71. Colossians 3:15-16
72. Exodus 14:13-14
73. Numbers 14:2-3, 28-29; Matthew 12:36-
    37; Mark 11:25-26
74. Exodus 20:4-6
75. Ecclesiastes 4:9-10
76. Joshua 1:7
77. Romans 8:37
78. 1 John 4:4
79. 2 Chronicles 20:15
80. Ephesians 5:2, 8, 15
81. Mark 9:29 KJV
82. 2 Thessalonians 3:3
83. Job 1:12
84. Isaiah 41:10
85. 1 Samuel 17:34
86. Numbers 13:26-33
87. Isaiah 61:1
88. Acts 26:18

STEP 8 - GO AND MAKE DISCIPLES
1. Romans 8:30, Ephesians 1:18
2. Ephesians 1:11 MSG

3. John 15:16 NCV
4. John 15:8 ESV
5. Romans 6:13
6. Romans 12:1 GNT
7. Philippians 2:15-16
8. John 17:18 MSG
9. Matthew 28:19-20
10. 2 Corinthians 5:18 GNT
11. Acts 20:24 NLT
12. John 20:21
13. Ephesians 4:4-14, 1 Corinthians 1, 1
    Corinthians 7:17, 1 Peter 2:9
14. Romans 7:4 GNT
15. 2 Corinthians 6:1 NCV
16. Galatians 6:10 ESV
17. Ephesians 5:16 NCV
18. Proverbs 3:27 GNT
19. Matthew 20:28
20. Romans 14:12
21. Mark 8:35, Matthew 10:39, Luke 17:33
22. Exodus 3
23. Genesis 6:5-14
24. Jonah 1-4
25. Acts 9:1-16
26. Proverbs 3:5
27. Romans 8:28
28. John 15:14
29. John 15:10
30. Mark 10:27
31. Isaiah 46:11b MSG
32. John 14:6
33. Genesis 12:1
34. Psalm 37:23 NKJV
35. Genesis 6:22
36. Genesis 12:1-8
37. 1 Samuel 16:1-13
38. Amos 7:14-15
39. Jonah 1-4
40. Matthew 4:18-22
41. Matthew 9:9
42. Acts 9:1-19
43. *Matthew Henry Commentary on the Whole
    Bible,* Bible Study Tools

44. Genesis 17:9-14
45. Barker, K. L & Kohlenberger, J. R. *The Expositor's Bible Commentary.* Zondervan.
46. Adapted from a list of obstacles that originally appeared in Jones, L. B. (1996). *The Path.* New York: Hyperion.
47. Exodus 3
48. 1 Samuel 9:21-27
49. Jeremiah 1:6-8
50. 1 Kings 11:1-12
51. Nehemiah 6:1-4
52. Luke 9:57-60
53. 1 Kings 19
54. Judges 6
55. Exodus 2:11-12
56. 1 Samuel 13:8-14
57. Matthew 16:21-23
58. Luke 9:52-56
59. Acts 8:14
60. 1 Samuel 17
61. Genesis 37-50
62. Numbers 11
63. Numbers 13-14, Deuteronomy 1
64. Judges 4-6
65. Matthew 25
66. Deuteronomy 28:1, 8
67. Luke 24:49
68. 1 Corinthians 12:7 NLT, Romans 12:4-8, Ephesians 4:8-15, 1 Corinthians 7:7
69. 1 Corinthians 12:11 NLT
70. 1 Corinthians 12:4-6
71. 1 Peter 4:10-11 NAS
72. Romans 14:7
73. Proverbs 18:1
74. 1 Corinthians 12:12, Ephesians 2:21-22, Ephesians 3:6, Ephesians 4:16, Colossians 2:19
75. 1 Corinthians 12:27, Ephesians 5:23
76. 1 Corinthians 12:18
77. Ephesians 4:13
78. 1 Corinthians 12:21
79. 1 Corinthians 12:18 NKJV
80. Colossians 3:14 ESV
81. Galatians 5:14
82. John 13:35
83. 1 John 2:9-11
84. 1 John 3:10
85. 1 John 3:14-15
86. 1 John 3:16-17
87. 1 John 4:7-8
88. 1 John 4:11-12
89. 1 John 4:20-21
90. 1 John 5:1-2
91. 1 Corinthians 13:13
92. 1 John 3:18 GNT
93. Matthew 22:14
94. Isaiah 6:8
95. 1 Corinthians 6:19
96. Matthew 25:21

UNIT 4: ABIDE
1. John 15:4 ESV
2. John 15:5
3. John 15:10
4. Luke 10:20

STEP 9 - HUMBLE YOURSELF
1. Proverbs 16:18
2. Luke 9:46, Luke 22:24
3. Mark 10:35-39
4. Isaiah 66:2
5. Proverbs 11:2
6. Proverbs 22:4
7. Matthew 20:26-27
8. Matthew 23:11-12, Luke 14:1-11, Luke 18:14
9. Matthew 18:4
10. Matthew 11:29
11. Matthew 5:3, 5
12. James 4:10 KJV
13. 1 Peter 5:5-6
14. Romans 12:16
15. 1 Corinthians 13:4-5 NKJV
16. Philippians 2:3 NKJV
17. Colossians 3:12
18. Philippians 2:5-9
19. John 6:38
20. John 8:28

21. John 5:19
22. John 14:10
23. John 5:30
24. John 8:50
25. John 5:41
26. John 17:22
27. Philippians 4:13
28. 1 Corinthians 1:31
29. 1 Peter 5:6
30. Daniel 4:37
31. 2 Corinthians 12:7 NLT
32. Numbers 20:10
33. 2 Chronicles 26
34. Luke 12:48 NCV
35. Luke 18:11 NLT
36. Isaiah 65:5
37. John 5:44 MSG
38. Galatians 5:26 MSG
39. Galatians 6:4
40. Galatians 5:21 MSG
41. John 21:20-22
42. Proverbs 25:23
43. Mark 7:22, Galatians 5:12, James 3:16
44. Isaiah 53:7
45. Philippians 2:7
46. Romans 8:28
47. 1 Peter 3:9
48. Daniel 4:4, 27
49. Philippians 2:4
50. Matthew 6:33
51. Ephesians 4:22
52. Luke 9:25
53. 1 John 2:15-16 MSG
54. 1 Thessalonians 2:6
55. Luke 16:15
56. John 10:41
57. Luke 7:28
58. 1 Corinthians 1:28
59. 1 Corinthians 1:27
60. Matthew 13:22
61. Philippians 3:8
62. Matthew 6:24
63. Matthew 6:19-21

64. Luke 16:11
65. John 12:42
66. John 9:18-22
67. 1 Kings 19:1-5
68. Genesis 12:10-13, 20:1-2
69. Revelation 3:16
70. Matthew 10:33
71. Genesis 6:9
72. 1 Kings 18:19
73. 2 Corinthians 5:14
74. 2 Corinthians 5:9
75. 2 Corinthians 10:13 NJKV
76. Matthew 25:14-30
77. 2 Corinthians 3:18 NLT
78. Psalm 39:4 NLT
79. Philippians 3:7 NLT
80. Proverbs 13:7 MSG
81. 1 John 2:17 NLT
82. 1 Peter 2:11 MSG
83. 1Timothy 6:6
84. John 3:30
85. Isaiah 42:1-5 MSG

STEP 10 - REST BESIDE STILL WATERS
1. Isaiah 30:15 NKJV
2. Psalm 32:7
3. Genesis 2:2
4. Matthew 14:23
5. Mark 6:31
6. Matthew 11:29
7. Ericsson, K.A., Krampe, R.T., & Tesch-Romer, C. (1993). The role of deliberate practice in the acquisition of expert performance. *Psychological Review,* 100 (3), 363-406.
8. Rath, T. (2013). Eat Move Sleep. Missionday.
9. 3 John 1:2
10. Roberts, F. J. (2002). *Come Away My Beloved.* Promise Press.
11. Matthew 6:25-34
12. Matthew 13:22 ESV
13. Matthew 11:28
14. Matthew 6:34

15. Philippians 4:7 MSG
16. Colossians 3:15
17. Philippians 4:7
18. Hebrews 12:1 ESV
19. John 10:11
20. For a comprehensive review of Psalm 23: Keller, W. P. (2007). *A Shepherd Looks at Psalm 23*. Grand Rapids, MI: Zondervan.
21. 2 Timothy 1:7 KJV
22. Philippians 4:11-13
23. Psalm 42:7
24. John 7:37
25. John 4:13-14
26. Jeremiah 2:13
27. Isaiah 35:6-7 NKJV
28. Isaiah 41:17-18 NKJV
29. Isaiah 58:11 NKJV
30. Isaiah 53:6
31. Philippians 2:13
32. 2 Corinthians 3:18 ESV
33. 1 Thessalonians 4:3 MSG
34. 1 Thessalonians 5:23
35. Isaiah 30:21
36. Matthew 28:20
37. 2 Thessalonians 3:3, 1 Corinthians 10:13
38. John 10:10
39. 1 Peter 1:4 NLT
40. Ephesians 1:18 NLT
41. 1 Thessalonians 5:10, 4:17
42. 1 John 3:2, 2 Corinthians 3:18
43. Revelation 21:4
44. Romans 8:17, Colossian 3:4, 2 Thessalonians 2:14, 2 Timothy 2:12, 1 Peter 5:1
45. Mark 9:41, 10:30, 1 Corinthians 3:8, Hebrews 10:35, Matthew 25:21-23
46. James 1:12
47. Revelation 1:8
48. 2 Peter 3:13, Revelation 3:12, Revelation 21:1-2
49. Joel 2:28
50. 2 Timothy 4:7
51. 1 Chronicles 28:20
52. Habakkuk 2:3 NLT
53. 2 Corinthians 3:18 MSG
54. Deuteronomy 7:22
55. John 16:12
56. Philippians 1:6
57. John 14:10
58. Psalm 46:5, Acts 20:24
59. Matthew 25:21
60. Psalm 37:23 NKJV
61. Mark 10:27
62. 1 Timothy 4:15
63. Hebrews 13:20-21

www.ingramcontent.com/pod-product-compliance
Lightning Source LLC
Chambersburg PA
CBHW080837120626
46553CB00009B/2459